SAGE was founded in 1965 by Sara Miller McCune to support the dissemination of usable knowledge by publishing innovative and high-quality research and teaching content. Today, we publish over 900 journals, including those of more than 400 learned societies, more than 800 new books per year, and a growing range of library products including archives, data, case studies, reports, and video. SAGE remains majority-owned by our founder, and after Sara's lifetime will become owned by a charitable trust that secures our continued independence.

Los Angeles | London | New Delhi | Singapore | Washington DC | Melbourne

'Kashmir' Avoidance and Subversion of Justice

Kashmir is another region in South Asia that has witnessed protracted conflict that remains unresolved even after two decades. It cannot be said that Kashmir is post-conflict or that transitional justice would have the same meaning there as in the other South Asian contexts. However, given the grievous abuses that have been committed during the conflict, transitional justice mechanism would necessarily have some relevance for Kashmir. The then Jammu and Kashmir Chief Minister Omar Abdullah had proposed the formation of a Truth and Reconciliation Commission to "heal the wounds of Kashmiris" who had hugely suffered during the conflict.

While the conflict is still ongoing in Kashmir with no signs of any political resolution to the issue, local human rights groups rightly apprehend that if the government forms such a Commission, it would be only used to further entrench impunity. The prevailing situation in Kashmir is such that there have been almost no prosecution of perpetrators of serious violations, the fate of the forcibly disappeared persons remains unknown, and extrajudicial killings and sexual violence continues. If the government is sincere about implementing transitional justice mechanisms, then it should begin by granting sanction for prosecution of security force personnel involved in human rights violations, repeal laws such as the AFSPA, Public Safety Act and ensure that the guilty are punished.

The insistence of the state government under the then Chief Minister Omar Abdullah, to form a Truth and Reconciliation Commission over other transitional justice mechanism, has meant that there is a political motive to impede justice processes through the normal courts by forming a TRC. Why doesn't the government instead invite the UN Working Group on Disappearances to ascertain the fate of the thousands who have disappeared, or ensure that there are swift prosecutions in cases of human rights violations?

Besides, the formation of a Truth Commission cannot be a replacement to the political resolution of the conflict. Neither can it replace the demand for punishment of the perpetrators of serious crimes including disappearances. Also, how could a TRC be feasible if human rights abuses continue to happen in Kashmir? Perhaps the

WOMEN AND POLITICS OF PEACE

Omar Abdullah government had envisaged the TRC as a never-ending process, which will shift the focus from the demands of justice. Cynicism as regards the sincerity of the TRC proposal is further reinforced by the context in which the Abdullah government mooted the idea. It is a context in which the government has repeatedly failed to demonstrate its commitment to the demands of justice. Moreover, at the time the Omar Abdullah spoke about TRC, public attention was centered on the mass graves unearthed by the State Human Rights Commission which is the government's own body. Indeed, there was a general sense in Kashmir that the concept of the TRC was put forward by the Omar Abdullah government to hoodwink public opinion.

Most importantly, why was the government not investigating and prosecuting the mass rapes of Konan Poshpora, a village in North Kashmir, carried out by the armed forces? Even when the District Judge reopened the investigation in 2013, 22 years after the incident, the concerned government agencies refused to investigate and submit a final report despite a court order to do so within three months. Moreover, when the successor PDP-BJP government led by Mufti Mohammad Sayeed took over in early 2015, the state government challenged the JK High Court granting compensation to the Konan Poshpora rape victims in Supreme Court. In the Shopian rape and murder case of 2009 also, there have been no authoritative investigations that have led to prosecution (International People's Tribunal on Human Rights and Justice in Kashmir 2009; Independent Women's Initiative for Justice 2009; Warisha 2013).

The variables of truth, justice, and reconciliation are not mutually exclusive and it is difficult to ascertain the order in which they form a part of any peace process. Like reconciliation, justice is a key component of lasting peace. There is no agreement on what reconciliation exactly means. Broadly, it entails an end to, and acknowledgement of the past historical injustice supplemented with measures to repair the wrong. A common experience of human rights abuse does not necessarily translate into a common way to deal with the past. Thus, reconciliation needs to address not only the conflicting historical narratives of different communities but also the way they want to deal with the past. But reconciliation should not become an excuse to subvert justice. Political transitions occur in many different ways and there is no one magical formula for these widely divergent contexts.

Thank you for choosing a SAGE product!
If you have any comment, observation or feedback,
I would like to personally hear from you.
Please write to me at **contactceo@sagepub.in**

Vivek Mehra, Managing Director and CEO, SAGE India.

Bulk Sales

SAGE India offers special discounts
for purchase of books in bulk.
We also make available special imprints
and excerpts from our books on demand.

For orders and enquiries, write to us at

Marketing Department
SAGE Publications India Pvt Ltd
B1/I-1, Mohan Cooperative Industrial Area
Mathura Road, Post Bag 7
New Delhi 110044, India

E-mail us at **marketing@sagepub.in**

Get to know more about SAGE

Be invited to SAGE events, get on our mailing list.
Write today to **marketing@sagepub.in**

This book is also available as an e-book.

WOMEN AND POLITICS OF PEACE

South Asia Narratives on Militarization, Power, and Justice

Edited by

RITA MANCHANDA

Los Angeles | London | New Delhi
Singapore | Washington DC | Melbourne

First published in 2017 by

 SAGE Publications India Pvt Ltd
B1/I-1 Mohan Cooperative Industrial Area
Mathura Road, New Delhi 110 044, India
www.sagepub.in

SAGE Publications Inc
2455 Teller Road
Thousand Oaks, California 91320, USA

SAGE Publications Ltd
1 Oliver's Yard, 55 City Road
London EC1Y 1SP, United Kingdom

SAGE Publications Asia-Pacific Pte Ltd
3 Church Street
#10-04 Samsung Hub
Singapore 049483

Published by Vivek Mehra for SAGE Publications India Pvt Ltd, typeset in 10.5/12.5 pt Baskerville by Zaza Eunice, Tamil Nadu, India and printed at Chaman Enterprises, New Delhi.

Library of Congress Cataloging-in-Publication Data Available

ISBN: 978-93-860-6262-8 (HB)

SAGE Team: Supriya Das, Neha Sharma, Niharika Sah and Ritu Chopra

Contents

13

Against Forgetting: Gendered Justice in "Post-conflict" Bangladesh

Dina M. Siddiqi

Mapping the Terrain of Gender Justice

In this essay, I map the terrain of gendered justice for women at the margins of the nation today, taking the abduction and as yet unresolved disappearance, over 20 years ago, of the outspoken indigenous rights activist, Kalpana Chakma,[1] as a signpost. The trajectory of her case points to the asymmetric political, historical, and cultural landscapes traversed by Pahari/Jumma women, imagined as "*outside* the Bengali nation," (emphasis added) in relation to their Bengali counterparts. Without wishing to overstate its significance, I also explore the multiple and continuing reverberations of this missing female body on mainstream feminist politics.

In a broader context, I assess the possibilities for justice in the post-Chittagong Hill Tracts Peace Accord period, that is, since 1997. I conclude that the situation has not altered dramatically in the interim. The "post-conflict" situation in the CHT is anything but conflict-free. Rather, the existence of the Accord renders invisible the ongoing militarization of everyday life in the area. In the circumstances, the

List of Abbreviations

AFSPA	Armed Forces Special Powers Act
AIHRC	Afghanistan Independent Human Rights Commission
ALP	Afghan Local Police
ANA	Afghan National Army
ANP	Awami National Party
ANP	Afghan National Police
ANAF	Afghanistan National Armed Forces
ANSF	Afghan National Security Forces
APDP	Association of Parents of Disappeared Persons
APRP	Afghanistan Peace and Reconciliation Program
APWAPS	Asia-Pacific Women's Alliance on Peace and Security
AWAW	Association of War Affected Women
BIWN	Bangladesh Indigenous Women's Network
BPFA	Beijing Platform for Action
BLPI	Bolshevik-Leninist Party of India
CA	Constituent Assembly (Nepal)
CEDAW	Convention on the Elimination of all Forms of Discrimination Against Women
CHT	Chittagong Hill Tracts
CID	Commission of Inquiry on Disappearances
CID	Criminal Investigations Department
CIEDP	Commission of Investigation on Enforced Disappeared Persons
COI	Commission of Inquiry
COIN	counter-insurgency
CPA	Centre for Policy Analysis
CPA	Comprehensive Peace Agreement
CPN	Communist Party of Nepal
CTF	Consultative Task Force
DDR	Disarmament, Demobilization and Reintegration
DGFI	Director General of Forces Intelligence

DIAG	Disbandment of Illegal Armed Groups
EPRLF	Eelam People's Revolutionary Liberation Front
EPW	Economic & Political Weekly
EVAW	Elimination of Violence Against Women
FATA	Federally Administered Tribal Areas
FCR	Frontier Crimes Regulation
FHH	Female Headed Households
FWLD	Forum for Women, Law & Development
GOI	Government on India
GR	General Recommendation
HBF/HBS	Heinrich Boll Foundation/Stiftung
HDI	Human Development Index
HPC	High Peace Council
HRCP	Human Rights Commission of Pakistan
HRH	Home for Human Rights
HRW	Human Rights Watch
HSZ	High Security Zone
HWF	Hill Women's Federation
ICCPR	International Covenant on Civil and Political Rights
ICES	International Centre for Ethnic Studies
ICJ	International Commission of Jurists
ICJ	International Court of Justice
ICG	International Crisis Group
ICT	Information and Communications Technology
ICT	International Crimes Tribunal
ICTJ	International Center for Transitional Justice
IDP	Internally Displaced Persons
IHL	International Humanitarian Law
IIGEP	International Independent Group of Eminent Persons
IMF	International Military Forces
IPKF	Indian Peace Keeping Force
ISAF	International Security Assistance Force
JSS	Jana Samhati Samiti
JVP	Janathā Vimukthi Peramuṇa
LGBTQ	Lesbian, Gay, Bisexual, Transgender and Queer
LLRC	Lessons Learnt and Reconciliation Commission
LSSP	Lanka Sama Samaja Party

LTTE	Liberation Tigers of Tamil Eelam
MoWA	Ministry of Women Affairs
MRG	Minority Rights Group
MWHRD	Mannar Women for Human Rights and Democracy
MWDF	Mannar Women's Development Federation
NAP	National Action Plan
NBA	Nepal Bar Association
NCPJ	National Consultative Peace Jirga
NEN	North East Network
NIB	National Intelligence Bureau
NGO	Non-Governmental Organization
NMA	Naga Mothers Association
NPMHR	Naga Peoples Movement for Human Rights
NSCN (IM)	National Socialist Council of Nagaland – Isak-Muivah
NTTP	Nepal Transition to Peace Initiative
NWFP	North West Frontier Province
OHCHR	Office of the High Commissioner for Human Rights
OISL	OHCHR Investigation on Sri Lanka
OMP	Office of Missing Person
ONUR	Office of National Unity and Reconciliation
PAWF	Pacific and Asian Women's Forum
PCICAD	Presidential Commission of Inquiry into Complaints of Abduction and Disappearances
PCJSS	Parbatya Chattagram Jana Samhati Samiti
PIPFPD	Pakistan–India Peoples' Forum for Peace and Democracy
PLA	People's Liberation Army
POP	Pre-orientation Program
PRT	Provincial Reconstruction Teams
PTRO	Peace Training and Research Organization
RAW	Revolutionary Association of the Women of Afghanistan
RSM	Resolute Support Mission
SAARC	South Asian Association for Regional Cooperation
SAFHR	South Asia Forum for Human Rights
SAWF	South Asian Women's Forum
SAWP	South Asian Women for Peace
SAWIPS	South Asian Women's Institute for Peace Studies

SCR	Security Council Resolution
SGBV	Sexual Gender Based Violence
SGI	Sub-committee on Gender Issues
SPA	Seven Party Alliance
SWDC	Suriya Women's Development Centre
TID	Terrorists Investigations Department
TRC	Truth and Reconciliation Commission
TTP	Tehriqi Taliban Pakistan
UML	United Marxist-Leninist
UNAMA	United Nations Assistance Mission in Afghanistan
UNFPA	United Nations Population Fund *formerly United Nations Fund for Population Activities*
UNHRC	United Nations Human Rights Council
UNIFEM	United Nations Development Fund for Women *now UN Women*
UNIRP	United Nations Interagency Rehabilitation Program
UNMIN	United Nations Mission in Nepal
UNSC	United Nation Security Council
UNSG	United Nations Secretary General
VDC	Village Defence Committee
VMLR	Verified Minor and Late Recruits
WAC	Women's Action Committee
WAN	Women's Action Network
WAF	Women's Action Forum
WAPPDCA	Women's Alliance for Peace, Power, Democracy and Constituent Assembly
WCDM	Women's Coalition for Disaster Management
WCW	World Conference on Women
WILPF	Women's International League for Peace and Freedom
WIPSA	Women's Initiative for Peace in South Asia
WISCOMP	Women in Security, Conflict Management and Peace
WMC	Women & Media Collective
WPS	Women Peace and Security
WRN	Women's Regional Network

Acknowledgments

This book has been a long journey, inspired by an assembly of women across the South Asian region, claiming a voice, challenging marginalization, and asserting their perspectives, but it would not have been possible without the unstinted support of Anne Stenhammer of the UN Women South Asia Regional Office, who shared that vision and boldly overcame national anxieties about engaging with the women, peace, and security agenda in the region. A special thanks to Roshmi Goswami, who constituted the UN Women-SASRO "Experts Group" which enabled the convening of the conference "The Changing Dynamics of Peace Building in South Asia: Recasting Women's Agency and Transformative Strategies" that provided the blueprint for the book. Special mention should be made on the continuing support extended by Rebecca Tavares, UN Women. Vital in backing research for the book project was Navsharan Singh, IDRC, who has been enthusiastic in supporting gender equality initiatives. Such an edited volume is a collective effort in both its conceptualization and translation into text, and my sincere appreciation to all the contributors for their willingness and patience in walking the long journey to publication. Also, I owe a debt of gratitude to the South Asia Forum for Human Rights (SAFHR) team, particularly Tapan Bose and editorial assistants Aarushi Prakash and Swati Prabhu. Finally, a special word of thanks to the SAGE Publications' editorial team, especially Supriya Das, and to the anonymous reviewer whose helpful comments made our arguments more robust.

Introduction*

Rita Manchanda

Women do a lot of the hard work, doing shuttle diplomacy—taking important messages from one party to another during the conflict, but are forgotten when the experts and politicians take over. We, as the mothers of missing soldiers, were responsible for brokering a ceasefire between the government and LTTE. The LTTE acknowledged our contribution, the government did not.

Visaka Dharmadasa, War Affected Women's Association, Sri Lanka

45,000 people have been killed and human rights defenders were being killed every day. Instead of confronting the Taliban, the Pakistan government was carrying on a dialogue with them. Nobody had asked Pakistani women about the ongoing talks with the Taliban.

Hina Jilani, Lawyer and UN Eminent Persons Group

Peace with Taliban will not to happen, soon. Too many forces national and international have a vested interest in the conflict continuing. For the Taliban we are part of the problem not the solution. Because we were not holding the gun we were forgotten then, now we are kept away from bringing peace to the country.

Sima Samar, Afghan Independent Human Rights Commission

---

*This chapter is deeply indebted to the South Asia Conference on "The Changing Dynamics of Peacebuilding in South Asia," Kathmandu, February 15–17, 2013 and the Conference Report edited by Anouhita Mojumdar, see www.safhr.org; the South Asia Women's Meet on WPS, New Delhi February 22–23, 2014 and APWAPS Forum and Asia-Pacific Regional Consultation for the Global Study UNSCR 1325, Kathmandu February 11–13, 2015.

The Regional Context

The stuttering on-again and off-again talks about talks with the "good" Taliban in Afghanistan and Pakistan since 2012–15[1] have finally foundered because of the Taliban's unrelenting offensive, but not because of the prescient warnings of Afghan and Pakistani women who question such peacemaking which far from ending violent extremism exacerbates militarization and terrorist activities. Women were convinced that such a "peace" would prove disadvantageous to their rights and life chances as had been the bitter experience of women in Swat and FATA, Pakistan. But evidently, such anxieties mattered little at the "peace table" where men concerned with power and domination sat with guns. Paradoxically, while these Afghan and Pakistani women work for peace, many are more worried about the crisis of the solutions being proposed and the prospect of a post-conflict political economy of violence that will disempower them further.

Transformative Peace with Women

When the moment of peacebuilding is unlikely to be transformative and is more of a restoration of status quo (which was part of the problem in the first place), how should women's collectivities—local, national, and regional—engage with peace processes that deliver a violent peace or at best peace as "pacification"? (Francis 2010). It is a dilemma that continues to splinter women's networks across regions and ethnicities in Nepal, the Chittagong Hill Tracts (CHT): Bangladesh and Sri Lanka. In post-war Sri Lanka, the continuing failure to bridge the justice and reconciliation gap has resulted in heightening the state's two antagonistic ethnonationalist ideologies (Uyangoda 2012:21) and created a context in which according to an interview-based study, Sinhala women dream of returning to the idyllic communal harmony of the pre-conflict time, while Tamil minority women demand transformative justice (Hernández-Reyna 2013:45–46). In Nepal and the CHT the moment of peacemaking divided the Maoist women leaders in the Himalayan state and split the Hill Women's Federation which had held aloft the human rights and peace front in the CHT.

In India's Northeast, the top-down Indo-Naga Framework Agreement (2015) has been signed, but the Naga Mothers and other social collectivities in the vanguard of the peace movement were kept out. Most likely then that the Agreement's provisions (still secret) will follow the script of earlier accords around identity conflicts, guaranteeing the community's customary laws, without reservation and ignoring international norms of protection of women's rights. How should women balance their identification with the struggle for the survival of community identity and challenge customary practices which are gender oppressive?

Gendered power shifts produced in the upheaval of conflict and the peace momentum open up empowering possibilities for women as evidence-based research has established, but only too quickly, tail into a patriarchal backlash (Manchanda and Bose 2015). The conflict "aftermath" brings back the gendered public–private divide, pushing women ideologically and violently back into the private sphere. Motherhood politics empowers women in conflict and disempowers them in "peacetime" (Kolas 2014: 41–48). The contingent situation may be different in Bangladesh or Northeast India but the gendered politics of being instrumentalized in power narratives is the same across regions and cultures (Meintjes, Thurshen, and Pillay 2002).

When peace agreements are negotiated, nobody asks women "what do you think"—be it the misogynist Taliban with its ideology of subjugating women or the gender "neutral" negotiators in Nepal, India's Northeast or Bangladesh's CHT. In Pakistan's Swat peace negotiations (2008–2009), when women lobbied to be included, insisting on "no peace talks about us, without us" and in a rare exception a woman minister was included in the Awami National Party delegation, the gender apartheid Taliban made her exclusion a deal breaker (Bushra Gohar, South Asia Women's Meeting on WPS, Delhi 2014). The Swat accord unleashed more violence and militarization.

How should women confront the multilayered sociocultural barriers that block their entry into public life so as to participate as equal citizens in rebuilding conflict affected societies and a stable and just peace? In Nepal and Afghanistan, the peace momentum delivered progressive policies but regressive practices. Gender quotas ensured that a third of the members in Nepal's Constituent Assembly were women, but numbers do not translate into power and authority when there is no inner party democracy and the post-conflict consensus rapidly gives way to a sharply divided polity. In Afghanistan, gender quotas seated women in the Constitutional Jirga and parliament, but increasing insecurity with impunity has made elected women more dependent upon conservative warlords who promote them as proxies, alienating them from the women's networks which had lobbied for their participation. Sri Lanka continues to resist gender quotas. Its profile of representation reveals the hostility of political parties to women in politics across ethnicities. After the initial strides of Tamil women into public office, Tamil men emboldened by the possibility of leveraging electoral victories in the North, have eased out the women.

Militarization, Security, and Violent Peace

Increasingly, women's efforts at peacebuilding in South Asia are coming up against the long-term effects of entrenched and expansive militarization in the region and the corrosion of access to justice and fundamental freedoms. How should women's rights activists respond to peace kept at gun point, that is, militarization of peace as in Sri Lanka and Kashmir? The morphing of hard militarization in post-war societies into "soft militarization" is normalizing militarization in peacetime as evidenced in the increasing penetration of the military into civilian, economic, and governance sectors in Bangladesh and Sri Lanka.

Militarization gets normalized when emergency laws that suspended fundamental rights in these "zones of exception" get incorporated into post-war—post-conflict legal regimes. Values and practices of militarization get routinized when in Jammu & Kashmir (J&K) local residents, driving past miles of permanent camps of security forces through the border district of Rajouri barely notice the slogan painted on the walls *ajeet hain, abheet hain!* (we are victorious, we are invincible), let alone question—victory over whom: their own citizens! (Women's Regional Network 2014: 31).

The use of new tools of militarization—surveillance technologies—is making for securitized societies with gendered consequences, especially for women's security, their livelihood options, welfare needs, and the social networks on which they depend. In post-war Sri Lanka, women embedded in the country's unresolved contradiction of two antagonistic ethnonationalist ideologies are under pressure to conform to gendered ethnocultural ideals. Accordingly, women have stepped back into even more domesticated spheres, grounded on identities such as the ideals of "[…] a good women, the nation of the good women, the patriotic women." (De Mel interviewed by Hernández-Reyna 2013: 56).

The ascendancy of extremist forces has created an ambivalent context for women, where they reject the strictures on their conduct imposed by misogynistic extremists but are desperate to protect their families and their communities from polarization and threat. Women peacebuilders are caught between the rising tide of extremism in their communities, and the constraints placed upon their work by counter-terrorism policies (UN Women 2015a:14). Women's rights activists are confronting strategies that instrumentalize women in the fight against extremists, and render them more vulnerable when "protectors" exit as in Afghanistan?

In the post-9/11 decade, women's rights groups in Pakistan were confronting a post-secularist lobby that valorizes a "different" kind of equality (nonliberal and non "Western"), and conflates with discredited western values, the possibility of "Muslim women being allowed to step out of their infantilized marital roles and pietist desires and be recognized as equal citizens" (Shehrbano 2015). While all sections of society are affected by the expanding sites and forms of militarization, the impact on women and their lives is disproportionate, given that militarism and patriarchy are conjoined ideological systems. Moreover, structurally entrenched gender inequalities in South Asian societies render women particularly vulnerable. The female body, in the name of protecting the "honor" of our women (and violating the honor of the other), becomes the front on which war is waged. In India, the hysteria around the myth of *love jihad* (the seduction of Hindu women by Muslim men) ignited the Muzaffarnagar (2014) communal violence including the sexualized attack on the Muslim women there.

How should women's collectivities confront the post-conflict, political economy of violence which as in the CHT targets women's vulnerability (through arson and sexualized violence) for land grabbing and forcible displacement, putting at risk lives, livelihoods and inhibiting women's agency? Should gender-equality activists promote jobs for women's in the militaries or resist it as expanding the militarization of society in India, Nepal, and Sri Lanka? How can feminist peace activists be strengthened in their work in reimagining an alternative discourse to war and militarism?

Justice, Reconciliation, and Reparations

The transition to a "post-conflict" situation hinges upon demilitarization and power sharing and crucially, truth, justice, and reconciliation for healing war-scarred societies, fighting impunity and reestablishing the rule of law and governance. In South Asia, transitional justice (TJ) mechanisms have got embedded in the tools of peacemaking in the region but "reconciliation" has overwhelmed truth, justice, and reparations. Perpetrators who continue to control the institutions of power decree blanket amnesties. In Nepal, TJ mechanisms are being used by political actors to shield those who were responsible for serious violations and not to account for past crimes, except to say that "reconciliation" must happen between communities.

In Sri Lanka, reconciliation has been overtaken by the focus on recovery and the material "reconstruction" of the war-torn infrastructure of the northern and eastern regions, with little attention to the social issues and gendered dimensions (ICAN 2013: 5) of problems facing local populations. A survey by the Jaffna-based Center for Women and Development estimates that there are in total 40,000 female-headed households (FHH) and 20,000 of them in Jaffna district alone (cited in ICAN 2013: 5). But the post-war reconstruction process has been directed at traditional family units with the assumption that there is a male head of household and decision-maker. There has neither been any attention to FHH nor to the fact that women's and men's needs, concerns, and skills may vary significantly.

Six years after the war ended, Sri Lanka's experiments with state managed TJ mechanisms via "Commissions of Inquiry" have failed to bring closure to the violent past in a deeply divided and unequal society. The aspiration to "move on" trips over the anguished need for truth and justice; and inhibits women's groups across regional and ethnic fault lines to work together to protect rights across ethnic regions and collectively heal (Hernández-Reyna 2013: 44). In Bangladesh, the government's institution of a War Crimes Tribunal (2010–) 40 years after the 1971 Liberation War, and the popular support for justice articulated in the Shabagh Movement, is a sharp reminder of the necessity of retributive justice for closure, but equally it is a reminder of the socially disrupting consequences of holding a Tribunal in a deeply polarized polity.

In Nepal and Afghanistan women's groups, human rights collectivities and victims groups are up against amnesties positioned as a deal breaker in political settlements. The May 2016 power deal struck between political actors in Kathmandu assures general amnesty to Maoist leaders and cadres accused of human rights violations. Victims are being forced to give us justice for a dubious reconciliation as part of the truth reconciliation (TR) process. When the state protector is the predator, from whom do women demand justice? Sexual violence is exempted from amnesty but the statute of limitation of 35 days for reporting war-time rape is a cruel joke.

Lofty normative frameworks commit the international community to hold accountable perpetrators of grave crimes against women through criminal justice proceedings, and to exclude amnesties especially for sexual violence. What difference has it made for survivors to access justice and reparations and to deter gender-based sexualized violence? The evidence from South Asia is distressing. Special security laws such as Armed Forces Special Powers Act[2] (AFSPA) in India have entrenched a socio-legal culture of impunity, resulting in denial of justice, social stigma, and economic distress. In the last 54 years, not a single member of the army or paramilitary has been prosecuted[3] for murder, rape, or destruction of property except in some rare instances, when under the Army Act, a court martial has been conducted (Verma Committee Report 2013).

The culture of impunity for crimes against women has lowered the social threshold for violence and sexualized abuse of women. While still a child you can be shot in the head or blown up by a mine on the way to school. Reproductive rights can be violated by extremist diktats and gendered insecurities can curb access to school, livelihood, and public office. UN Human Rights Council reports continue to raise concern on the increasing incidence of violence with impunity against girls/women as a common feature of transitional and "post-war" societies (OHCHR 2015).

Justice mechanisms, including truth and justice processes remain gender-insensitive to women's priorities. Navanethan Pillay, the UN Human Rights Commissioner had warned: "Experience shows that in most transitional justice scenarios there is a chronic problem of gender inequality and systemic discrimination against women" (2009). TJ mechanisms in Bangladesh, Nepal, and Sri Lanka reflect these persisting gender gaps, especially in understanding "what is justice" for women. It is both contextual and gendered, a Nepali woman activist emphasized, "just offering justice and punishment for the perpetrators is not enough, as many women want reparation and rehabilitation, without which they won't come forward" (UN Women 2015a:109).

These above concerns, perspectives, and questions were voiced by the region's women politicians, scholar–activists, gender-equality campaigners, women peace mentors, human rights defenders, and women political leaders at a series of regional conclaves in Kathmandu (2013), Delhi (2014), and Kathmandu (2015). Women focused on the changing dynamics of the multiple threats to peace and security and its consequences for redefining the women, peace, and security (WPS) discourse in the region. These regional conversations were opportunities to audit our states' implementation of UN Security Council Resolution 1325 (2000) which magisterially established the relevance and value of linking WPS. It was an exercise in transnational feminist solidarity.

The intensity and richness of transnational experiential sharing and knowledge production provided the impetus and organizing framework for this South Asian volume. Also, the logic behind driving the book project was that in the UN Women compendium Sourcebook and Handbook, missing from the evidence-based global mapping of WPS were the experiences of the women of a region where a third of the world's women live (UN Women 2012b). Additionally, the region has some of the worst gender indicators in the world.[4] Feminist scholars have pointed to the crucial linkage between women's low social status and gendered vulnerabilities, that is, the continuum of the "the mundanity of rightlessness" pre-conflict, conflict, and post-conflict (Pereira in Hossain and Mohsin (edited), Zubaan 2016).

Thinking Regionally: Working Across Borders

Many of the challenges facing the South Asian countries are common. The opportunities for strategic intervention predicate working regionally, sharing lessons learned, exchanging good practices, recognizing centres of excellence, setting common standards, developing model regional accountability indicators and mechanism.

Anne Stenhammer, UN Women, Kathmandu 2013

Underpinning these regional conclaves and indeed the book project was the understanding that women across South Asia share a struggle with decades of interstate and intrastate conflicts, the roots and consequences of which increasingly connect the region's diverse histories and societies. They confront a common pattern of gendered vulnerability and opportunity rooted in the low status of women in the region, though the contingent situation will be different. The future stability of the region reflects the regions interconnectedness. For instance, the Afghanistan transition post-2014 directly affects "peace" and democratic rights in all the neighboring countries. Peace in the region is contingent upon curbing the competition and confrontation of regional (and global) hegemons and abandoning the self-destructive strategy of using proxy armed groups.

Deficits of governance, development, and democracy have produced conditions for extremists to spread violence within and across national boundaries. Self-serving elites, weak governance institutions, and the contagion of the socio-legal culture of impunity has unleashed vigilante violence targeting secularists, dissenters, human rights defenders, minorities, and women who dare to "step out." Women across the region voiced their anxiety at the transnational contagion of ascendant extremist ideologies and the growing culture of intolerance, violent vigilantism, and nonaccountability.

What is striking at these cross-border dialogues is the effulgent experience of transnational solidarities in confronting shared crisis. For instance in Kathmandu (2013), there was a crisp indictment of geostrategic global interests which exacerbated tensions and produced conditions for extremists to create division and conflict in the region. But equally, women were critical of the destabilizing activities of their own and neighboring states and alluded to the historical and contemporary dynamics of the production of political violence and war atrocities, for example, Pakistan: "East Pakistan"/Bangladesh 1971 war; India: Sri Lanka 1987; Pakistan: Kashmir/India; and the Pakistan: Afghanistan: India triangle of cooperation and confrontation.

Women introspected on what should be their responsibility vis-à-vis their state's hegemonic activities in destabilizing neighboring states, especially when such actions have direct implications for the rights of women with whom we avow solidarity? A benchmark in "herstory" of women's peace activism, in this volume, is the symbolic significance of Pakistani women apologizing for the war crimes perpetrated by Pakistan soldiers on Bangladeshi women. Pakistan Government has not apologized, although the established war narrative of the 1971 war is being challenged by military voices in Pakistan exposing the army's role in systemic and widespread use of sexual torture and forced pregnancy.[5]

Myriad initiatives at cross-border peacebuilding and democracy building activities have shown the importance and value of regional thinking and regional strategizing. Institutional initiatives such as SAARC may be flaccid, but as the quintessential regionalist Tapan Bose remarked, "the regional identity of South Asia is not state driven but people driven. The task is to push our national security states to transform themselves to respond to people's needs. Here women's movements have been amongst the strongest in transforming state and society relations" (SA Women's Conference 2013). More recently, cross-border gender-accountability initiatives got a new impetus with women's groups using the Convention on Elimination of Violence Against Women (CEDAW) reporting mechanism to demand accountability for India violating Sri Lankan[6] and Nepali women's rights.[7]

Three of the region's leading women peace activists Goswami, Khan, and Samuel in mapping "herstory" of the region's WPS narrative in this volume, posit that the range of cross-border networks of women's peace activism and especially the interventions of the region's leading peace women, have created sufficient momentum to produce a South Asian women's peace movement and a recognizable regional WPS discourse. An important caveat is added by a Pakistan feminist scholar Nighat Khan, reminding us of the divisions among women's groups and indeed against homogenizing women and privileging women as a category. "We need to recognize that women have multiple identities and at what point their identity as a woman is privileged over the religious, caste or other identities issues" (UN Women SA Conference 2013).

UNSCR 1325 and WPS Agenda in South Asia

The advocacy work of South Asian women's groups has been an integral part of the global mobilizations that resulted in the historic advances for women's human rights as reflected in the successes of the women's treaty CEDAW, World Human Rights Conference, the World Conferences on Women, including the Beijing Platform for Action (BPFA) which identified "women and armed conflict" as one of the 12 critical areas of concern. Five years later, the UN Security Council gave formal recognition to the linkage between WPS by adopting UN Security Council Resolution 1325 in 2000.[8]

The narratives of production of UNSC 1325, as Laura Shepherd deconstructs, arise from the two sites of power (institutions) which claim authority over the adoption of Resolution–Security Council and the NGO Working Group on Peace and Security 2000 (Tryggestad 2009: 396).[9] These two narratives derived from the women peace and security discourse are competitive; one is state centric, militarist and masculine, and at home in the UN Security Council, the other is socially transformative, emphasizing the participation of women in prevention, rebuilding and recovery. But the dominant logic in the two discourses of gender peace and security is compatible, for implicit in the image of war-torn societies being rebuilt is the global neoliberal governance agenda that converges with the concepts of state and sovereignty emerging from the UNSC. Shepherd, importantly, reminds that NGO activity at the global level was dominated by the industrialized countries situated in the zones of peace, a domination that has choked the production of alternative narratives in the zones of conflict.

This edited volume from the zones of conflict in South Asia realigns the WPS discourse closer to the global south as indeed does the UN Women "Global Study" (2015a). In documenting the region's narrative of the production of the WPS discourse, Chapter 3 "herstory" argues that from the outset there was a disconnect between the discursive trajectories of (a) the global south women's rights movements and (b) the coalition of transnational advocacy networks of women and human rights groups. That coalition drove the WPS agenda in the all-boys club, the Security Council (Tryggestad 2009).

Goswami, Khan, and Samuel allude to their diffidence about the campaign of some "northern NGOs" to have a WPS resolution adopted by the Security Council, an exclusivist forum with an "unfortunate history" of punitive military interventions targeting the "underdog." The preference was for the more inclusive General Assembly resolution or incorporation in the CEDAW mechanism. The authors contend that the trajectory of the WPS resolutions was diverging from the women's rights and the social-equality agenda. Significantly, 1325 and its affiliate WPS resolutions 1820, 1880, and 1889 do not invoke the CEDAW framework of substantive-equality. "Of the 988 resolutions since the year 2000, when the Council took up the WPS agenda, only 10 resolutions mention CEDAW" (Asling Swaine cited by Leslie Davis in GIWPS 2016).

Housed in the Security Council, the WPS resolutions gain on symbolic importance but lose on ownership. Attention to the WPS agenda in the Council depends upon committed individuals in members states and the UN Secretariat. The NGO–Working Group in mapping WPS in the Security Council in 2013–14 concluded that the Security Council has "not truly internalized the WPS agenda. When considering crisis situations (post-electoral violence, spurt in violence against civilians) in countries that have peacekeeping or political mandates it rarely addresses WPS concerns, despite its consideration of WPS in its regular discussions on these countries."

The tension between the two trajectories of WPS & CEDAW burst into the open at the Kathmandu meeting of the Asia-Pacific Women's

Alliance on Peace and Security (APWAPS) when the women exhorted Coomaraswamy, helming the Global Study on UNSCR 1325 (UN Women 2015a), to guard against 1325 becoming "more a management tool of making wars and conflicts safe for women rather than addressing the root causes and politics of wars and conflicts."[10]

These divergences in perspective contribute to the limited impact of the WPS resolutions in the region and its value to civil society for promoting peace with women. Indeed, the gendered and disproportionate impact of conflict on the lives of the region's women remains largely overlooked by national and international policymakers in the region. UNSCR 1325 has had little influence in protecting or promoting women as key drivers in peacebuilding (Paffenholz, Potter, and Buchanan 2015). Women, as a social group, have been marginalized in peace processes of the region, for example, CHT, Northeast India SWAT & FATA: Pakistan, as well as internationally facilitated and monitored ones: Sri Lanka, Nepal, and Afghanistan (Bell and O'Rourke 2010).

The governments of India, Pakistan, and Sri Lanka are wary of mechanisms that trail international accountability for human rights, including women's rights, in internal conflicts. For example, India supports 1325 but denies the existence of internal "armed conflicts," and the relevance of 1325 to "disturbed" areas of the Northeast and J&K.[11] Even in instances where some gender-active policymakers have slipped into the country's five year plans, references to the special concerns of "women in disturbed areas" and explicitly called for gender review of AFSPA, neither 1325 nor any other international mechanism is invoked as a norm (India Planning Commission Five Year Plans: XI 2005–11& XII 2012–17, 54–56). In India's expanding overseas assistance when claims are made on gender inclusiveness (e.g., Sri Lanka–India Housing Project), there is no reference to the international benchmark—CEDAW or 1325 (Manchanda 2015).

In Nepal's internationalized peace process, the framework of 1325+ has proved more influential (Banerjee et al. 2010). Nepal adopted a National Action Plan (NAP) on 1325 and 1820, and as leading women's rights advocate Bandana Rana emphasized the international profile of 1325 helped them leverage the support of key ministries and include 75 women in the NAP Steering Committee. However, as with other country experiences, Nepal's NAP is "napping" as the new political forces in control have little stake in earlier commitments (Buchanan et al. 2012).

In Afghanistan, another internationalized peace process, protecting and promoting Afghan women's rights in post-war Afghanistan was a mantra but it was not till 2009 that NATO took on a gender advisor. Ten years into the peace process, Afghanistan began discussions on a 1325 NAP driven by the INGO Inclusive Security. In 2015, Afghanistan adopted a NAP on 1325. On NAP's effectiveness, Afghan Women's Network assessment is bleak (Karlidag 2014). The resurgence of the Taliban and the international community's quit strategy has not only deprioritized women's rights, but produced a willingness to barter rights for a "peace" deal. Disillusionment over the ineffectiveness of 1325 is reflected in Sima Samar, ex-Minister Women's Affairs, comments, "It recognizes us (women) but it doesn't include us."

In South Asia, "it is our own initiatives and movement building in the region that gives us our energy and provides more solace than the UN," asserted Hina Jilani, the former UN Special Rapporteur. "Let us build on 1325. Whatever you have on hand you use to your advantage. But it cannot be the center of our focus." Echoing this ambivalence, Sheba George, a human rights defender working with anti-Muslim pogrom survivors was blunt,

> In Gujarat, every national machinery and international mechanism was harnessed. An incredible number of feminists, human rights experts and activists made representations before a host of national and international fora including CEDAW committee. Yet it was mostly through the Court that truth was established and justice rendered to the extent possible. (SA Women's Conference Report 2013)

In contrast, the adoption of CEDAW GR 30 (CEDAW General Recommendation 30, 2013) was welcomed by women's groups in the region as a "game changer." Importantly, GR 30 defines "conflict" as spanning foreign occupation to communal violence, its analysis stresses structural inequalities and unlike 1325, the treaty body has an accountability mechanism. Even before GR 30, women's groups in India have used the CEDAW (North East Network 2008) reporting mechanism to leverage international accountability on sexual gender-based violence

(SGBV) in the Gujarat massacre, and AFSPA in the conflict troubled Northeast (CEDAW 2014; Hazarika 2014: 175).

Women's groups have used the available opportunities[12] to leverage international mechanisms to establish state accountability for women's rights in conflict and peacebuilding. It is worth remembering that CEDAW, 1325, and BPFA have large and sustained civil society constituencies as was evidenced during the Beijing +20 civil society review (UN Women 2014). In Nepal, as Mandira Sharma in this volume highlights, human rights organizations brought in vetting measures by lobbying the Department of UN Peacekeeping Operations to recall UN peacekeepers accused of human rights violations in Nepal. Human rights defenders have invoked the Rome statute (International Criminal Court) to indict rape as a "war crime" and a "crime against humanity" in informal and formal systems of justice. Sexualized violence in the 1971 war played a key role in the provenance of the international legal discourse on rape as a weapon of war.

Book's Vision, Structure, and Methodology

The essays in this volume are held together by the vision of women as equal citizens determined to be part of processes that control their life chances, and build a transformative peace reworking unequal relations. As Afghanistan's Human Rights Commissioner Sima Samar reminded the community of women and men in Delhi (2014), "during 35 years of war Afghan women because they weren't carrying guns were voiceless and forgotten, peace will be possible when women are seen not as part of the problem but the solution."

The edited volume is designed to bring together the region's experiences and feminist expertise and to tease out the particularities of a complex South Asian WPS discourse. Giving coherence to this collection of spatially diverse and varied experiences is the argument that there is a recognizable South Asian WPS discourse derived from the specific complexities of the region's context of colonialism, caste, ethnicity, religions, and gender and shaped by the perspectives, and peace work of the local women in the region. By foregrounding the region's experiences and analytical expertise, the book seeks to bridge a critical gap in the global discourse.

The South Asian landscape of war and peacebuilding is both internationalized, that is, Afghanistan, Nepal, (and Sri Lanka 2002–05) and local and national, that is, India, Bangladesh, and Pakistan. This provides opportunities for rare comparative analysis and comparative assessment of the effectiveness of leveraging WPS resolutions. The book builds upon the region's rich stream of feminist scholarship on women, war, and peace narratives in a context of nation and state building struggles. It builds a longitudinal analysis of peace politics, to interrogate settled assumptions in view of the changing dynamics of militarization, violent peace, and persisting impunity.

The volume represents a leap forward in the scholarly research and policy analysis of WPS by its focus on the aftermath moment of the conflict cycle, of post-war/post-conflict transitions in the region. The common aftermath experience of elusive even violent peace challenges lazy assumptions about the notion of "post-conflict" and posits the continuum of pre-conflict of conflict and post-conflict situations.

In mapping a South Asian scape on the logic of a regional coherence in the community of experiences and policies, the volume challenges our partitioned academies that have dictated country-specific analysis. The book's argument of a SA–WPS discourse is a significant contribution to the body of knowledge.

Diversity and Disparity of Styles

Few scholars in the region have cross-border expertise on conflicts and peacebuilding and to distill comparative and conceptual theorizing. It remains an underdeveloped research field. The compromise was a thematic overview chapter which in broad strokes unpacks the dynamics of the theme knitting together the varied country experiences and analytically teasing out theory. Brief field notes and participant's analysis follow which focus on the country context.

The design melds scholarly with participatory analysis. The macro level overview of the theme is written by an eminent scholar and expert in the field. For the field notes and participant analysis, I reached out to some established scholars, but importantly, a new generation of writers, including human rights defenders, judges, and politicians from conflict-affected areas. Evidently, the design predicates disparity in style of presentation. The gain is in authenticity of voice by having former judge and development practitioner Judge Najla Ayubi, human rights defender Huma Safi, educationist Noreen Naseer, and coordinator of The International CHT Commission Hana Shams Ahmed, speak for themselves.

There is also the singularity of "herstory", derived from a conversation among three women who inspired and gave intellectual direction to women's peace movements, and challenged "peacebuilding as an apolitical engagement and to use (sic) peacebuilding as a transformative agenda that questions both the patriarchal nature of states as well as the patriarchal development paradigms set in motion in post conflict reconstruction" (UN Women S-SARO Regional Open Day 2011). It is a personalized recalling of moments and remembering of "friends" met on myriad pathways that converged to produce a South Asian WPS discourse.

Arguably, we will have to wait for a comprehensive analytical narrative of the making of the South Asian women and peace architecture, but "herstory" identifies the signposts on the way and whets our appetite to explore the contribution made by South Asia's peace women in shaping the global, regional, and local WPS discourse. What makes for the "particularity" of the region's peace activism? First generation feminist scholar–activist Kumari Jayawardene suggested that the robustness of the region's movements for women's rights and peace lies in its close linkages with grassroots struggles for socioeconomic justice and equal rights (Jayawardene 1986). Three decades later, feminist peace activist Kumudini Samuel in mapping what are the possible contours of peacemaking in the current imbalance of political and military power in Sri Lanka, singles out the value of the interconnectedness of women's peacework with issues of structural injustice and armed conflict in coalition building across different identity belongings. Such a coalition across ethnic fault lines would leverage not "shared oppression" but "citizenship rights and demanding a stake in determining post war development strategies…"

Themes

The book is organized around three themes: (a) women's political participation in building a transformative peace, (b) militarization, security, and violent peace, and (c) justice, reconciliation, and reparations. These are interlinked themes. Continuing militarization, the casual and routineness of political violence has implications for women's security and freedom of movement, constraining women's life enhancing access to education, livelihood, and participation in public life. The persistence of a political economy of violence and a culture of impunity pushes women back into restricted gendered roles. Several essays grouped under militarization should be read with an eye on women's participation such as Anuradha Bhasin Jamwal's essay which discusses the complexity of women negotiating personal and public roles in militarized Kashmir.

Women's Political Participation in Building a Transformative Peace

This thematic segment plays out against the backdrop of the crisis of solutions proposed to end conflict, and the post-conflict political economy of violence that disempowers women, despite their being vaulted into public space during conflict and its aftermath. Invariably, the gatekeepers to the "peace table" give entry to those who have an army, represent a political party, or political community. As a recent study noted, "as the power related reasons for women's inclusion are not there; so the women are not there, if they do not lobby for their inclusion" (Paffenholz et al. 2015: 4).[13] Such a strategic emphasis on one structural change—women's participation assumes women participate as "women." It is a problematic assumption. For instance, Maoist women in India and Nepal deprioritize tackling patriarchy in their political party and oppose affirmative action, identifying with the movement's political ideology.

Swarna Rajagopalan sets the frame through a broad mapping of four-country post-conflict transitions and the struggle to leverage the peace momentum and promote women's meaningful participation in the patriarchal bastion of public affairs. Drawing a continuum between conflict and post-conflict, and "apart from conflict" situations, Swarna reflexively identifies the promoters and inhibiters to women's political participation and provides insights on the comparative effectiveness of gender quotas, but is skeptical of state interventions, pulling down the walls of patriarchal attitudes. Rita Manchanda, in a complementary chapter, explores the scope and gendered dynamics of women's participation in peace processes and peacebuilding and examines how and why peace politics are empowering and disempowering building on a five-country analysis. In an ironic tease, in the section, Gendered Perspectives on "Why I am afraid of peace!" she examines the paradox of peace women opposing peace processes that are likely to deliver a violent peace.

Bringing in a "Participant Analysis" perspective is Goswami, Khan, and Samuel's essay, "herstory" on the contribution of the region's peace women to realigning the global WPS discourse of peace with social justice. Kumudini Samuel, a member of the region's sole gender consultative mechanism in a peace process (Sri Lanka 2002–03), in an essay encapsulating 30 years of peace activism in Sri Lanka, reflects on the prescience of the Liberation Tigers of Tamil Eelam (LTTE) women in insisting upon gender quotas in the face of the setbacks women encounter in politics.

Militarization, Security, and Violent Peace

This section tracks women's experiences of militarization through the conflict—peace cycle—"Transition" in Afghanistan, ceasefire-pacification hiatus in Kashmir, "post-war" in Sri Lanka and "post-peace accord" in Nepal, Bangladesh, and Northeast India. The peace delivered is more akin to internal domination. Military strength is rarely downsized, but as Anuradha Chenoy (2002), the region's leading scholar on women and militarization in the region examines, militarization morphs its forms, and shifts its sites. "This heavy securitization is felt differently by women who are at risk of being sexualized subjects and targets of control." Unpacking the relationship of patriarchy and militarism as mutually reinforcing ideologies, Anuradha emphasizes that militarization constructs a particularly aggressive and homogenized form of masculinity and power that spills over into public spaces and impacts social relations in the intersection of conflict–post-conflict. Demilitarization is necessary to end violence against women, she argues.

In the clutch of field notes, Bhasin–Jamwal's essay on Kashmir joins issue with the global discourse on women and extremist movements, and warns of women's vulnerability to being instrumentalized by both extremist ideologues and security forces as they become "easy targets for both sides for co-option as informers and spies." Sri Lankan academic, Neloufer de Mel unravels "soft" militarization in the conflict-affected zones in North, six years after the military defeat of the LTTE. The government's hi-tech strategy of digital surveillance for managing "risks" to the nation-state, particularly focuses on the rehabilitated LTTE women who remain under intense surveillance and are socially ostracized. The indifference to gendering disarmament, demobilization, and reintegration (DDR) programs, including in internationally monitored peace processes is stark in Nepal where the majority of the Maoist women cadres have fallen through the cracks of gender blind rehabilitation programs as Upreti and Shreshta analyze.

The failure to seriously address demilitarization and demobilization processes for reasons of political expediency has entrenched post-conflict political economies of violence in India's Northeast, Afghanistan, and the CHT producing increased criminality and less controlled violence. In Afghanistan, Huma Safi confronting a deteriorated security and human rights situation blames the policy choices of the international community and the Afghan Government of appeasing warlords and working through irresponsible armed groups affiliated to warlords and jihadi-parties, many of whom enjoy the overt and covert support of governmental agencies and the international community.

Justice, Reconciliation and Reparations

In the liberal peacebuilding template, the focus is on TJ mechanisms to address human rights crimes, to bridge the gap in the breakdown of the legal system, and to redress discriminatory laws. As the UN Human Rights Council Report on Sri Lanka bluntly said, "years of denials and cover-ups" mean that the Sri Lankan system is "not yet ready to handle these types of crime" (OHCHR 2015). TJ is not without its critics and various TR mechanisms in the region are mired in controversy over slipping up on a minimum standard for TJ, balancing truth telling with retributive justice, and confronting the struggle of memory against forgetting with the pressure to "move on."

Warisha Farasat, a former practitioner of TJ with the Centre for International Transitional Justice in Nepal, in her lead essay mapping TJ initiatives explores the contradictory and competing pulls inherent in the South Asian praxis of TJ. The victims perceive TJ as delivering truth justice and reparations to them, while the political class does not see it in its interest to hold itself accountable. Within this overall contradiction is the gender gap, for while there have been advances in international jurisprudence setting, implementation remains weak. UN Human Rights Commissioner, Navinethan Pillay in anguish observed, "A gender and women's human rights perspectives are vindicated when perpetrators of sexual violence are brought to account." The field notes in this volume and elsewhere (Zubaan-IDRC Sexual Violence and Impunity Papers 2016; UN SG Report on Conflict Related Sexual Violence 2015) document that sexual violence in conflict and the aftermath is a widespread routine and even systematic; silence on sexual violence persists on the part of community and state, and there is a systematic lack of accountability of perpetrators.[14] Exceptional but heartening is the Jaffna High Court's judgement (2015) sentencing four soldiers to 25 years imprisonment who were found guilty of gang rape of a Tamil woman in a Kilinochchi resettlement camp in 2010.

In India, some advances have been made in jurisprudence and in amendments to the rape law (2013), such as inclusion of armed forces under the category of aggravated sexual assault category but the effect of AFSPA coupled with the Army Act (1950) has ensured impunity for widespread sexual violence. Consequently, in Kashmir, out of the 25 cases of sexual assault since 1990, partial legal process was possible only in two cases—Konan Poshpora mass rape (1990; Mushtaq et al. 2015) and the Shopian double rape (2009; International People's Tribunal on Human Rights and Justice in Indian-administered Kashmir 2009). Evidence-based research is establishing that unless the culture of impunity against SGBV is uprooted, the social deterrent against such crimes carries over to post-conflict societies. Jamwal's field analysis shows that in Kashmir, military and militancy have spawned a social culture of violence evidenced in rising domestic violence and incest. Najla Ayubi in "No peace, without justice" argues that the impunity with which women have been killed, kidnapped, and publicly harassed by armed groups and the failure of the official justice institutions to investigate these cases has made women much more vulnerable to violence.

Amnesties have subverted the possibility of establishing rule of law. In Afghanistan, the AIHRC's "Call for Justice" (2005) was foreclosed by the adoption of the Peace and Reconciliation law which offered blanket amnesty. Anjum Ara Begum, a legal activist from India's

Northeast decried the offer of amnesty to armed groups as part of ceasefire agreements. "The victims of human rights violations, a majority of whom are women, have not been consulted about these amnesties, let alone about broader plans for transitional justice…" (SA Women's Conference 2014).

Nepal's accountability commissions trail an amnesty clause (but exempt sexual crimes).[15] However, as legal advocacy campaigner Mandira Sharma reveals the TRC process has been used as an alibi to evade due process of law by Maoists and Nepal army and police. Nepali civil society has used parallel justice initiatives—such as UN Treaty special procedures to file cases of sexual war crime in the UN Human Rights Council and so on. Impunity persists in Bangladesh through erasure of memory. Academic Dina Siddiqi focuses on the Kalpana Chakma disappearance case as symbolic of gender-based human rights crimes of the Bangladesh army against the "other," the CHT hill people and analyzes the Bengali ethnic state's subtle strategy of systematically erasing her disappearance and even that of her military abductor from political memory.

This book is testimony to the value of women's peacemaking and to their democratic right to seize peacebuilding as an opportunity for building a just and inclusive society. Importantly, the volume is a product of feminist researchers redefining militarization, security, peace, and justice. It intervenes at a critical cusp in the region's dynamics and the reshaping of the international peace and security order.

Notes

1. Peace talks initiated in July 2015 by Afghanistan's Ashraf Ghani government with Taliban representatives in Pakistan, and backed this time by the country's powerful military have run aground as a result of the power struggle within the Taliban and renewed offensive. The road to peace with the Taliban is strewn with deadly mines as former Afghanistan President Karzai learnt in efforts at talking peace to Taliban leaders since 2012. Across the border, Pakistan President Nawaz Sharif since taking over power in 2014 extended overtures to the *Tehiriqi Taliban*, Pakistan till its devastating attack on Karachi airport precipitated the launch of *Zarb-e-Azb* military operation to eliminate all terrorists.

2. The Armed Forces (Special Powers) Act (AFSPA), (1958) grants special powers in what are termed "disturbed areas." It was introduced as a legally enabling framework for the army and para-military forces to combat insurgency in Nagaland

and since has been extended to the Northeast and J&K. The fourth and sixth sections of the Act ensure no criminal prosecution against any person who has taken action under this act without prior sanction, including sexual violence.

3. In response to an RTI filed by Khurram Parvez, coordinator of J&K Coalition of Civil Society, the J&K Home Department replied: "no sanction for prosecution has been intimated by the Ministry of Home Affairs and Ministry of Defense to the State Government from 1990–2011 under the J&K Armed Forces Special Powers Act." See Home/RTI/15/2012/1213.

4. See also UNDP Gender Inequality Index; World Economic Forum Global Gender Gap.

5. Major General Khadim Hussain Raja (2012) "*A Stranger in My Own Country: East Pakistan, 1969–1971* cited by Khalid Ahmed in Military voices now challenge the established narrative of the Bangladesh war in *Indian Express*, January 9, 2014.

6. The CEDAW Committee in its "Concluding Observations" urged an immediate review of India's housing project in Sri Lanka.

7. Nepal and Indian civil society networks invoked extraterritorial obligations in the context of the Laxmanpur Dam on the India–Nepal border. The CEDAW Committee urged GOI to redress concerns about displacement, loss of livelihood, housing, and food insecurity (FIAN 2013).

8. UNSC resolutions 1325 has been followed by a succession of WPS resolutions 1820 (2008), 1888 (2009), 1889 (2009), 1960 (2010), 2106 (2013), 2022 (2013), and 2242 (2015).

9. NGO Working Group in 2000 comprised Hague Appeal for Peace, Women's International League for Peace and freedom, International Alert Amnesty International, Women's Commission for Refugee Women and Children.

10. AWAPS Recommendations to the Global Study on Implementation of UNSC 1325, Kathmandu April 2015.

11. Indian Government has been hostile to women's groups from the Northeast raising AFSPA with the CEDAW committee and other international for India's Ambassador to the UN, Hardeep Puri's strongly protest against the inclusion of India's Naxal-affected areas under the rubric of "armed conflict" in the 2010 *Report on Children in Armed Conflict* (*The Times of India* 2010).

12. For example, women's groups in India cutting across region, ethnicity, caste, and class came together in the Wing initiative (2010) in the context of UN SC 1325 to discuss women confronting militarized situations, gender-repressive customary laws, social discriminatory structures, and violence. In Pakistan, in May 2010, the Women's Parliamentary Caucus enabled the holding of a National Convention of Women Parliamentarians on the "Role of Women in Peace, Security and Reconciliation."

13. UN Women estimated in 2012 that women comprised 4 percent of signatories, 2.4 percent of chief mediators, 3.7 percent of witnesses, and 9 percent of negotiators between 1992–2011. See UN Women (2012).

14. Justice was possible in the Bilkis Bano rape case and in the successful prosecution of Gujarat's former state Minister Maya Kodnani in the Naroda Patia case for incitement to riot, rape, and massacre. Ten years later in the Kandhamal communal assaults, out of the 41 cases of sexual assault and abuse, only the case

of Sr Meena was justice possible and largely due to sustained campaigns by human rights defenders.

15. See HR Commissioner Navi Pillay's critical comments on amnesties comments. Accessed December 19, 2016, http://www.ohchr.org/EN/NewsEvents/Pages/DisplayNews.aspx?NewsID=14510&LangID=E

Bibliography

Banerjee, Paula et al. 2010. *Women, Peace and Security Implementation of UN Security Council Resolution 1325 in the Context of Finnish Development Policy with case studies from Kenya, Nepal and North-East India.* Finland: Ministry for Foreign Affairs.

Bell, Christine, and Catherine O'Rourke. 2010. "Peace Agreements or Pieces of Paper? The Impact of UNSC Resolution 1325 on Peace Processes and Peace Agreements," *International Comparative Law Quarterly*, 59(4): (941–80).

Buchanan, Cate et al. 2012. "From Clause to Effect: Gender in Peace Agreements." *Centre for Humanitarian Dialogues.* Accessed December 24, 2016, http://www.hdcentre.org/uploads/tx_news/24ClausereportwebFINAL.pdf

CEDAW General Recommendation 30. 2013. *Women in Conflict Prevention, Conflict and Post Conflict.* Accessed November 30, 2016, http://www.ohchr.org/Documents/HRBodies/CEDAW/GComments/CEDAW.C.CG.30.pdf

CEDAW. 2014. *Concluding Observations on the Combined Fourth and Fifth Periodic Reports of India*, July 24 C/IND/CO/4-5. Accessed December 18, 2016, http://tbinternet.ohchr.org/Treaties/CEDAW/Shared%20Documents/1_Global/INT_CEDAW_SED_58_22164_E.pdf

Chenoy, Anuradha. 2002. *Militarisation and Women in South Asia.* New Delhi: Kali for Women.

Davis, Leslie. 2016. "Enhancing Accountability for Women, Peace & Security." *Georgetown Institute of Women Peace and Security.* Accessed November 30, 2016, http://blog.giwps.georgetown.edu/enhancing-accountability-for-women-peace-security/

Enloe, Cynthia. 2000. *Maneuvers the International Politics Militarising Women's Lives.* Berkeley, California: University of California Press.

FIAN. 2013. *Annual Report 2013*, accessed November 30, 2016, www.fian.org/fileadmin/media/publications/Publications_AR/FIAN_Annual_Report_2013_eng_web_rz.pdf

Francis, Diane. 2010. *From Pacification to Peacebuilding.* London: Pluto Press.

Government of India. 2012. "Twelfth Plan 2012–2017." *Social Sectors* III: 54–56. Accessed November 30, 2016, http://planningcommission.gov.in/plans/planrel/12thplan/pdf/12fyp_vol3.pdf

Hernández, Reyna S. 2013. *Reconciliation in Post-Conflict Sri Lanka: An Inside Perspective of War Affected Women* (Master's Thesis). Accessed November 30, 2016, https://www.academia.edu/8299516/Reconciliation_in_Post-Conflict_Sri_Lanka_An_Inside_Perspective_of_War_Affected_Women

Hazarika, A. et al. 2014. "GR30," in *India 4th–5th NGO Alternative Report on CEDAW* by NAWO, 160–184. New Delhi.

International People's Tribunal on Human Rights and Justice in Indian-administered Kashmir. 2009. *Militarisation with Impunity: A Brief on Murder & Rape in Shopian, Kashmir.* Accessed November 30, 2016, http://www.kashmirprocess.org/shopian

Kolas, Ashild. 2014. "Mothers and Activists in the Hills of Assam." *Economic & Political Weekly* XLIX (43–44): 41–48.

ICAN (International Civil Society Action Network). 2013. "Elusive Peace, Pervasive Violence: Sri Lankan Women's Struggle for Security and Justice." Issue Brief No. 8, Washington DC. Accessed December 16, 2016, http://www.icanpeacework. org/wp-content/uploads/2013/06/Slanka-final.pdf

Jayawardene, Kumari.1986. *Feminism and Nationalism in the Third World.* London: Zed Press.

Karlidag, Melika. 2014. *UN Security Council Resolution 1325 in Afghanistan: Civil Society Monitoring Report 2014.* Kabul: AWN. Accessed December 19, 2016, file:///C:/ Users/Rita/Downloads/1421230851UN%20Security%20Council%20 Resolution%201325%20in%20Afghanistan%20-%20November%2018,%20 2014.pdf

Manchanda, Rita. 2001. "Where are the Women in South Asian Conflicts," in *Women War and Peace in South Asia,* edited by Rita Manchanda, pp. 9–42. New Delhi: SAGE Publications.

———. 2015. *Expert Briefing on India and Gender Peace and Security.* London: SAFERWORLD.

Manchanda, Rita, and Tapan Bose. 2015. *Making War Making Peace: Conflict Resolution in South Asia.* New Delhi: SAGE Publications.

Meintjes Shiela, Meredith Thurshen and Anu Pillay. 2001. 'There is no Aftermath for Women', in *The Aftermath: Women in Post Conflict Transformation,* edited by Meintjes Shiela, Meredith Thurshen and Anu Pillay, pp. 3–17. London: Zed Press.

Mushtaq, Samreen et al. 2015. *Do You Remember Kunan Poshpora.* Delhi: Zubaan Books.

North East Network. 2008. "CEDAW: Concluding Comments of the Committee on Elimination of Discrimination against Women: India 37th session 15 Jan–2 Feb."

OHCHR. 2015. *Report of the OHCHR Investigation on Sri Lanka (OISL)A/HRC/30/ CRP.2.* Accessed December 18, 2016, www.ohchr.org/EN/HRBodies/HRC/ RegularSessions/.../A.HRC.30.CRP.2_E.docx

Paffenholz, Potter, and Buchanan. 2015. "Fresh Insights on the Quantity and Quality of Women's Participation in Peace Processes." Policy Brief May, CMI, Geneva.

Pereira, Fustina. 2016. "The Unbreakable Tedium of Rightlessness", in *Of The Nation Born, Zubaan Series on Sexual Violence and Impunity in South Asia,* edited by Hameeda Hossain and Amena Mohsin. Delhi: Zubaan.

Pratt, Nicola, and Richter-Devroe, Sophie. 2011. "Critically Examining UNSCR 1325 on Women, Peace and Security." *International Feminist Journal of Politics,* 13(4): 489–503.

Raja, Khadim Hussain. 2012. *A Stranger in My Own Country: East Pakistan, 1969–1971.* New Delhi: Indian Express.

Sajjad Hassan. *Survivors of Mass Communal Violence in Muzaffarnagar: Profiles of Loss, Dispossession, and Recovery.* A Report (unpublished) by Misaal and Centre for Equality Studies, New Delhi.

Samuel, Kumudini. 2010. *The Centrality of Gender in Securing Peace: The Case of Sri Lanka* (WISCOMP). Delhi: Rupa Publications.

Shepherd, Laura J. 2008. "Power and Authority in the Production of United Nations Security Council Resolution 1325." *International Studies Quarterly*, 52(2): 383–404.

Shehrbano, Afiya. 2015, August 04. "Is Pakistan Male?" *The News International*, (Pakistan).

South Asia Women's Conference. 2013. "The Changing Dynamics of Peace building in South Asia," Kathmandu, February 15–17. Conference Report edited by Anouhita Mojumdar. SAFHR/UN Women. Accessed December 19, 2016, www.safhr.org

Steinberg, Donald. 2010. "Beyond Words and Resolutions: An Agenda for UNSCR 1325." Accessed December 18, 2016, http://www.crisisgroup.org/en/publication-type/commentary/steinberg-beyond-words-and-resolutions-an-agenda-for-unscr-1325.aspx

Tryggestad, Torun. 2009. "Trick or Treat: The UN and Implementation of Security Council Resolution 1325 on Women Peace and Security PRIO." *Global Governance*, 15(4): 539–557.

The Times of India. 2010, June 19. "Naxal Problem not an Armed Conflict." Accessed December 18, 2016, http://timesofindia.indiatimes.com/india/Naxal-problem-not-an-armed-conflict-India-tells-UN/articleshow/6063604.cms

UN Secretary General. 2015. *Conflict Related Sexual Violence.* Report of the Secretary-General to Security Council, March 23, 2015, S/2015/203, p 33. Accessed December 19, 2016, http://www.un.org/en/sc/documents/sgreports/2015.shtml

UN Women S-SARO Regional Open Day. 2011, September 27–28. *Partnerships for Peace. Women's Perspective in Conflict Resolution, Peace Making and Peacebuilding in South Asia,* New Delhi: UN Women.

———. 2012a. *Women's Participation in Peace Negotiations: Connections between Presence and Influence* (2nd edition).

———. 2012b. *Sourcebook on Women Peace and Security.* New York. Accessed November 30, 2016, http://www.unwomen.org/ru/digital-library/publications/2012/10/un-women-sourcebook-on-women-peace-and-security

———. 2014. *India Civil Society Beijing Platform for Action: 20 Year Review,* compiled by Rita Manchanda with Shivani Vaishnava. New Delhi: UN Women.

———. 2015a. *A Global Study on Implementation of UNSCR 1325.* New York: UN Women.

———. 2015b. *Guidebook on CEDAW General Recommendation No. 30 and the UN Security Council Resolutions on Women, Peace and Security.* New York: UN Women.

Uyangoda, J. 2012. "Healing after War: Thinking beyond the Solitudes," in *Healing the Wounds: Rebuilding Sri Lanka after the War,* edited by D. Herath and K. T. Silva. Kandy: International Center of Ethnic Studies (ICES).

Verma Committee. January 23, 2013. *Report on Amendment to Criminal Law.* Justice Verma, L. Seth, G. Subramanium, New Delhi. Accessed December 18, 2016, http://www.prsindia.org/uploads/media/Justice%20verma%20committee/js%20verma%20committe%20report.pdf

Women's Regional Network, Denver: Colorado USA. 2014. *Unequal Citizens: Women's Narratives of Resistance Militarisation Corruption and Security,* compiled by Rita Manchanda, Delhi.

PART I

WOMEN, PARTICIPATION, AND PEACEBUILDING

1

Peace with Women: Political Participation in Post-conflict Contexts

Swarna Rajagopalan

This chapter explores the political participation of women in peacebuilding and politics in four South Asian post-conflict settings—Afghanistan, Bangladesh, Nepal, and Sri Lanka. It opens by briefly defining its terms of reference—"political participation" and "post-conflict" settings. Four case studies of South Asian post-conflict states are given here. In each of these, two avenues of women's engagement will be surveyed, that is, women's participation in the peace process, including the writing of new constitutions, and women's participation in formal political institutions. It concludes with a discussion of women's participation—in polities ostensibly at peace, in conflict zones and in post-conflict areas—and what enables or inhibits such participation.

Definitional Notes

Women's participation in public affairs is intrinsically important in every setting; the ability and willingness of women to be a part of policy and political life is a real measure of democratic politics. Conversely, the absence of women—common to most political cultures—is indicative not just of their alienation and disempowerment but of the inequitable nature of social structures and a lack of political commitment to equality. Following Shirin Rai, we identify participation and representation as two dimensions of access to decision-making, approximating the input and output sides of the political process (Rai 2005: 3). There is a third, which is having an actual seat at the table without being silenced.

The point of departure for this essay is the view that women should be involved in decision-making in their communities, local or national, in peacetime, during conflict and in the post-conflict period, and interest in women's political participation is essentially an interest in their political involvement. Participation should be meaningful. Women whose views were included in a 2010 Nepal study had a very broad view of what that meant (Abdela 2013: 12). Women should be included in the peacebuilding process on "equal or better" terms than men; as they put it, "… there should be 51% women rather than 33%."

A quick review of several "post-conflict" situations highlights how problematic the term is. In most countries, peace, conflict, and post-conflict conditions co-exist. Conflicts do not have open and shut beginnings and endings, and in any society, multiple conflicts may wage at a particular moment. The term "post-conflict" is applied when one of them—the oldest or the most violent or the most internationally visible—ends, but to the others, no end may be in sight. Furthermore, even as a polity might move to "post-conflict" status with a new constitution and allegiance to new and more gender-equitable values, society changes at a slower pace. Finally, the "post-conflict" label applies poorly where conflict—albeit long-standing, intense, and deeply destructive—remains local to particular places and communities. Elsewhere, in the same polity, things continue as before, and this is what most reports and statistics on women's participation capture—not information specific to the post-conflict context.

In this chapter, both the narrative and analysis move back and forth between conflict and post-conflict—and "apart from the conflict"— because it is so often hard to separate these circumstances. This applies not just to the discussion of the case studies but also to the closing discussion of what enables or inhibits participation.

Gendered Profiles: State, Politics, and Society

Afghanistan

Afghan history recalls many heroic women, and for over a century the modernizing Afghan elite have supported human rights. The years of communist rule following the Soviet occupation reinforced this, placing women in the spotlight. Growing conservatism about women's participation in the public sphere was a part of the growing anti-Soviet sentiment. This culminated in the misogynistic climate between 1996 and 2001 when the Taliban took control of Afghanistan's government. The point made is that prowomen policies or provisions in the post-2001 dispensation were a restoration and not an introduction of Afghan women's rights and participation (Hunt and Amiri 2002).

Peace Process

Women's absence from formal peace processes between 1979 and 1988 Geneva Accords does not reflect the reality that decades of modernization had built leadership potential among Afghan women. This was in part because of the flight of so many Afghan families into exile. At the December 2001 meeting in Bonn, there were two women among the Afghan signatories, a reflection of the role that women's rights had played in rallying support for the American intervention. The two women, Amena Afzali and Sima Wali, came to the conference with a track record of working on education and women's rights. For women, the positive outcomes of the 2001 Bonn Agreement lay in the mandate to ensure women's representation in the Emergency Loya Jirga and the appointment of a woman as one of the five vice-chairs of the Interim administration, in charge of women's affairs and public health.

The Emergency Loya Jirga convened in June 2002 provided space for 160 women to articulate their experiences and aspirations; the Constitutional Loya Jirga that followed in December 2003 had 102 women out of 500 members. Two of the nine members of the Constitutional Drafting Committee and seven of the 35 members of the Constitutional Review Commission were women. They produced a constitution which provided a quota for women's representation.

In June 2010, Afghan women were part of the National Consultative Peace Jirga. Three hundred and thirty four women and 1,334 men took part in these consultations to develop a strategy to end conflict in Afghanistan. Women used the opportunity to demand that the participation gains made since 2001 be protected from reversal. Sustained lobbying ensured that a forum of activists participated in the follow-up Kabul Conference, which endorsed the reintegration of the Taliban but with a nod to preserving women's gains.

Following the Peace Jirga, a High Peace Council (HPC) was formed to oversee the Afghanistan Peace and Reconciliation Program (APRP). Nine women are members of the 70-person HPC. Its women's committee held meetings with women from across the provinces, including women members of the Provincial Peace Councils. However, the HPC's "Peace Process Roadmap to 2015" contains no reference to women's rights. As Orzala Ashraf Nemat writes, "One point that is increasingly clear for Afghan women is that the Taliban are not the only group trying to deny women an active role (Nemat 2011: 20–21)." An embassy official is quoted as saying "Women's issues are important but they are not our top priority" (Oxfam 2011: 20–21).

In the 2011 International Afghanistan Conference in Bonn, only five Afghans addressed the assembled foreign ministers and officials from around the world; of these, one of the two civil society representatives was a woman, Selay Ghaffar, and she got three minutes to speak. Excluded from the main meeting, women activists traveled to several key capitals including Bonn to press their case (Wheeler 2012). As Noorjahan Akbar of Young Women for Change stated, "Women want peace but not at the cost of losing our freedom again" (Oxfam 2011: 2).

Indeed, outside of formal peace processes, the agency of women is hard to miss. The efforts on the ground of women activists and women's organizations and the transnational networks they accessed, sometimes through Afghan women in the diaspora, created awareness worldwide of what Afghan women experienced in the decades after 1979. The honor roll of Afghan women's groups and activists is long, with many working under threat to their lives. Revolutionary Association of the Women of Afghanistan (RAWA), founded in 1977, worked as part of a suppressed democratic resistance first during the Soviet years, then the Taliban and now religious fundamentalism (RAWA 2013). The Afghan Women's Educational Centre (2012), set up in 1991, worked on both sides of the Afghanistan–Pakistan border and was both a meeting place for refugee women and the venue for classes in English, computer usage, tailoring, and even basic literacy. Established in 1995, the high-profile Afghan Women's Network includes 103 NGOs and 5,000 individuals which networks and coordinates with key governmental, international, and nongovernmental players.

Political Institutions and Political Processes

The Ministry of Women Affairs (MoWA) was set up at the 2001 Bonn Conference and Sima Samar was the first woman to hold this portfolio. Locating itself in the historical context of women's activism in Afghanistan, the Ministry's twin objectives are to "secure and expand" women's legal rights and "to ensure the rule of law" in women's lives. The National Action Plan for the Women of Afghanistan is the main policy document of the MoWA (Ministry of Women Affairs 2008). In the face of skepticism of the discourse of gender sensitivity and in spite of its high profile, the embattled department is seriously underfunded.[1]

The 2004 Afghan Constitution recognizes the equality in law of all its citizens, "women" and men (emphasis added). It lays the foundation of a system of quotas to ensure women's representation in politics. Sixty-eight seats are reserved in the lower house of parliament. In the upper house, one-sixth of the members of the upper house must be women. The provision to reserve 25 percent of the provincial council seats was amended to lower this quota to 20 percent in July 2013. Quotas function more as a ceiling than a minimum requirement, with the highest vote-getter still being relegated to a quota seat (Independent Election Commission and UNIFEM 2009: 11).

Among the many presidential candidates in 2004, one was a woman, Massouda Jalal. In 2009, there were two female candidates in a pool of 41. In the 2005 general elections, 344 women contested elections to parliament and 285 women contested the provincial council elections. Forty-four percent of newly registered voters were women. Three hundred and thirty three women contested the 2009 provincial elections, but a decline in female voter turnout was observed in many areas, with some polling stations having virtually no female voters. In the 2010 parliamentary elections, 422 women contested elections, the number of male candidates dropped. A quarter of the women ran in the Kabul area, and at least three women ran from every province. Voter turnout was low. In 2014, there were no female presidential candidates and only 308 out of 2,713 provincial council candidates were women (IECA 2014). About 36–38 percent women voted in the two rounds of elections (Athayi 2014).

The most important factor affecting political participation of women in Afghanistan is the declining security situation (Independent Election Commission and UNIFEM 2009: 7–10; National Democratic Institute for International Affairs 2009: 2, 32). Violence impedes the mobility of women, and it also deters women from working as polling station agents, further deterring women voters (Donati and Arghandiwal 2013). Also, since women are not obliged to have their photographs on their voting card, proxy voting was possible. Moreover, security concerns resulted in polling stations being relocated to areas where it was hard for women to travel. A low rate of literacy among Afghan women meant many could not correctly use the ballots. Scheduling the elections just before Ramadan when homemakers are very busy was listed as another deterrent to participation.

For candidates, too, security was the major impediment, and the provision of security hotlines and security protection did not help enough (National Democratic Institute for International Affairs 2009: 30, 33). Cultural factors also placed women candidates at a disadvantage; they required the endorsement of family or village elders for their campaign to be credible. As in every other part of the world, women in Afghanistan also find it very hard to raise funds for their campaigns. Apart from participation in Parliament, in some parts of Afghanistan, there is a tradition of women's councils (*shuras*), which the government is trying to revive as a resource for rural development. But many of the same challenges limit women's participation in these councils, including intimidation (Grenfell 2004: 22–25).

Access to Justice

Women's access to justice poses specific challenges. A 2013 Oxfam report states that women make up less than 1 percent of the police. The high prevalence of sexual and gender-based violence within the home makes it particularly vital that women police officers are available to record complaints. The presence of women police at checkpoints would facilitate the mobility of women, to say nothing of stopping men from masquerading as women to carry out attacks. But prejudice within government circles, low salary, and night shifts deter women from joining the police (Oxfam 2011: 15).

It is estimated that 300 women lawyers work as defence lawyers, and there are virtually no women lawyers in 31 provinces (Hakimi 2013). A September 2013 conference of female judges, discussing the obstacles women faced in getting justice emphasized that women judges are targeted and stigmatized for doing their work. The result is that there are provinces which have no female judges. Also, there is no woman judge in the High Council of the Supreme Court.

The Law on Elimination of Violence against Women, which was passed as a presidential decree in 2009, went to the Afghan Parliament for ratification in May 2013, to have the vote deferred indefinitely after a mere two-hour debate. Very few women have access to the formal justice system, and this reinforces the culture of impunity around violence against women and human rights violations (Oxfam 2011: 14). The number of female prisoners has been on the rise, and a majority of female prisoners are held for "moral crimes," which include running away from an abusive husband, premarital or extramarital affairs, and rape.

Bangladesh[2]

The struggle of those who live in the Chittagong Hill Tracts (CHT) to preserve their identity, their lands, and their autonomy from a Bangladeshi state predicated on a single Bangla identity on one side and people from the plains looking for "living room" backed by the coercive authority of that state on the other illustrates the oft-used metaphor of the "matryoshka" doll to describe nested nationalisms. Reinforcing this is land acquired by the development state, which in building the Kaptai dam displaced hundreds of thousands who had always lived in this area.

Ironically, Bangladesh came into being in 1971 as an expression of linguistic nationalism, asserting that one hegemonic cultural identity could not be imposed on a multination state encompassing many diverse histories. And the Bangladeshi state went on to do just that—identifying Bangladeshi with Bengali to the exclusion of the other communities that lived within the same state. The hill people of the CHT in the southeastern part of the new country sought autonomy within the new state. Women activists played an important and visible role in the CHT struggle for autonomy (Guhathakurta 2001: 252–93).

Political Institutions and Political Processes

In the history of women's activism in CHT, an important marker is the formation of the Parbatyo Chattagram Mohila Samity in 1975 to raise awareness among women about the CHT struggle (Halim 2010: 186). In 1977–78, about 150 women were given arms training and a women's regiment of the Jana Samhati Samiti was formed. Participants were mostly educated women who remained politically active after the regiment was disbanded in 1983. Women were active also in student organizations like the Pahari Chhatra.

In 1988, the Hill Women's Federation (HWF) was founded, prompted in large measure by the rape and sexual harassment of women by the security forces. Also, there were few women combatants, most of whom were involved in providing the *Shanti Bahini* auxiliary services like cooking, nursing, and serving as informers (Mohsin 2005: 244).

Membership of the HWF overlapped with other organizations like the Pahari Gono Parishad and the Pahari Chattra Parishad. HWF is listed on the Parbatya Chattagram Jana Samhati Samiti (PCJSS) website as a "Wing Organization (2013)." While women activists drew attention to the insensitivity of the male-dominated leadership to their concerns, they agreed that these gender related concerns could only be addressed with self-determination and autonomy of the hill peoples (Chakma 2001: 281–84).

The CHT peace process lasted over two decades, during which time, two women held the office of Bangladesh Prime Minister. Yet, there were no women representatives involved in the negotiations on either side—the PCJSS or the government (Mohsin 2005: 236). In spite of the role of the HWF in making known human rights violations in the CHT, not one woman represented the CHT side.

The CHT Accord (signed before UNSC 1325) has been criticized as a "gendered" accord (Mohsin 2005: 246). The Accord created Hill District Councils for Rangamati, Bandarban, and Khagrachari, to control the transfer and lease of lands, forests, hills and waterbodies. It created a regional council to oversee these. The administrative arrangements provide for quotas—three women at the district and regional councils—two tribal and one nontribal. The Accord makes no quota provision for tribal women in the national parliament or the Advisory Council to assist the Ministry of CHT Affairs. It provides for recruitment from CHT to the police, but there is no quota for recruiting female constables or officers.

The CHT Accord mentions human rights in the preamble but overlooks the history of human rights violations by security forces in the CHT. The amnesty provided in the Accord was meant for JSS cadres and contingent upon them surrendering arms. It speaks of the rehabilitation of those who fled their homes during the years of fighting, but it does not address women's experience of forced conversion, eviction, abduction, rape or persecution. It says nothing about the sexual violence that was rampant in the years of conflict, nor anything about violent excesses by soldiers. It is estimated that between 1991 and 1993 over 94 percent of reported CHT rape cases were by security personnel and more than 40 percent of those raped were under the age of 18 (Mohsin 2005: 246).

The Accord does not take into account tribal women's property rights. For the PCJSS this is a problematic question, because of the fear that women marrying outside the community will take property out of the community. There is no requirement that the governing Councils consult both men and women in their decision-making.

Reparation and rehabilitation provisions are not gender sensitive (Buchanan et al. 2012: 53–54). The provision for educational scholarships does not specifically include women and girls. No mention is made of female-headed households in the context of rehabilitation, employment or credit facilities. It is well-established that unless otherwise specified, benefits do not accrue to women. The JSS also overlooked the work of women in compiling their surrender list, listing only two, instead of 50 (Halim 2010: 184).

The Accord provided for the phased withdrawal of paramilitary and army camps to their permanent bases and the occupied land to be returned to owners. This has not happened. There is a discrepancy between the government's claim to have withdrawn 172 camps and their communication to the PCJSS that they have withdrawn 31 camps. Some of these have since been redeployed. The previous military operation under a martial law situation like "Operation Dabanal" has been replaced by "Operation Uttoran" but with the same everyday impact (PCJSS 2013).

One consequence of militarization is restricted mobility. The large numbers of security personnel in the countryside means that wherever women need to go in order to gather water, fuel, and fodder, they face the risk of sexual violence (Halim 2010: 185). Incidents of sexual and other violence by Bengali settlers also seem to have gone up since the Accord, because they are no longer confined to isolated settlements (Chakma 2012). The climate of impunity which discourages women from making complaints contributes to their insecurity. Naher and Tripura makes the additional point that men in the community, angry and frustrated as a result of losing their land and livelihood, are resorting to violence within their families (Naher and Tripura 2010: 194).

A JSS leader, Shantu Larma, is quoted as saying that as long as institutions in the CHT are dominated by Bengalis, there can be no justice for women (Halim 2010: 187). In his view, even 18 years after the signing of the CHT Accord the Hill District Councils and the Regional Council do not enjoy enough autonomy or authority to ensure an end to impunity. Bangladesh set up an International Crimes Tribunal in 2009 for crimes against humanity including sexual violence during the 1871 war for independence, but impunity for the same behavior during counter-insurgency operations continues in the CHT.

Women's participation in peace work in post-conflict CHT is framed by the broader Bangladeshi context. Women's participation in local government has been a Fundamental Principle of state policy since the Bangladesh Constitution was first enacted in 1972. Quotas for women exist at both the local and the national government levels in Bangladesh (International IDEA 2007). As per the 15th Amendment (2011), the Bangladesh constitution reserves 50 out of 350 seats in Parliament for women. Sixty-nine women actually sit in Parliament, making up about 20 percent of the members. Over four decades this number has doubled, making it one of the oldest quota systems. Since 1997, three seats are reserved for women in each union parishad—the lowest tier of government.

In spite of having two female prime ministers who are the leaders of Bangladesh's main political parties and a female Speaker, women's political participation in Bangladesh falls short. Sheikh Hasina is quoted as saying, "Women candidates could not survive in the election politics of violence and money. Moreover, the popular belief is that nominating a woman for a seat is the other name of losing it" (Chowdhury 2013: 2). Ironically, political analysts such as Chowdhury rule out religion as a deterrent, for the religious parties are most active in mobilizing women. It is the male control of the public and private spheres that matters.

> In the public sphere, women have to contend with *mastan* culture ... the availability of illegal arms, accessibility to black market money and fear of sexual harassment.... In the private sphere, women have to cope with a lack of control over their own income, family involvement and non-cooperation of husbands. (Chowdhury 2013: 4)

For the women of the CHT, in spite of their activism during the conflict years, when it came to the peace process, the CHT women were invisible even to their partners in the struggle. The post-Accord years have not opened up for them the arenas of politics and policy. If anything, the public sphere has become more fraught with risk—both because of a shrinking democratic space and the deteriorating safety in CHT villages, where institutional arrangements are facilitating the incremental inclusion of women in the mainstream of politics, CHT women are excluded by virtue of both of ethnicity and gender. In 2012, women from the CHT formed the "Bangladesh Indigenous Women's Network" to increase women's participation and end the oppression experienced by women.

Nepal

For 10 years, between 1996 and 2006, Nepalwas ravaged by internal war between the Communist Party of Nepal (Maoist) and the Government of Nepal. Over the decade of conflict, Nepal's women saw their world change in dramatic ways (Gautam, Baskota, and Manchanda 2001: 214–51) as evidenced by women making up one-third of the Maoist forces. It made women visible in politics as never before. "[T]he ordinary village women who joined the Maoist Army learned a new 'liberation vocabulary' that encouraged them to question traditional gender roles" (Upadhyaya 2011: 92; 2010: 99).

For women in Nepal, peace was not just the absence of conflict. It meant,

> [A] combination of economic security (having an assured basic income), food security (physical and economic access to food), health security (access to basic health care), environmental security (access to clean water, clean air, ecological security), personal security (freedom from physical violence

and threats), right to human dignity and freedom of a person, community (cultural integrity) and political security (protection of civil rights and freedom and responsibilities). (Baechler 2010: 3–5; Rajbhandari 2008: 108)

Peace Process

A large number of women had engaged in different kinds of peace work in the years preceding the Comprehensive Peace Agreement (CPA), yet, none was included in the final negotiations (Paudel 2003). Masses of women had participated in the prodemocracy movement to exert pressure on the Seven-Party Alliance and the Maoists to come to terms, but the peace was negotiated at the elite leadership level on both sides (Upadhyaya 2011: 93). In the course of the several stages of peace negotiations in 2001, 2003, 2005, and 2006 only Anuradha Koirala was involved in 2003 and in a note-taking role. Gender was not a concern, and human rights only received attention in 2006.

The CPA (2006) makes general references to women and gender. The first, in the Preamble, which pledges a "forward-looking restructuring of the state by resolving the prevailing problems related to class, ethnicity, regional and gender differences." This is reiterated in Articles 3.4 and 3.5 on equal rights for women. Article 7.1.1 in the section on Human Rights explicates that both sides agreed that gender, among others, was not a ground for discrimination. A single section is devoted to "Rights of women and children" and Article 7.6.1 commits both sides to protecting the rights of women and children, including putting an end to violence against them.

A Centre for Humanitarian Dialogue project examines the CPA and finds multiple entry points or missed opportunities for making it a more inclusive agreement (Buchanan et al. 2012). The CPA's references represent women "as people whose problems need resolving, rather than as productive contributors to the new society (Buchanan et al. 2012: 42)." The CPA does not reference the Convention on the Elimination of all Forms of Discrimination Against Women (1979) and it ignores women's right to land ownership and inheritance in its land reform provisions (Buchanan et al. 2012: 43–44, 50). None of the institutions set up by the CPA—the Interim Legislature, Constituent Assembly, National Peace and Reconciliation Commission, and High-level Truth and Reconciliation Commission—were designed to be gender-inclusive (Buchanan et al. 2012: 38–39, 71).

Political Institutions and Political Processes

What the CPA omitted, the Interim Constitution (2007) remedied. This was a result of lobbying by women's groups and high-profile women activists with the support of UN agencies. Women were members of the peace task force, which had "representatives of political parties, the Peace Secretariat, local facilitators and international advisers (Buchanan et al. 2012: 100)." Since then, there has been some watering down of these rights (Manchanda 2010: 7–8).

The Interim Constitution in Article 20 recognized four specific rights of women:

(1) No discrimination of any kind shall be made against the women by virtue of sex. (2) Every woman shall have the right to reproductive health and reproduction. (3) No woman shall be subjected to physical, mental or any other kind of violence; and such act shall be punishable by law. (4) Sons and daughters shall have the equal right to ancestral property.

Most importantly, Article 63 (5) mandated that one-third of the members of the constituent assembly be women, ensuring that they would have a say in drafting the mandate of the state and the design of its institutions.

In 2006, Women's Alliance for Peace, Power, Democracy and Constituent Assembly (WAPPDCA), an NGO, compiled a "Who is Who of Nepali Women," listing over 3,000 qualified Nepali women able to participate in political and peace processes (Suthanthiraraj and Ayo 2010: 40). The 2008 elections to the Constituent Assembly returned 191 women members—30 directly elected, 161 through proportional representation, and 6 more were nominated. Subsequently, in the 2013 Constituent Assembly elections, the category "third gender," available to Lesbian, Gay, Bisexual and Transgender (LGBT) candidates, was introduced (LGBTQ Nation 2013). However, in the direct election process for 240 seats, only 10 women were directly elected—4.2 percent, the remainder of the quota to be made up through allocation of the proportionate representation seats.

What was women's experience in the Constituent Assembly 2008–13? Old patriarchal ways seem to have resurfaced in the post-conflict moment and women's descriptions of their experience do not inspire hope. Women feel that they are still treated as less competent and as supplicants, and that senior leaders do not listen to what they have to say (Bhusal 2011; Manchanda 2010: 8; Rai 2008). It is reported that in the post-conflict period, alliances between women's organizations are unravelling (Suthanthiraraj and Ayo 2010: 40–41).

While the quota provisions go toward meeting the goal of women's political participation, two challenges remained. The reintegration of the Maoist women combatants and supporters remains a challenge even after the integration process has been otherwise completed (Colekessian 2009). The second is support to the women entering politics at the grassroots level, in particular, the Local Peace Committees set up in 2007 with a requirement that 33 percent of the members should be women.

Undeterred by these challenges and constraints, women have continued to organize and to use every avenue available; including for instance, in influencing security sector reform (DCAF 2011: 78). Two hundred senior officials received training on human rights, especially the rights of women and children in 2003. In 2004, the creation of a training manual for field personnel was supported by the NGO Save the Children, the military police, the police, and the prime minister's office.

Most significant was the National Action Plan for UN Security Council Resolution 1325, adopted in 2011. The drafting process is considered exemplary because it was very inclusive (Rana 2012, v; Sundman [n.d.]). Over 3000 women and organizations participated. Key government agencies, NGOs, and international development organizations were involved in the drafting. It was finalized after consultations with conflict-affected women and girls, local peace committees, local government authorities and civil society organizations, and individuals working on women's rights and gender equality(Government of Nepal and Saathi 2012: 1) (see Table 1.1).

Table 1.1 Women's Participation Indicators, Nepal, 2006–12

Sphere	Number	Percentage
Political Parties and Constituent Assembly (2008)	197	33.2
Council of Ministers (2009)[a]	6	14
Constitution-making—Interim Constitution 2007	4	25
Cabinet (2007)	3	13
Constituent Assembly Committees[b]	–	15.21–65
Justice Sector (across levels), most at Appellate Court Level	6	1–4
Nepal Bar Association (across levels)	491	7–12
Constitutional Bodies[c]	34	15–100

Sphere	Number	Percentage
Nepal Army Officers (across levels), most at Captain Rank[d]	258	6.78
Nepal Army Soldiers (across levels), most at Sergeant Rank[e]	1266	1.47
Nepal Police (across levels), most at Constable Rank (2227)	3457	5.77
Armed Police Force (constable Rank: 739)	996	3.22
Peace Keeping Missions Deployed by Army (2011–12) (all levels)	217	1.63
UN Peace Keeping Missions Deployed by Nepal (2007–9)[f]	115	–
Senior Positions in Civil Service (2011)[g]	790	6.49
Peace Negotiating Teams and Agreements (Govt. and Other)[h]	19	–
Major Political Parties Central Working Committees	107	14
Local Peace Committees	484	29.2
Private and NGO Sector (Central Committee Members)	58	28

Source: Government of Nepal and Saathi (2012: 8–20).

Notes: [a] Has varied between 2006–2009, from 11.1 percent in 2006, to 14 percent in 2009, with a low of 9.1 percent in 2007 (Government of Nepal and Saathi 2012, 8).
[b] Has ranged from 15.21 percent in the Natural Resources, Financial Rights and Revenue Sharing Committee to 64.40 percent in the Women, Children and Social Welfare Committee. Women are only 24.19 in the Constitutional Committee, 27.90 percent in the Fundamental Rights Directive Principles Committee, 25 percent in the National Interest Preservation Committee and the Security Special Committee. In other words, the division of subjects replicates the gendered division of labor in society (Government of Nepal and Saathi 2012, 11).
[c] The 100 percent female membership statistic is for the National Women's Commission (Government of Nepal and Saathi 2012, 12).
[d] 234 out of 258 women officers in the Nepal Army in 2012 ranked between the levels of Lieutenant and Major. This means that in years to come, they could hopefully constitute a critical mass, as they rise through the ranks, visible as role models (Government of Nepal and Saathi 2012, 13).
[e] 937 Sergeants, 107 Followers and 99 Warrant Officers First Class and Recruits form the bulk of the 1266 soldiers (Government of Nepal and Saathi, 2012, 13).
[f] The total number of Nepali women in Peace Keeping Missions is 197, but just between 2007–2009, the number is 115, counting both Police and Armed Police units (Government of Nepal and Saathi 2012, 15).
[g] Four women at Secretary level, 9 at Joint Secretary level, 97 at Under Secretary level and 680 at Section Officer level. There are fewer women in the pipeline than one would expect (Government of Nepal and Saathi 2012, 17).
[h] 12 women and 19 men participated in the peace process from the Government side and 7 women and 74 men on behalf of other negotiating parties (Government of Nepal and Saathi 2012, 18).

Sri Lanka

In the early decades after decolonization, Sri Lanka made pathbreaking developmental choices that led to some of the region's most enviable human resource indicators on health and education. The good human resource indicators and the high-profile activism of women, however, did not spare them the usual travails of war—bereavement, displacement, trauma, sexual violence and loss of livelihood—over two generations. The International Crisis Group's (ICG) recent report summarizes:

> There were many forms of violence. The LTTE forcibly recruited women and girls to join the insurgency and did not hesitate to threaten or kill Tamil women who challenged the Tigers' authority. Government security forces and the IPKF were responsible for many cases of rape, torture and killing of Tamil women. Both sides abducted or disappeared women's husbands and other family members, increasing economic and social vulnerabilities. (ICG 2011: 4)

Significantly, *Women Under Siege* singles out an important difference:

> But what sets Sri Lanka's conflict apart from many others is that sexualized violence was not used by all sides. While government, paramilitary, and rebel forces all violated human rights, the Liberation Tigers of Tamil Eelam (LTTE), or the Tamil Tigers, successfully trained their fighters not to rape, according to multiple sources. The LTTE, famous for suicide bombings, ethnic cleansing, displacement, forced recruitment of child soldiers, and murder, reportedly did not use sexualized violence as a weapon. (Hirsch 2013)

During the war, women's agency was most dramatically exemplified by the role that women in the Liberation Tigers of Tamil Eelam (LTTE) played. The experience of women in militant groups also differs from our stereotypes. It is often said that women join militant groups following the experience of sexual violence or in search of a feeling of empowerment. Researchers found that women in the LTTE felt empowered but did not necessarily have a say in decision-making within the organization (Ramachandran 2005: 154–76); Rajasingham–Senanayake (2001: 102–30) describes women's agency in conflict situations as "ambiguous empowerment."

In recent interviews by Ambika Satkunananthan, women from other militant groups spoke about the experiences that drew them into public life (like attending funerals of slain leaders) and about the challenges of continuing family strictures on movement (2012: 629). Women from the Eelam People's Revolutionary Liberation Front (EPRLF), for instance, did mainly political work but were sidelined from decision-making. They did take up issues like violence and abuse, but not with the support of the men in the organization. Women cadres faced social and familial disapproval and felt doubly vulnerable when the LTTE banned the EPRLF, but the latter did nothing to help women's safety (Satkunananthan 2012: 643–46).

Peace Process

There have been many moments in Sri Lankan history when peace talks have taken place and through all these moments, women have been active as peace and human rights activists. Women and Media Collective's *Strategic Mapping of Women's Peace Activism* (Emmanuel 2009: 7–9) identifies 20 spheres of such activism. Typically, peace work was placed in the context of other struggles, as for instance, the Sarvodaya Movement did, engaging and empowering groups across ethnic lines. When targeted for taking positions on the war and in support of peace negotiations, coalitions like Women's Action Committee recast themselves around more traditional roles like motherhood, that is, Mothers and Daughters of Lanka, the Southern Mothers' Front, the Northern Mother's Front (Satkunananthan 2012: 656–57) and the Association of War Affected Women.

Women's groups have undertaken practical work at the grassroots level to promote peace: from canvassing for women's land rights— Suriya Women's Development Centre; to running a preschool for Muslim and Tamil children so that they can be friends and their parents can interact—Muslim Women's Research and Action Forum; to building dispute resolution skills—*Samadanam*; to consultations on drafting laws on violence against women—Women and Media Collective; to counseling women affected by war and sexual violence in Jaffna—*Poorani* (Satkunananthan 2012: 652–54; Women and Media Collective 2009: 30–32).

These decades of women's activism were surely a factor in the creation of the sub-committee on gender issues (SGI) in December 2002 (Samuel 2010: 41–54). The objective of setting up the SGI was to include gender concerns in the peace process. Five women from the government (actually, women activists from civil society) and five from the LTTE made up the committee which was facilitated by a Norwegian woman minister. The SGI met twice formally, and both times in Kilinochchi, then the LTTE headquarters.

Barely had the SGI finalized its terms of reference to include: sustaining peace process, resettlement, personal security and safety, infrastructure and services, livelihood and employment, political representation and decision-making, and reconciliation, that the breakdown of the peace process in April 2003 aborted this process.

The 2008–2009 military campaign created a humanitarian crisis on a scale that was described by some as "genocidal" and questions of accountability remains on the table. The report of the Lessons Learnt and Reconciliation Commission (LLRC) did not devote a separate section to gender issues, leave alone the question of sexual and gender-based violence. Only one of the eight members was a woman. Many women who approached the LLRC were denied permission to testify, reinforcing discrimination against them (United Nations 2011: para 330).

Political Institutions and Political Processes

Three concerns dominate post-war Sri Lankan politics. The first is the humanitarian crisis that followed conflict and displacement—the rehabilitation of those who fled their homes, militarization in northern Sri Lanka, and a climate of shrinking space in the public sphere. These are also factors that affect women's participation.

Thirteen women were elected to Parliament in 2010; they made up 5.7 percent of the legislature. In 2015, 556 women contested elections and only 11 won (Jeyaraj 2015). The Sri Lanka Shadow Report to CEDAW stated in 2011, "In our analysis, the main obstacle to women's equal political representation remains within Political Parties, since they do not nominate an equitable number of women to contest elections" (Women and Media Collective 2010: 12). The government in its report to the CEDAW Committee claims that women are reluctant to engage in active politics despite a women's quota at the nomination level. After the war, especially in the north and east Sri Lanka women will outnumber men for at least one generation (ICG 2011: 18–22). Tens of thousands of women have been widowed, in a society that regards them as inauspicious. Many are very young. They struggle to support their families and contend with stigma and sexual harassment. Common to conflict zones everywhere, it has fallen largely to women to search for missing family members who may be held in detention by either side, lost or dead. The search for missing family members and the struggle for livelihood takes a toll on women, emotionally and physically. Locating relatives in detention centers brings emotional relief, but the physical and financial responsibility of visiting them weighs heavily. The assumption that anyone detained by security forces was also subjected to sexual violence adds to fear and stigma in their lives.

Militarization has a very everyday face in northern Sri Lanka where military camps and checkpoints surround civilian settlements and military personnel are involved in local businesses and building infrastructure. The military visits homes in the name of checking on demobilized LTTE cadres and there is a view that militarization is the new vehicle for internal colonization that will create demographic change. The ICG describes Sri Lanka's post-war culture as a "masculine, militarised" one (ICG 2011: 11).

In official pronouncements on women and women's rights, the tone is paternalistic—placing women on a pedestal, speaking of their protection and valorizing conciliation in the event of violence. On domestic violence, for instance, the president is repeatedly quoted as saying, "Anger between husband and wife is only until the pot of rice gets cooked." The government response to acts of violence perpetrated against women and children by current and former soldiers is merely that they will "delist" military deserters and "pursue the 'few dozen' allegedly involved in serious crimes (ICG 2011, 13–14)."

Disasters and donor fatigue have slowed down government-led recovery processes in both north and east Sri Lanka. Women's livelihood choices are limited, and they have ended up in competition with Tamil men for limited resources and opportunities (ICG 2011: 23–24). This has reinforced the sexist view that working women must be immoral. The war is blamed for a breakdown in values.

Violence against women in politics comes as no surprise. Thuggery and voter intimidation happen during elections, and sometimes "gender-specific and sexualized forms of violence" are witnessed (Women and Media Collective 2010: 15). In the north and east, human rights activists were always at risk under LTTE control, and in the post-war period, the space for difference and dissent has shrunk across the island. Women human rights defenders continue their work in the face of threats from multiple state and nonstate quarters (Minority Rights Groups International 2013: 17). Their activities include bearing witness and documenting human rights violations; helping grassroots women in their work and making sure that grassroots accounts inform national and global activism. In return, they face surveillance, military inspection, and harassment from various official and nonofficial quarters. Relatively unknown, they receive no protection and have no income security, and their work isolates them from traditional support systems.

Enablers and Inhibitors: Women's Political Participation

One of the most striking political features of the South Asian region is the presence of so many female heads of government and heads of state. Most of these women leaders come from politically influential families; observers often use the term "Widow–Orphan syndrome" to describe their rise but the successful consolidation of their position and influence speaks to both their skill and an accepting electorate (Table 1.2).

A 2012 study of regions across Asia identified the following key enablers and obstacles (True, Niner, Parashar, and George 2012: 12–16). Private sphere responsibilities keep women out of the public sphere; at the same time, when women enter the workforce, their workload doubles. Much depends on the unpaid domestic work of women. Cultural attitudes and expectations need to change so that women's nature and capabilities are not stereotypically seen as limiting their potential for public life. Women's education is essential although

Table 1.2 Number and Percentage of Women in National Legislatures of South Asia

State	Women in National Legislatures Number and Percentage
Afghanistan	Lower House: 69/249 (27.7%), September 2010 Upper House: 18/102 (17.6%), January 2015
Bangladesh	70/350 (20%), January 2014
Bhutan	Lower House: 4/47 (8.5%), July 2013 Upper House: 2/25 (8%), April 2013
India	Lower House: 65/545 (12%), April 2014 Upper House: 31/243 (12.8%), January 2014
Maldives	5/85 (5.9%), March 2014
Nepal	177/599 (29.5%), November 2013
Pakistan	Lower House: 70/340 (20.6%), May 2013 Upper House: 19/104 (18.3%), March 2015
Sri Lanka	11/225 (4.9%), August 2015

Source: Interparliamentary Union, Women in Parliaments: World Classification, As on July 1, 2013. Accessed December 19, 2016, http://www.ipu.org/wmn-e/arc/classif 010713.htm, accessed August 15, 2013 to September 22, 2015.

not enough on its own to draw women into political life. Finally, the study echoes others in identifying the role played by electoral systems and quotas; for each electoral system, there are quotas that help enhance women's participation and representation.

On the determinants of women's participation, Shvedova writes of three categories of obstacles: political, socioeconomic and psychological (Shvedova 2005: 33–44). Political obstacles begin with what she terms a "masculine model" of political life, which predicate political activity on men's lifestyles making it harder for working mothers or other women to network and balance politics with caregiving roles. Political parties fail to provide financial support to women for the increasingly expensive political enterprise, and they are also accused of applying more stringent standards to the selection of women. Moreover, women are often not as well-networked with civil society organizations like trade unions. Finally, political scientists have found that the nature of the electoral system matters. Single-member, first-past-the-post systems work less in favor of women than does proportional representation with multimember constituencies.

The second layer of obstacles comes from the various socioeconomic challenges faced by women in both advanced industrial and developing countries. Echoing the old idea that development aids democracy, Shvedova finds a positive correlation between development and women's representation levels which she attributes to their growing literacy and presence in the workforce. Also, while some cultures seek to limit women's participation in the public sphere, women perceive politics as a "dirty game." This last may account for their willingness to enter the public sphere in other ways, whether through traditional charity work or through modern nongovernmental organizations, emphasizing development, health care or welfare activities.

Two debates about political representation are also salient to women's political efficacy. The first is the question of whom or what is being represented by the representative. Women politicians often stress that they are politicians who happen to be women. It challenges the assumption that women will bring feminist or even women's special concerns to the table. The second debate concerns the use of quotas and on the whole, scholars, policymakers and activists appear to agree that they serve a useful purpose. (Dahlerup and Freidenvall 2005: 26) (Table 1.3).

In the post-conflict context, lack of security can be a serious deterrent to women's participation. Democracy, with or without gender equity and women's participation, is not possible without minimum standards of physical security. During conflict and repression, women could claim to "political space" as mothers looking for missing children which authoritarian governments found hard to repress as they placed motherhood on a pedestal as an ideal for women. The same factor worked to undermine women staking a claim to a decision-making role or to place feminist/gender issues on the agenda (Waylen 1994: 327–54). Their political engagement was predicated on "difference" and an outlook that Franceschet describes as "political motherhood"—"the ideal that politics is about acting selflessly and acting for others" (2001: 213). Waylen argues that where the democratic transition has included a move toward market liberalization, eroded social security and increased violence, women's political participation has declined (Waylen 1994: 344–53).

Table 1.3 Quotas Applied in South Asian States

State	*Quota Types*
Afghanistan	Legislated quotas for the Single/Lower House
	Legislated quotas for the Upper House
	Legislated quotas at the Subnational level
Bangladesh	Legislated quotas for the Single/Lower House
	Legislated quotas at the Subnational level
Bhutan	-
India	Legislated quotas at the Subnational level
	Political party quotas (Indian National Congress 15%)
Maldives	-
Nepal	Legislated quotas for the Single/Lower House
	Legislated quotas at the Subnational level
Pakistan	Legislated quotas for the Single/Lower House
	Legislated quotas for the Upper House
	Legislated quotas at the Subnational level
Sri Lanka	-

Source: Quota Database, Data grouped by quota type, http://www.quotaproject.org/country.cfm, accessed August 15, 2013.

Concluding Reflections

The 2011–12 "Progress of the World's Women Report" by UN Women optimistically pointed to two positive changes wrought in post-conflict contexts. First, the changing international legal environment which is making it harder to overlook sexual violence in conflict. In at least three instances—Yugoslavia, Rwanda, and Sierra Leone—transitional justice has included prosecution and conviction for sexual crimes. Second, post-conflict constitutional quotas helped increase women's representation in the legislature. This is especially true where the UN has been engaged in crafting the post-conflict moment. Afghanistan and Nepal exemplify this. In both cases, constitutional quotas have brought women into parliaments. In both cases, tradition has continued to marginalize them even within those spaces. In post-war Sri Lanka, the space for democratic politics is shrinking and women activists and human rights defenders are also affected by this change.

Traditional misogynistic attitudes illustrate the limits of outside intervention. UN agencies and resolutions, backed by international donors and even foreign military and diplomatic forces, might promote gender equality as a value, even making it a funding condition. But patriarchy's walls seem to survive. Women who are highly visible in the peace process become invisible thereafter, and find it hard to sustain the momentum of change. The reduction of quotas and the reversal on the domestic violence law in Afghanistan and the drop in numbers of elected women in Nepal are ominous. Even the most interventionist state's most determined decisions cannot force a change in the way that people think in the intermediate term.

Notes

1. Editor's Note: In June 2015, President Asraf Ghani's government adopted Afghanistan's National Action Plan for UNSC 1325 on Women Peace and Security (2015–18). The nodal overseeing authority is "Directorate of Human Rights and Women's International Affairs" under the supervision of the Ministry of Foreign Affairs.
2. Indebted to Dr Meghna Guhathakurta for this section.

Bibliography

Abdela, Lesley. 2010. "Case Study—Nepal: United Nations Security Council Resolution 1325: Women's Meaningful Participation in Peacebuilding and Governance. CARE/ Australian Development Corporation, Vienna/Kathmandu. Accessed November 9, 2016, http://www.ideas-int.org/documents/docs/CARE%20Report%20Nepal.pdf

Athayi, Abdullah. "From Transition to Transformation - Women, Peace & Security," Heinrich Böll Foundation, Gerda Werner Institute, 2014. Accessed December 19, 2016, http://www.gwi-boell.de/sites/default/files/uploads/2015/07/from_ transition_to_transformation_edit.pdf

Baechler, Günther. 2010, August. "A Mediator's Perspective: Women and the Nepali Peace Process." *Asia-Pacific Opinion*. Centre for Humanitarian Dialogue. Accessed November 9, 2016, http://www.peacewomen.org/portal_resources_resource. php?id=864

Buchanan, Cate, et al. 2012, December. "From Clause to Effect: Including Women's Rights and Gender in Peace Agreements," in *Women at the Peace Table Asia Pacific*. Geneva: Centre for Humanitarian Dialogue. Accessed December 19, 2016, https://www.hdcentre.org/wp-content/uploads/2016/07/24ClausereportwebFINAL-December-2012.pdf

Bhusal, Savita. 2011. "Nepal's women have a voice in politics but no one is listening." Poverty Matters Blog, May 27. Accessed December 12, 2016, http://www.

theguardian.com/global-development/poverty-matters/2011/may/27/nepal-women-in-politics

Chakma, Kalpana. 2001. Quoted in Meghna Guhathakurta, "Women's Narratives from the Chittagong Hill Tracts," in *Women, War and Peace in South Asia: Beyond Victimhood to Agency*, edited by Rita Manchanda. New Delhi: SAGE.

Chakma, Kabita. 2012, June 13. "Sexual Violence, Indigenous Jumma Women and CHT, Bangladesh." Parts 1 and 2. *South Asia Citizens' Web*. Accessed November 9, 2016, http://www.sacw.net/article 4727.html

Chowdhury, Farah Deeba. 2013, June. "Women's Participation in Local Governments: Bangladesh and India." Commonwealth Secretariat. Accessed November 9, 2016, http://secretariat.thecommonwealth.org/files/256105/FileName/WomensparticipationBangladeshandIndiaJune2013.pdf

Colekessian, Ani. 2009. "Reintegrating Gender: A Gendered Analysis of the Nepali Rehabilitation Process." INSTRAW Gender, Peace and Security Series Working Paper.

Dahlerup, Drude, and Lenita Freidenvall. March 2005."Quotas As a 'Fast Track' to Equal Representation for Women: Why Scandinavia Is No Longer the Model." *International Feminist Journal of Politics* 7 (1): 26–48.

DCAF. 2011. *Gender and Security Sector Reform: Examples from the Ground*. Geneva. Accessed December 19, 2016, http://www.poa-iss.org/kit/Gender-SSR-E.pdf

Donati, Jessica and Miriam Arghandiwal. 2013. *Afghan Women may be Denied Vote because of Female Security Force Shortage*. Reuters. Accessed December 19, 2016, http://uk.reuters.com/article/2013/08/28/uk-afghanistan-women-idUKBRE97R0IL20130828

Emmanuel, Sarala. 2009. *Strategic Mapping of Women's Peace Activism in Sri Lanka*. Colombo: Women and Media Collective.

Franceschet, Susan. March 2001. "Women in Politics in Post-transitional Democracies: The Chilean Case." *International Feminist Journal of Politics* 3(2).

Gautam, Shobha, Amrita Banskota, and Rita Manchanda. 2001. "Where There Are No Men: Women in the Maoist Insurgency in Nepal." In *Women, War and Peace in South Asia: Beyond Victimhood to Agency*, edited by Rita Manchanda. New Delhi: SAGE Publications.

Government of Nepal and Saathi. 2012. *Nepal National Action Plan on Implementation of the UNSCRs 1325 and 1820: First Year Monitoring Report*. Kathmandu: Ministry of Peace & Reconstruction.

Grenfell, Laura. 2004. "The Participation of Afghan Women in the Reconstruction Process." Human Rights Brief No. 12. Accessed November 9, 2016, http://www.wcl.american.edu/hrbrief/12/1grenfell.pdf

Guhathakurta, Meghna. 2001. "Women's Narratives from the Chittagong Hill Tracts." In *Women, War and Peace in South Asia: Beyond Victimhood to Agency*, edited by Rita Manchanda. New Delhi: SAGE Publications.

Hakimi, Asar. 2013. "Afghan Female Lawyers: Providing Hope for Female Detainees" (Interview with Najla Rahib). Accessed December 19, 2016, http://www.bamdad.af/english/story/2256 on September 12, 2013.

Halim, Sadeka. 2010. "Insecurity of Indigenous Women." In *Between Ashes and Hope: Chittagong Hill Tracts in the Blind Spot of Bangladeshi Nationalism*, edited by Naeem Mohaiemen. Bangladesh: Drishtipat Writers' Collective.

Hirsch, Michele Lent. 2013. Women under Siege, Conflict Profiles: Sri Lanka. New York: Women's Media Center. Accessed November 9, 2016, http://www. womenundersiegeproject.org/conflicts/profile/sri-lanka

Hunt, Swanee, and Rina Amiri. 2002. *Transition within Tradition: Restoring Women's Participation in Afghanistan.* Conference Report. Cambridge, MA: Harvard University. Accessed November 9, 2016, http://www.swaneehunt.com/articles/ TransitionWithinTradition.pdf

ICG (International Crisis Group). 2011, December. "Sri Lanka: Women's Insecurity in the North and East." Asia Report No. 217. Accessed December 19, 2016, https:// d2071andvip0wj.cloudfront.net/217-sri-lanka-women-s-insecurity-in-the-north-and-east.pdf

Independent Election Commission of Afghanistan. 2014. Frequently Asked Questions: Women as Candidates. Accessed December 19, 2016, http://www.iec.org.af/pdf/ factsheets-014/eng/faq_woman_and_candidate.pdf

Independent Election Commission and UNIFEM. 2009. "One Step Forward, Two Steps Back? Lessons Learnt on Women's Participation in the 2009 Afghanistan Elections." Resource Centre for Women in Politics, Gender Unit of the Independent Election Commission and UNIFEM. Accessed November 9, 2016, http://www.unifem.org/ afghanistan/docs/pubs/10/IEC_UNIFEM_Report_Afghan_Elections_2009.pdf

International IDEA. 2007. *Political Parties in South Asia: The Challenge of Change.* South Asia Regional Report. Accessed December 19, 2016, http://www.idea.int/sites/ default/files/publications/political-parties-in-south-asia-the-challenge-of-change.pdf

Jeyaraj, DBS. 2015, August 22. "Only 11 out of 556 Women Candidates Elected to Parliament Despite 52% of Population Being Female." Sunday Times. Accessed December 19, 2016, http://dbsjeyaraj.com/dbsj/archives/42814

LGBTQ Nation. 2013. LGBTQ Nation.com. "Nepal Opens Up National Elections to Members of 'Third Gender.'" Accessed December 19, 2016, http://www. lgbtqnation.com/2013/10/nepal-opens-up-national-elections-to-members-of-third-gender/.

Manchanda, Rita. 2010. "Nepali Women Seize the New Political Dawn: Resisting Marginalisation after Ten Years of War." *Opinion.* Accessed November 9, 2016, http://www.hdcentre.org/uploads/tx_news/47Nepaliwomenseizethenewpolitic aldawnFINAL.pdf

Ministry of Women Affairs. 2008. "National Action Plan for the Women of Afghanistan, 2008–2018." Government of Afghanistan, Kabul. Accessed December 16, 2016, http://mowa.gov.af/Content/files/TABLE%20OF%20CONTENTS.pdf

Minority Rights Groups International. 2013. "Women's Rights Defenders." In *Living with Insecurity: Marginalization and Sexual Violence against Women in North and East Sri Lanka.* Accessed November 9, 2016, http://www.minorityrights.org/download.php?id=1297

Mohsin, Amena. 2005. "Gendered Nation, Gendered Peace," in *Peace Processes and Peace Accords*, edited by Samir Kumar Das. New Delhi: SAGE Publications.

Naher, Ainoon, and Prashanta Tripura. 2010. "Violence against Indigenous Women." In *Between Ashes and Hope: Chittagong Hill Tracts in the Blind Spot of Bangladeshi Nationalism*, edited by Naeem Mohaiemen. Bangladesh: Drishtipat Writers' Collective. Accessed November 9, 2016, http://www.academia.edu/2482097/Chittagong_Hill_Tracts_ in_the_blind_spot_of_Bangladesh_nationalism

National Democratic Institute for International Affairs. 2009. *The 2009 Presidential and Provincial Council Elections in Afghanistan,* September. Accessed December 19, 2016, http://www.ndi.org/files/Elections_in_Afghanistan_2009.pdf

Nemat, Orzala Ashraf. 2011. "Afghan Women at the Crossroads: Agents of Peace—Or Its Victims?" A Century Foundation Report. Accessed November 9, 2016, http://www.peacewomen.org/assets/file/Resources/NGO/hr_afghanwomenatthecrossroads_march2011.pdf

Oxfam. 2011, October 3. "A Place at the Table: Safeguarding Women's Rights in Afghanistan." Oxfam Briefing Paper No. 153. Accessed November 9, 2016, http://www.oxfam.org/sites/www.oxfam.org/files/bp153-womens-rights-afghanistan-03102011-en.pdf

PCJSS (Parbatya Chattagram Jana Samhati Samiti). 2013. *Hill Women's Federation.* Accessed November 9, 2016, http://pcjss-cht.org/index.php?option=com_conte nt&view=article&id=58&Itemid=27

Paudel, Samira. 2003. "Women's Role in Peace Building in Nepal." *Democracy Nepal: Gateway to Nepali Politics and Civil Society.* Nepal: Friedrich Ebert Stiftung. Accessed December 19, 2016, http://www.nepaldemocracy.org/gender/role_women_peacebuilding.htm

Rai, Shirin. 2005, October 24–27. "Equal Participation of Women and Men in Decision-making Processes, with Particular Emphasis on Political Participation and Leadership." United Nations Department of Economic and Social Affairs (DESA) Expert Group Meeting Report No. EGM/EPWD/2005/BP.1. Accessed December 19, 2016, http://www.un.org/womenwatch/daw/egm/eql-men/docs/BP.1%20 Background%20Paper.pdf

RAWA. 2013. "About RAWA." Accessed December 18, 2016, http://www.rawa.org/rawa.html

Rai, Dewan. 2008. "Sarala's Struggle," *Nepali Times.* Issue No. 422. Accessed December 22, 2016, http://nepalitimes.com/news.php?id=15322

Rajasingham-Senanayake, Darini. 2001. "Ambivalent Empowerment: The Tragedy of Tamil Women in Conflict," in *Women, War and Peace in South Asia,* edited by Rita Manchanda. New Delhi: SAGE Publications.

Rajbhandari, Renu. 2008. "Gender-balanced Peace Building," in *Building New Roads to Peace,* edited by Günther Baechler, Nilamber Acharya, Peter Dammann, Renu Rajbhandari and Bishnu Raj Upreti. Lalitpur, Patan: Jagadamba Press.

Ramachandran, Sudha. 2005. "Dying to be Equal: Women Militants and Organisational Decision-Making," in *Women, Security, South Asia: A Clearing in the Thicket,* edited by Farah Faizal and Swarna Rajagopalan. New Delhi: SAGE.

Rana, Bandana. 2012. "Preface and Acknowledgments," in *Nepal National Action Plan on Implementation of the UNSCRs 1325 and 1820: First Year Monitoring Report.* Kathmandu: Government of Nepal and Saathi.

Samuel, Kumudini. 2010. "The Centrality of Gender in Securing Peace: The Case of Sri Lanka." In *WISCOMP Revisioning and Engendering Security Series.* New Delhi: Rupa Publications.

Satkunananthan, Ambika. 2012. "Whose Nation? Power, Agency, Gender and Tamil Nationalism," in *The Sri Lankan Republic at 40,* edited by Asanga Welikala. Colombo:

Centre for Policy Alternatives. Accessed November 9, 2016, http://republicat40.org/wp-content/uploads/2013/01/Representation-in-Politics1.pdf

Shvedova, Nadezhda. 2005. "Obstacles to Women's Participation in Parliament," in *Women in Parliament: Beyond Numbers*, edited by Julie Ballington and Azza Karam. Stockholm: International IDEA.

Sundman, Helena. n.d. "A Good Example—Nepal," in *Operation 1325*. Accessed November 9, 2016, http://operation1325.se/en/projekt/a-good-example-nepal

Suthanthiraraj, Kavitha, and Christina Ayo. 2010. *Promoting Women's Participation in Conflict and Post-Conflict Societies: How Women Worldwide Are Making and Building Peace*. Global Action for Peace, NGO Working Group on Women, Peace and Security, and Women's International League for Peace and Freedom, New York.

True, Jacqui, Sara Niner, Swati Parashar, and Nicole George. 2012. "Women's Political Participation in Asia and the Pacific." *SSRC Conflict Prevention and Peace Forum*. Accessed November 9, 2016, http://artsonline.monash.edu.au/thebordercrossingobservatory/files/2013/02/UNDPA-Women%E2%80%99s-Political-Participation-in-Asia-and-the-Pacific.pdf

United Nations. March 2011. "Report of the Secretary-General's Panel of Experts on Accountability in Sri Lanka." New York: United Nations. Accessed December 19, 2016, http://www.un.org/News/dh/infocus/Sri_Lanka/POE_Report_Full.pdf

UN Women. 2012. "Progress of the World's Women 2011–2012: In Pursuit of Justice." Accessed November 9, 2016, http://progress.unwomen.org/pdfs/EN-Report-Progress.pdf

Upadhyaya, Reecha. 2011. "Nepal," in *Peacemaking in Asia and the Pacific: Women's Participation, Perspectives and Priorities*, edited by Cate Buchanan. Geneva: Centre for Humanitarian Dialogue.

Waylen, Georgina. April 1994. "Women and Democratization: Conceptualizing Gender Relations in Transition Politics." *World Politics* 46(3): 327–54.

Wheeler, Travis. 2012. "Afghan Women See an Opportunity at Bonn." Inclusive Security Blog. Accessed April 19, 2016, http://blog.inclusivesecurity.org/afghan-women-see-an-opportunity-at-bonn/

Women and Media Collective. 2010. "Sri Lanka Shadow Report to the Committee on the Elimination of All Forms of Discrimination against Women." Colombo. Accessed November 9, 2016, http://www2.ohchr.org/english/bodies/cedaw/docs/ngo/WMD_SriLanka48.pdf

2

Gender, Power, and Peace Politics: A Comparative Analysis

Rita Manchanda

Interrogating Peace Politics

Three years ago, at an assembly of women leaders, activists, and scholars at a South Asia conclave on women transforming the politics of peacebuilding confidently asserted,

> We are resolved to open spaces for women's participation at every level and aspect of peace building.... Women have an equal stake in building peace and stability, in constructing dialogue and discourses for peace. Women shall take the initiative to politically transform peace processes to ensure equality in all power relations especially the relations between women and men. Kathmandu Declaration: *The Changing Dynamics of Peacebuilding*, February 2013.

The words of women resonated with resolve, confidence, and conviction. In the countries of South Asia, the social upheaval of conflict, mobilization in resistance politics, and the peace momentum toward transforming power relations had created openings for women and advocacy groups to make gains in women's equal rights, especially when backed by UN Security Council Resolution 1325 (UNSCR 1325), and gender levers in international aid and security programs. Since then, the dangers of increased insecurity, persisting militarization, extremism, aggressive intolerance, and the retreat of democratic accountability have increased in the region. Peace processes that had held aloft the promise of transformative peace and scope for reworking unequal gender relations are facing a cascade of setbacks—shrinkage of democratic space, conservative backlash, extremist vigilantism, regressive orthodoxies, and women's increasing socioeconomic vulnerability and targeted assaults. Across South Asia's multiple peace processes, women are confronting the complexity of engaging with peace politics that run the risk of disempowering rather than empowering marginalized and vulnerable groups. Women are at risk of getting co-opted in these processes, and worse, getting instrumentalized in strategies supporting or opposing violent extremism. Post-war/post-conflict transitions are producing situations of violence that are unpredictable, a politics that is uncertain and regressive and governance that is weak.

In Nepal, women who were in the forefront of the struggle for challenging institutionalized exclusion and for equality as articulated in the Comprehensive Peace Agreement (CPA; 2006), have in less than a decade voted back to power the political forces of status quo. In the process they have undermined the potential of the politics of change associated with the Maoists of reworking unequal and exclusionary power relations, including gender relations. In Afghanistan and Pakistan, women are confronting peace processes promoted by national governments and the international community which are not only exclusionary of women, but likely to roll back women's rights. Pakistan's experience with the collapsed Swat Peace Agreements in Swat in 2008, 2009 (Human Rights Watch 2009) is an ominous warning of the danger of human rights and particularly women's rights getting positioned as a transactional commodity, to be traded in a deal with the Taliban. Afghan women's sense of disillusionment and betrayal as they confront the exit strategies of the International Security Assistance Force (ISAF) was stark at the SA Women's Meet on Women Peace and Security in New Delhi, 2014. "You helped make the mess, you can't just walk away," was the accusatory cry of Judge Najla Ayubi, voicing the anger and anxiety of women human rights defenders who had been emboldened by development and aid agencies to act, and now stand alone, exposed, and targeted.

In neighboring Bangladesh in the Chittagong Hill Tracts (CHT), 18 years after an executive Peace Accord was signed, core questions of demilitarization, land and Bengali transmigration programs remain unresolved, the vulnerability and poverty of indigenous peoples has intensified, and women and girls' security has deteriorated in the context of a violent peace. The consequences of a victor's peace in Sri Lanka are evident in the country's post-war militarization, and the failure to heal a war scarred society and reconcile a deeply divided polity. In India's northeast the long awaited Indo-Naga Framework Agreement was signed in 2015, but can it bring peace to five decades of the Naga peoples struggle (Bhushan 2015; Bose 2015) especially when the secret deal excluded Naga civil society including the Naga Mothers' group which constituted the core of the peace constituency. Would the participation of women at the peace table have made a difference to a power driven agenda? Do women privilege their gender identity over their community identity? (Paffenholtz, Prentice, and Buchanan 2015).

Most peace deals are power sharing arrangements and have little to do with a socially transformative agenda. Feminist scholar activists contend that women's participation in peace processes should be transformative, redefining security, justice, power, and development paradigms. Peace as a transformative moment is exhorted in the UN Global Study on Implementation of UNSCR 1325 2015 and echoed in the UN Secretary General's Report on Women Peace and Security (UN SG Report on WPS 2015). But the peace moment in most conflict resolution processes is more likely to focus on ending violence and returning to normalcy. In Nepal and the CHT, as the peace process became an exercise in status quo and retreated from stated goals, many of the tallest women leaders in the struggle withdrew or aligned themselves with the anti-peace accord lobby.

In India, Kashmiri political activist, Zamrooda Habib and Hameeda Nayeem rejected the peace platitudes offered by President Pratibha Patil, if peacemaking failed to engage with justice. As "Sisters of Peace," a Kashmiri women's delegation had come to Delhi's Presidential Palace Rashtrapati Bhavan on September 29, 2010, to appeal as "mothers" to the president, to end violence and killing in Kashmir. They demanded "azadi," which Nayeem translated as freedom from repression and militarization.[1]

Women continue to be marginalized and ignored in formal peace negotiations, by state and nonstate political forces. In state power politics, regardless of women occupying high public office, governments negotiating peace ignore women and gender concerns. For instance, Bangladesh is dominated by women at the top in government and in the opposition, and gender quotas ensure a third of women in the national assembly and local government. But at the 1997 CHT peace negotiations in Dhaka, entry was confined to those with power, military, or political—all men.

The paper explores the scope and gendered aspects of women's participation in peace processes and examines how peace politics are empowering and disempowering in South Asia. I use, as a point of entry, the contextual constraints and inhibitors that for instance, produced the Nepal paradox of "We (women) had the numbers, but we felt disempowered" in the Constituent Assembly.

The paper probes the tension in women's mobilization in ethnic identity conflicts in Bangladesh and India that valorize safeguarding community identity based on customary laws and practices that tend to be socially oppressive of women. As scholars of gender and ethnicity have explored, women's democratic struggles are embedded in the ethnonational movements of which they are an integral part (Cockburn 1998; Das 2008: 56; Enloe 1993: 280). The survival of community identity depends upon safeguarding customary laws and practices, but it also involves women confronting customary practices which are socially exclusionary of women in public affairs, and gender discriminatory on women's rights to property.[2]

It is not accidental that political formations derived from identity mobilizations tend to be hostile to the entry of women in formal political processes. This is manifest in the persisting absence of women in the "post-conflict" institutions of representative governance, traditional and modern, in Northeast India (Manchanda and Bose 2015: 156–58). Indeed, the fierce backlash against Naga women's demand for their entitlement to women's quota in elected urban bodies draws attention to the limits of gendered power dynamics in ethnonationalist peace politics.

This paper draws upon my conversations with Afghan women in Kabul (July 2013), Nepali women in Kathmandu (October 2013), Naga women in Kohima (April 2014), and the voices of South Asian women in a series of regional conversations including Kathmandu (2013) and Delhi (2014). In addition I draw upon my recent writing on Gender and Ethnicity in *Making War, Making Peace* (Manchanda and Bose 2015).

I

> [T]here is now unquestionable body of evidence proving that women's meaningful participation increases the effectiveness of humanitarian assistance, the credibility and quality of peacekeeping, the pace of economic recovery in post conflict settings, and the sustainability of peace agreements.
>
> —UN SG Report on WPS 2015

Peace Politics and Gendered Power

Feminist research and advocacy has established and the club of the world's most powerful men—the UN Security Council—has acknowledged in the WPS resolutions that women suffer disproportionately from the impact of armed conflict and its gendered consequences. Women bear the brunt of managing the survival of families impoverished and shattered by the disappearance, torture, disablement and death of husbands, sons, and brothers; women and their dependent children comprise the majority of refugees and internally displaced persons. The female body is the ground on which war is fought and "honor" of communities sullied. Evidence-based studies have shown that women's exclusion from formal peacemaking is inextricably linked to the political economy of power which positions women as irrelevant (Paffenholz et al. 2015).

Its corollary is the notion of the continuum of gendered violence spanning the everyday experience of violence against women (VAW), its heightened intensity in conflict, and the consequences "post-conflict" for increased VAW, especially in the context of the carryover of impunity for sexualized violence in conflict. This aftermath continuum is sharply evident in the post-accord CHT, characterized by continuity in high levels of sexualized abuse of tribal women. Bina D'Costa in a recent study singles out the practice of impunity as the most important factor responsible for post-conflict sexual abuse of women largely by

"Bengalis—settlers, school teachers or staff of the forestry department or members of the armed forces" (D'Costa 2014: 39). Gender-based violence is used for "land grabbing" ethnic engineering (forced marriages and conversions) and to push back women out of the public sphere. Alongside violent conflict's socially destructive impact, participatory research has established that, the societal disruption of war opens up spaces for women, civilian and combatant, to take on nontraditional roles, obliging them to assume multiple burdens but expanding possibilities for an "ambivalent empowerment" (Rajasingham 2001). In Nepal, rural women in households without men broke through gendered taboos around the plough and thatching; in Sri Lanka's north and east, female-headed Tamil households took up fishing in the lagoons; in the CHT it was the women who took decisions on displacement and cross-border migration (Meintjes, Pillay, and Thurshen 2002: 7). The exigencies of resistance politics in India's Northeast and Kashmir, Nepal, Sri Lanka, CHT, and Pakistan's Balochistan—saw the mass entry of women into the public sphere of men. Women joined armed resistance struggles and the state's militaries overturning gender stereotypes. As men retreated from the public spaces, women assumed positions of local public authority[3] constituted the humanitarian and human rights front line and promoted peace and reconciliation.

The paper continues the logic of this inquiry into gendered power shifts to explore in the Transition, the scope for translating the moral authority and status of women consolidated through their peacework in conflict, into structures of formal politics? Can Motherhood politics socially premised on the self-abnegating role of the mother be a vehicle for women becoming political subjects and agents shaping more inclusive and just post-conflict societies?

Women's Peacework: From Moral Authority to Claiming Public Voice

In the map of local women's peacework, Irom Sharmila of Manipur has emerged as South Asia's peace icon. She's been on hunger strike since 2000 protesting the abuse of power under AFSPA[4] which mandates shoot on suspicion and entrenches a culture of impunity (She is force fed in custody). Meanwhile, her sisters, the Meira Paibis (torch bearers) keep nightly vigils in their neighborhood, performing resistance in mass "sit ins" and rallies against enforced "disappearances" and AFSPA (Mehrotra 2009). In 2004, the Meira Paibis staged a naked protest before the gates of the headquarters of the Assam Rifles in Imphal, outraged at the rape, torture, and killing of Manorama Devi by state paramilitary forces, and demanded repeal of AFSPA (Judge Upendra Singh Report of Judicial Commission of Inquiry into Manorama's death, n.d.).[5]

Less dramatic but no less bold for women oppressed by multiple bonds of sociocultural restrictions, two dozen Baloch women marched for a month over 700 km to Karachi to seek justice for their brothers, sons, and husbands who have disappeared, allegedly at the hands of Pakistan's security services.[6] Human rights activist Sabeen Mehmud dared to organize a discussion forum in Karachi on "Un-silencing Balochistan" hosting the founder leader of the Voice for Baloch Missing Persons. She was killed in a targeted attack after the seminar (Ali 2015).

At the grassroots is where women in the many conflicts and peace processes of South Asia are found and confined. Amongst them, the profile of Naga women in peacemaking is singular because you glimpse the potential of women peace makers with established moral authority in the "informal" grassroots sphere of politics asserting their right to participate in the decision-making public sphere. Traditionally, Naga women were institutionally excluded from tribal decision-making structures. However the conflict created the social context for local women's agency in peacework,[7] that is, mediating between warring factions; managing community survival by patrolling the night streets and sounding alerts; using kitchen politics to appeal to "rebel" groups to avert reprisal attacks against communities; negotiating the release of "boys" taken away by state and nonstate armed groups; defending human rights and protesting violations, especially sexual gender-based violence; building reconciliation between divided communities; providing indirect channels of communication between armed "national" leaders and monitoring ceasefire violations and redefining the ground rules to include civilian security (Manchanda 2004b).

Naga women's role in peace politics expanded with the widening of the middle space for civil society activism during the long ceasefire 1997–2015. Moreover, over 60 years of protracted militarized conflict and multiple cycles of peacemaking, Naga society has undergone rapid social and economic changes. In particular, state and market penetration and 18 years of the cold peace tailing into the Indo-Naga Framework Agreement 2015 have produced realignments in the structures of traditional power and authority. The coexistence of traditional and "modern" representative institutions of the state has chipped away at the power of traditional tribal hierarchies. This has been reinforced by the increasing privatization of the communitarian land holding which has weakened the structural foundation of tribal authority. New circles of power, the emergence of classes and the growing inter linkages—local, national, and international—have transformed Naga society and polity. Integral to this social churning is the unsettling of gender relations as a fundamental aspect of the realignment of power and control in Naga society (Manchanda and Bose 2015).

Expectedly, there is a fierce patriarchal backlash. "All these social changes, the inclusion of women in decision-making authorities, will destroy our identity, our communities. It's against our customary law and practices," protested Yansathung Lotha, chairperson of the village tribal authority, Wokha. Women's self-sacrificing, self-abnegation roles give power and social legitimacy to Mothers' Groups but disempowers their assertion as citizens with equal rights. So, while Naga society has come to expect that Naga women will have a place in influential civil society peace initiatives such as Forum for Naga Reconciliation 2008—translating local women's peace activism in the informal sphere of politics into authority in the formal sphere of representative politics ("modern" and traditional) has produced a gendered confrontation.

It has got catalyzed around Naga women organizations—Naga Mothers, Watsu Mongdang, Lotha Eloe—claiming the right to 33 percent reservations in metropolitan and town councils in accordance with the national policy on gender quotas. That provision was formally incorporated as law by the Nagaland state assembly in 2006.[8] Women's claim to representation in the public sphere is contested as threatening Naga identity and in violation of Art 371A which guarantees upholding customary laws and practices. The polarizing debate has dragged in property rights for women, also denied under customary law (women readily admit absence of property right holds women back in contesting elections).

So socially divisive has been the women's demand, that the Ao apex tribal body excommunicated the Ao women's organization Watsu Mongdang for nearly a year on a specious charge. Watsu leads the demand for reservations in the suspended Mokokchung elections. The Naga apex tribal body, Naga Ho Ho also opposes women's quota. Under pressure from traditional patriarchies, the Naga state assembly has repealed the 2006 law extending gender quotas in urban bodies to Nagaland. The women took their case to the Supreme Court, transgressing yet another red line. A well-known Naga scholar journalist in Dimapur said, "We should have resolved this within our own institutional structures."

The social significance of the women's challenge can be measured by the Naga tribal bodies and the Naga state assembly invoking Article 371 A. According to Banu Jamit, Nagaland's senior most woman civil servant, Nagas have invoked Article 371 A only twice—once, in asserting Nagaland's claim to its special rights over natural resources, (Suan 2013), the other, on quotas for women in urban and metropolitan councils.

Nagaland is walking the familiar social tract of other conflicts— once the guns are silenced, and "normalcy" restored, the gendered public–private divide hardens and women are ideologically and coercively pushed back into the private sphere, of and for women. Their agency in the official narratives of the struggle is erased (Guhathakurta 2010). The contingent situation may be different in Guatemala, Kosovo, Liberia, Bougainville, Nepal, India, Bangladesh, and Nepal, but the gendered politics of being instrumentalized in the power narratives are the same across regions and cultures and history (Chaterjee 1989).

For instance, the dynamics of resistance politics amidst militarization and militancy in Kashmir obliges Zamrooda Habib to join and politically affiliate her organization Muslim Khawateen Markaz with the separatist coalition Hurriyat, but she has no illusions about the Kashmir movement's instrumental use of women's involvement.

> Women have been at the forefront during the protests and have suffered though more passively than actively, though some have been killed and crippled for life during the present agitation (and) during insurgency raped, molested and rendered destitute, widowed... but the nation isn't aware of their sacrifices and contribution.[9]

Zamrooda has reason to be bitter. A member of the Hurriyat since 1993, she had expected that when she was arrested in 2003 and jailed under anti-terrorist laws, the Hurriyat leadership would support her. However, as she reveals in her memoirs *Qaidi no 100*, the Hurriyat disowned her.

Kuki gender equality activists in Manipur echoed a similar sentiment of being used in the struggle for a Kuki (tribal) homeland.

> [W]e were let down by our committee members and leaders. Women did all the work during the blockade—we put up the barriers, we went on hunger strikes, we were the ones who dealt with and were abused by security forces. But when it came to having an understanding with the government, the men quietly went and signed the papers without consulting us. Vachin Haikop, Sadar Hills District Demand Committee, Manipur.[10]

The roots and aims of these struggles may have been to transform the nature of inequality, exploitation, and exclusion, but too often, these ethnic elite directed movements become struggles in which the "people" (especially women) become pallbearers of a movement to seize power and maintain control (Manchanda and Bose 2015). Samir Das, a student of peace accords, reminds us:

> Women's democratic struggle are in many ways embedded in ethnicity and ethnic movements and the success of their struggle depends not so much on their ability to stand alone (for that is what seldom happens in any society) but very much on how they steer and negotiate their way through conflict between their gender identities as women and as members of some particular ethnic communities. (Das 2008: 56)

Amena Mohsin succinctly captures this ambivalence, "They (CHT indigenous women) call for their rights to property currently denied to them in their customary laws. But the preservation of their customs and culture is critical for them" (Mohsin: SACW 2012).[11] In neighboring Nagaland, their indigenous sisters are resisting marginalization. Rosemary Dzuvichu, who has been co-steering the Joint Women's Front for Naga women's right to gender quotas is determined that this time, women's rights will not be ignored in the guaranteeing customary laws and traditions. "We women, have never had a voice in any of the negotiations for these peace agreements, that's why customary laws have been guaranteed without any reservation, ignoring international norms of protection of women's rights," Roesmary declared (Northeast Dialogues SAFHR and HBF, Delhi, November 2015). It is important to remember when extolling the democracy of the Naga village republics that Naga women did not vote in the historic 1951 Naga plebiscite. This exclusion of women from public life of the tribes has spilled over to resisting women's participation in the "modern" institutions of representative governance.

Ethnic Quotas

In several peace agreements involving indigenous groups, the position of women is specifically addressed by providing quotas in power sharing arrangements in the CHT, Bodoland—Assam, Guatemala, Aceh, Mindanao, and Bougainville. The CHT Accord reserved three seats for women in the two tier hill district and regional self-governing councils in the tribal inhabited area. Two are to be elected from the tribal population, and one from the nontribal population. Not only is there the unintended consequence of capping women's representation, but extending tribal or ethnic quotas to women is quite problematic. As Bell and O'Rourke's gendered analysis of peace agreements indicates, "Quotas for women are sometimes provided as a subpart of what is assumed to be an overarching ethnic or clan identity meaning that women may well be viewed as being present as ethnic and clan members first and foremost." It undermines "the potential for cross-identity organization of women to promote women's equality within new government structures" (Bell and O'Rourke 2010).

It is a timely reminder that women are not a homogenous category, their identity qua women is intersected by other competing affiliations and identities. Also, it cannot be assumed that women will prioritize their gender identity (Cockburn 1998). Gendered audits of the working of the CHT accord have shown that women have no significant influence on decision-making (D'Costa 2014: 33). (Currently there is only a single woman representative in Rangamati District Council.) Indigenous hill women's poor political representation limits their lobbying and advocacy opportunities, effectively excluding them from law and policymaking processes. The gendered consequences of this exclusion is evident in the persisting high levels of sexualized violence with impunity, not as before by the armed forces but largely by Bengali settlers against girls/women in schools, work sites, and the market in an overall militarized situation (D'Costa 2014).

Nepal Women: From Invisibility to Protagonism

> Today, the image of tired malnourished women carrying children at one end and rearing cattle at the other end has been transformed into the image of dignified fighting women with guns. Hisila Yami (Comrade Parvati)

Nepal's conflict and conflict resolution momentum saw huge shifts in gendered power as a result of the convergence of—(a) the mass mobilization of women in a revolutionary struggle with an ideological thrust toward women's equality, (b) women's upsurge in the democratic Jana Andolan II to rid authoritarianism, (c) the organizational activism of women's rights NGOs, and (d) the international community's support for gender inclusion. It vaulted Nepal to the top of the region's GDI for political participation, with the historic achievement of women accounting for a third of the members in the Constituent Assembly and that too from the excluded castes, janajati, and Dalit and Muslim communities.

Several studies have tracked the empowering and disempowering experience of women's participation in the Maoist movement mobilized around an equality and equity ideology which consciously emphasized women's rights (Arino 2008; Manchanda 2004a; Ogura 2009; Pettigrew and Shneiderman 2004; Yami 2007). The 10 years "Peoples War" 1996–2006 created the context for the mass visibility of poor, rural, illiterate women, the majority from oppressed castes and indigenous communities. Women and girls were said to constitute 40 percent of the movement, not only in the mass fronts and propaganda units but also the people's militias and the People's Liberation Army. Anthropologists Pettigrew and Shneiderman found in their encounter with two women Maoists, a Dalit and a Chettri, the scope for flexibility in caste and gender relations. The two were found cleaning their guns. "They did not help in preparing food or in repairing uniforms, both of which jobs were done by men" (2004).

According to a Survey undertaken by the CPN–Maoist women's department, more than 40 percent of women respondents coveted working in the PLA, viewed as a vehicle for rapid sociopolitical mobilization. Sixty-one percent sensed gender discrimination in promotions and 58 percent felt their abilities were doubted (Yami 2007). However, with the majority of the women in the movement aged 14–18 years, capacity for asserting agency was limited. Significantly, findings showed 65 percent were motivated to join because of class oppression, 16 percent indicated gender discrimination.

The reinforcing layers of caste, ethnic, economic, and gender oppression was the material condition of most Nepali and especially rural women's lives. (Amnesty International points to 118 gender discriminatory provisions in 54 different laws in 2007.) The opportunity to escape from the harsh feudal living conditions, the pull of the Maoist liberation rhetoric and campaigns in support of women's rights drew many volunteers (Arino 2008; Manchanda 2004a; Saferworld 2010). Maoist party chairman "Prachanda" admitted the party was caught by surprise at the overwhelming response of women. It brought in its wake social churning on questions of marriage, love, and family relations (Onesto 2005: 195), and rejection of socially degrading menstrual taboos, support for widow remarriage, proscriptions against polygamy, dowry and so on.

The decade of "Peoples War" 1996–2006 radically altered Nepal's society and polity. Maoist women leaders claimed that the locus of Nepali women's movement shifted from urban centers to rural areas, from middle class women to the janajati and lower caste women (Parvati 2003). In 2001, discriminatory restrictions on women's right to inherit parental property was debated, the right to abortion law passed in 2003 and changes demanded in discriminatory citizenship laws. But already in 2004, the gender alert was sounded of the dangers of slipping back to the old ways of servitude of—"cooking, cutting grass and carrying wood, of becoming invisiblized again, of doing nothing," as a young Maoist cadre said (Manchanda 2004a).

There were no women in the 2004 ceasefire negotiations? The Maoists had judiciously put together a negotiating team which reflected their multiple constituencies, for example, janajati (indigenous) and Madhesi (regional) but no women.

> At all the political negotiating tables I have seen in Nepal during the peace process, not once have I seen a woman at the table. So far in the peace process, decisions are being made by men for women. (Ian Martin UNMIN)

The CPA (2006) in the preamble to the road map of peace, incorporated motifs of "inclusiveness, proportionality and participation" and a general reference to ending discrimination on the basis of class, caste, ethnicity, and gender in the restructuring of a more inclusive state. But both the Committee for drafting the Interim Constitution and the Ceasefire Code of Conduct Monitoring Committee were dominated by upper caste hill men. Lobbying by an interpolitical party women's alliance, supported by women activists and backed by UN agencies, resulted in their inclusion. Advocacy by UNFPA led to the inclusion of gender in the UNMIN mandate and the appointment of a gender advisor.

The 2007 interim constitution reflected major gendered power shifts. The high mark was the provision of a third of all positions in public bodies for women. The Maoist decision to nominate women for 73 of their seats proved a game changer in the elections, producing a constituent assembly in which a third were women and significantly, many from oppressed social groups. Major advances were made in recognizing women's reproductive and property rights. Nepal led South Asia in adopting a National Action Plan on 1325 and 1820 (Buchanan et al. 2012).

However, against the backdrop of a fast vitiating "national" consensus, gender as a cross-cutting category got elided by other group interests. The surge in the politics of ethnicity divided women along ethnic and regional affiliations. None of the four Cabinets during the first CA process appointed the promised quota of 33 percent women Ministers. Within the Maoist movement, gender became a casualty of the internal Prachanda versus Baidya struggle for dominance, and security sector reform and the future of 3,846 women combatants in the cantonments—was marginalized.

"When there is difference between the parties, the possibility of asserting a cross-party gender sensitive agenda shrinks," observed

Sarita Giri, a member of the drafting committee of the Constitution. Consequently on statutory rights for women regarding citizenship and property rights, cross-party alliance building proved too weak. Sapana Malla, a leading NGO campaigner for women's legal rights, and UML nominee in the CA, regretted the dilution of rights in comparison with the Interim Constitution. Kalpana Rana (2012), coordinator of the women's caucus in the first CA summed up their experience,

> We feel women (in the CA) are still supplicants—that position has not changed. Earlier, men made laws for women which were imbued with patriarchal values. Now we are 33 percent in the CA. We have our own negotiating power. But we forget that we are not in the political decision making bodies, the high level political committees. Women were not consulted when citizenship and the electoral system were decided (to women's disadvantage) despite our year-long campaign. The CA kept back all disputed issues to the last minute which meant they did not receive enough time.

More importantly, the polarization of politics marginalized the constitutional assembly process which hinged on consensus.[12] Political decision-making retreated from the democratic, transparent forum of the CA to high-level "male" political committees and informal secret parleys in smoke filled backrooms. It is a reminder of women's disempowering limits in accessing "all male patronage networks" where decisions are taken.

The context of the rapid unravelling of the Maoist social revolution undermined the agency of women in public sphere. Nowhere was this more visible than in the experience of the former Maoist women combatants (Saferworld 2010, Upreti and Shrestha in the volume). Yami had warned, "sons will be welcomed back with open arms, but for daughters there can be no return" (Manchanda 2010).[13] Today they face social stigma and rejection for flouting cultural norms. And what do they go back to—the house, the kitchen and grass cutting? In Nepal, the absence of a gender plan as a part of the DDR process saw the self-demobilization of the most vulnerable.

Moreover, Nepal's new constitution after nearly 10 years of delay and two CAs, has rolled back some of the significant gains made, especially on equal citizenship rights. With citizenship not a right but at the discretion of the state, Nepali mothers, especially single mothers, have to prove the father is not a foreigner and the child was born in Nepal. In case of a Nepali woman married to a foreign man, she can confer only naturalized citizenship to her child, whereas a Nepali father can confer the citizenship by descent. This has huge exclusionary implications for Nepal's Madhesi population, given the customary practices of cross-border co-ethnic caste marriages.

Afghanistan—Against all Odds: Enhancing Women's Rights

Protecting Afghan women—after three decades of civil war and the Taliban's gender apartheid years—was projected as morally legitimizing the international invasion of Afghanistan. Enhancing the rights of Afghan women was an integral part of the internationally backed state-building project. Advocacy by Afghan women's rights activists, the international media and influential international NGOs such as the "Feminist Majority" got six Afghan women to the Bonn Conference 2001. It paved the way for women to make up 20 percent of the voting delegates in the Constitution Jirga (2003). The result was a Constitution which guaranteed 27 percent reservations for women in parliament, access to health care and education and importantly women as equal citizens.

> We thought it better to specify men and women and not just all citizens. We felt that if we didn't, men would say this is a male-dominated society, so the term all citizens does not apply to women. (Masooda Karokhel, MP, Herat)[14]

Breaking the cultural taboos about politics and women, in the 2004 election, a woman stood for president, and two for vice president. The conservatives were in retreat and opportunities opened up for women as governors and mayors, in the bureaucracy, the judiciary, police force, in business, NGOs, the professions, and the provincial peace committees. By 2013, women were 25.5 percent in the national civil service and nearly 13 percent in the provincial services, though short of National Action Plan for Women of Afghanistan target of 30 percent (Ministry of Women Affairs 2008: 9). Expectedly, more women work in the social ministries. Families are more comfortable with their women working among other women. Few are in decision-making. Women continue to confront attitudes of ingrained social prejudice, and insensitivity, for example, indifference to providing women separate toilet facilities in a rigidly gender segregated social environment.

> He (the male administrator) gave me a kettle, to make tea in and pee in! (Women employee in provincial service, Kandahar)

President Ghani's efforts to break through blind prejudice on women's participation and nominate the first woman judge in a nine member Supreme Court met with a wall of opposition from conservative clerics and MPs. Judge Anisa Rasouli's nomination failed in parliament (one member objected to a menstruating woman touching the Quran).[15]

In the security sector vital for ensuring women's access to security and justice, women's profile is abysmal—Afghan National Police: 1.3 percent, Afghan National Army 0.4 percent (Karlidag 2014: 15). Cultural sensitivities constrain Afghan women, especially the most disadvantaged, from speaking to a man unrelated to them, including a male police officer, let alone reporting violence. The targeted assassination of high-profile women in the police force has been a demoralizing deterrent to women joining the police force. In September 2008, the Taliban murdered Lt. Colonel Malalai Kakar, head of the department of crimes against women in Kandahar. In July 2013, Islam Bibi, a senior female officer in southern Helmand province was assassinated. Two months later Nigar, her successor, was killed. Few families are willing to send their daughters to work in the predatory male-dominated ethos of the Afghan police, especially in view of reports of sexual harassment at the hands of the male officers (Human Rights Watch 2013; International Crisis Group 2013).

Quotas ensured 28 percent of the seats in the Wolesi Jirga for women (50 percent of the appointees to the Upper House are women). In 2005, 12 percent of the Wolesi Jirga candidates were female, by 2010 the number had increased to 16 percent. The proportion of women amongst the candidates running for seats in the provincial councils has also increased, from 5 percent in 2005 to 12 percent in 2014. This has now dropped significantly to 97 women following the 2014 provincial council elections. A major reason for this was the 2013 election law that reduced the proportion of seats reserved for women from 25 to 20 percent.[16]

While quotas help women access power, women's rights activists were concerned that women MPs lacked real decision-making power. Also the rewards of power have politicized and divided the once more cohesive powerful women. "Men are using the divisions amongst us—ethnic, sectarian, religious—to divide us," said Mabooba Saraj co-founder Afghan Women's Network. "Political women are not prepared or willing to trust us (women's groups) and work for enhancing women's rights," especially in a high-risk security environment. "Women in parliament feel that we cannot assure their security. "They see two Deputy Ministers of Women's Affairs (Najia Sediqi and her predecessor Hanifa Safi) killed in Lahman province," said parliamentarian Shinkai Karokhail (Interviews, Kabul, April 2013). However, Ghani's coalition government has sought to promote women in public life and has appointed three women Cabinet Ministers and two women as provincial governors. But there is skepticism about their effectiveness in an environment of clashing warlords, and stiff opposition to their appointments.

In the tumult of the transition, the ISAF's exit and the weak governments confronting contentious warlords and the Taliban retaking territory, the signposts of a roll back on women's rights are ominous. The electoral law guaranteeing seats for women in provincial assemblies has been cut from a quarter to a fifth. Earlier, in 2012, the Ulema Council of Afghanistan issued a derogatory statement about women being "inferior and secondary to men," justifying grounds for restrictions on their movement. The statement was uncritically showcased on the presidential office website. Despite protests, the Dari and Pashto versions remained on the website. The historic Elimination of Violence Against Women (EVAW) law (2009), a law that for the first time stipulated that the state was legally bound to protect women from violence, criminalized rape, child marriage, forced marriage and the giving away of a girl to settle a dispute—was threatened, with conservative members in parliament denouncing it as unIslamic.

EVAW law remains valid but the attention its detractors have received has undermined its already limited use. Moreover, President Karzai declined to speak in the law's favor. His successor, President Ghani voices support for women's rights and promises greater representation in governing institutions. But the sharply deteriorating security situation and the impunity with which women are targeted is pushing women out of public life.

II

Gendered Perspectives on "Why I am Afraid of Peace!"

The irony of a war weary Nigerian telling peace researcher and theorist Jean Paul Lederach—"I am afraid of 'peace'" (Lederach 1999) is a chilling reminder of the consequences of failed or "bad" peace accords. Roger Mac Ginty is one of the few in the stream of peace research, who boldly asserts that "a peace accord that fails to deliver positive social and economic change, perpetuates inter group hostility and is accompanied by a crime surge—is in need of revision" (2006: 106). Does that explain why in Nepal seven out of eleven of the Maoist women in the Central Committee of the Party opted out of peace process and joined the rejectionists, the radical Baidya faction of the movement, which continued to voice the rhetoric of revolutionary transformation?

Can this analysis help us to understand why in the CHT the vanguard of the HWF and their Dhaka-based civil solidarities allied with the "anti-accordists"? What counsel does it hold for the Afghan or Pakistani women who are fearful of a peace with the Taliban in which they stand to lose their rights? What does "peace" mean in the Northeast for the Bodo tribes women for whom peace is an interregnum between recurring cycles of conflict? What does it mean for their Muslim or Santhal women neighbors in Assam, violently uprooted not once but several times to IDP camps in the wake of ethnic peace accords that relentlessly reproduce exclusionary identity politics? What kind of peace is the Indo-Naga Framework Agreement capable of delivering for indigenous women, mobilized in the struggle, constantly pushed back post-conflict into the limited niches of their ethnic, caste or tribal communities to be governed by local patriarchies?

The changing and complex dynamics of peace processes call for a reflexive approach to the assumption of a "post-conflict" situation, as women and men confront peace processes that have become a continuation of militarization by other means and in which human rights and justice are sacrificed in the pragmatic pursuit of ending violence in deals brokered by "external" conflict managers. What should be women's role vis-à-vis peace deals that seriously disadvantage and disempower them? Should Afghan and Pakistani women support peace talks with an extremist misogynist force like the Taliban that is ideologically opposed to the notion of women as having human rights?

In 2008–09 in Swat, Pakistan the secular government of NWFP/Khyber Pakhtunkhwa, the Awami National Party, sought to buy peace with Taliban outfits in Pakistan, agreeing to impose their interpretation of the *Shariat* in the Swat valley in the hope of removing the people of Swat from the direct line of fire of the militants and the military. The appeasement accords were concluded at a time when Talibanization was already sweeping Pakistan. Within weeks of the February 2009 accord, Tehriqi Taliban Pakistan (TTP) emboldened by the government's concessions took military control of three neighboring districts. The ceasefire collapsed. The army resumed operations. The Taliban rulers of Swat, signaling their brand of justice—publicly flogged a woman. A two minute mobile telephone video of a veiled screaming face down on the ground as two men held her down and a third whipped her, went viral. Public outrage drove the people of Swat to resist the Taliban (Human Rights Watch 2009).

The ANP government faced bitter criticism for doing a deal with the Taliban which threatened not only greater violence but placed women's right and lives at greatest risk. Ironically, Taliban leader Maulana Fazlullah had effectively won over the women through his radio broadcasts and they had contributed financially to the cause.[17] Women's subsequent opposition to the Taliban in Swat was instrumental in effecting the Taliban's retreat. In 2012, Taliban leader Maulana Fazlullah would order Malala Yousafzai to be killed in Swat. In 2013–14, the Nawaz Sharif government put out peace overtures to the TTP, wanting to talk peace with it.

Women in Pakistan and even more so in neighboring Afghanistan are anxious that in the current moves to strike deals with the Taliban, their rights be not bartered away. Under these circumstances, the international community's promise of protecting women and enhancing women's rights reiterated in the multilateral donor frameworks in London (2010) and Tokyo (2012), has become long on rhetoric and short on commitment. Significantly, the international community's engagement in Afghanistan is held up as an example of gender sensitivity, in design planning and implementation. The UN SG Report on WPS (2015) extols the use of gender expertise in NATO in Afghanistan—

> For example a well-functioning network of gender advisors and focal points is now in place across civilian and military elements of NATO institutions and field commands. The Planning Process of Nato's 'Resolute Support Mission in Afghanistan,' the first mission where allies and partners made the required gender expertise available at all levels from the start of the Mission illustrates that integrating gender is an integral part of the entire mission planning cycle. (UN SG Report WPS 2015: para 110)

In comparison, Afghan women rights activists are critical of ISAF's over emphasis on the military dimension as opposed to investing in the rebuilding of social infrastructure. They point to the militarist orientation of ISAF's interventionist profile including the militarization of aid. Indeed the Global Monitoring Report on 1325 in 2009 had criticized NATO as having no clear strategy or approach to protecting women and girls and said it had failed to use UNSCR 1325 as a tool or reference, to entrench peace and security for women.

Afghan women are divided about the initiatives for building a framework of peace, especially in a rapidly deteriorating security situation in which the writ of the state's ANAF and ANP is shrinking before the reassertion of military control of the Taliban and armed opposition groups over Afghanistan (WRN 2013). Some women are seizing opportunities for participating in processes such as the government convened National Consultative Peace Jirga (340 women in 1600 NCPJ). But Judge Najla Ayubi was skeptical of the value of the participation of women nominated by the government. Shinkai Karokhel, an MP and women's rights activist was equally skeptical about the women in the HPC, the formal mechanism for overseeing the APRP (2010). Male committee members did not share information with them. Similar exclusions are evident in the Provincial Peace Committees. "It is mere tokenism," Karokhel said. "The women were handpicked by the government. We (women's groups) didn't choose them. They don't feel they need to be sensitive to our concerns."

Conclusion

Evidence-based analysis indicates that conflict and the conflict resolution momentum open up spaces for subtle shifts in gendered power. The contingent situation will be different in different contexts and between domestic (Northeast: India, Swat, and FATA: Pakistan, CHT: Bangladesh) and internationalized processes (Afghanistan, Nepal, and Sri Lanka). For instance, internationalized processes provide scope for mediators to encourage gender sensitivity, yet the high stakes involved relating to a global threat to peace and security, also drive the need to end violence quickly and rush through a peace deal, notwithstanding that it sacrifices human rights. However there are other instances where the international community has worked with a broad alliance of local women activists (e.g., in Afghanistan, Sudan, Somalia, DRC, and Nepal) to secure the inclusion of gender perspectives and consolidate women's participation.

Alongside, there is the common pattern of backlash by resurgent conservative patriarchal forces pushing out women. "Women are taking the seats of men against our traditional values, while their space is at home" an Afghan male delegate declared in the NCPJ. He was echoing the sentiments of his colleagues in the Nagaland state assembly. Also, the changing dynamics of peace process that are a continuation of militarization, confront women with growing insecurities that constrain their mobility.

Also, presence does not mean "participatory inclusion" and where there is little or no internal party democracy, there is likely to be "participatory exclusion." As the Nepali Congress chief whip said to CA member Arzu Deuba, "aren't you happy to be seen, why do you want to be heard!" Also, as discussed above, we cannot assume women will identify with women qua women and not privilege their other party or ethnic affiliations. As the Naga, CHT, and Afghan contexts remind us, women are embedded in their community identities and invested in community struggles. Women pursuing an autonomous agenda—promoting peace or aggressively reworking unequal power relations—are likely to be rejected as "outsiders." The CHT, Naga, and Bodo women's capacity for realizing a gender empowering politics depends not on standing outside the social community, but by balancing their gender identities as women and as members of particular ethnic communities.

In Afghanistan and Pakistan, women are confronting the challenge of peace deals that are certain to threaten their life chances. Their participation—direct and indirect—needs to be bounded within their particular community structures. Sans the inclusion of women's voice, there will be little possibility of incorporating gendered concerns in sociopolitical process that will shape their futures and that of their communities.

Notes

1. The Indian NGO "Women's Initiative for Peace in South Asia" (WIPSA) had taken the initiative for a group of Kashmiri women activists across the political spectrum from human rights defender Parveena Ahangar to Zamrood Habib to appeal to India's woman President Pratibha Patil for an end to military repression. Styling themselves as "Sisters for Peace," the Kashmir women's delegation represented mobilization derived from the logic of motherhood politics.
2. Tribal Customary Law and Women's Status National Commission for Women. See http://ncw.nic.in/pdfReports/Customary%20Law.pdf
3. In El Salvador, during conflict, a number of women took charge of political institutions in El Salvador, for instance, 33 out of 262 mayors elected during 1985–88 were women. See Kumar (2001). In Nepal, in areas most affected by the conflict, the Maoist heartland. As men went underground, women took over positions in local representative institutions, for example, ward members and the phenomenon of all women wards emerged (see Gautam, Banskota and Manchanda 2001).
4. Armed Forces Special Powers Act—AFSPA (1958; Introduction Note: 5).
5. See http://www.hrln.org/hrln/images/stories/pdf/report-of-commission-of-the-judicial-inquiry-manorama-death.pdf (accessed November 16, 2016).
6. "Baloch families march 700 km to seek justice for missing relatives", AFP, *The Express Tribune* (Pakistan). Accessed December 18, 2016 http://tribune.com.pk/story/635060/baloch-families-march-700-km-to-seek-justice-for-missing-relatives/
7. The Naga armed struggle has drawn in significant numbers of women into the fighting ranks as well as administrative cadres, including the appointment of Women Kilosners in the NSCN I–M shadow government. But unlike in neighboring Nepal, the social impact has been very limited.
8. In 2001, the Nagaland government enacted the Nagaland Municipal Act, extending the 73 and 74 constitutional amendments (1992) to Nagaland for setting up metropolitan and urban councils. Five years later, 33 percent reservations for women were incorporated in the Nagaland Municipal (First Amendment) Act, 2006. Since its adoption, no elections have been held despite the expiry of the terms of the 19 existing councils.
9. See Zamrood Habib's interview in October 2010 on *Koshurputa.blog*.

10. Sadar Hills District Demand Committee (SHDDC) is struggling for autonomy of the Kuki tribes dominated Sadar hills in Manipur. Kuki women who were the visible face of the 94 days blockade found themselves bypassed when the male leadership of the SHDDC negotiated a political deal with the Manipur state government on October 31, 2011, lifting the blockade on the promise of upgrading the Sadar Hills to a district (see Roy 2012).

11. Mohsin, Amin. 2012. South Asia Citizen's Web. Accessed December 19, 2016, http://www.sacw.net/article2574.html

12. A time sheet of hours spent in the CA reveals the minimal importance of the CA process for politically significant political leaders across parties (Chautari 2013). Accessed December, 16, 2016, http://himalaya.socanth.cam.ac.uk/collections/journals/mcpb/pdf/MC_PolicyBrief_04_ENG.pdf

13. "Nepal Women Seize the Political Dawn", Centre for Humanitarian Dialogues, Geneva Dec, Opinion. Accessed December 19, 2016, www.hdcentre.org/uploads/tx.../47NepaliwomenseizethenewpoliticaldawnFINAL.pdf

14. Personal communication, April 2013, Kabul.

15. See http://www.theguardian.com/world/2015/jul/08/afghan-supreme-court-female-nominee-anisa-rassouli (accessed December, 16, 2016).

16. See http://www.cmi.no/publications/file/5301-womens-rights-and-political-representation.pdf (accessed December, 16, 2016).

17. Interview with lawyers and women's rights activist Rukhshanda Naz, Islamabad August 21, 2015.

Bibliography

Abdela, Lesley. 2010. "Women's Meaningful Participation in Peacebuilding and Governance." Case Study. CARE Nepal. Accessed December 12, 2016, http://gender.care2share.wikispaces.net/file/view/CARE%20Report%20Nepal%20-%20Final%20-forbrussels.pdf/295571080/CARE%20Report%20Nepal%20-%20Final%20-forbrussels.pdf

Ali, Imtiaz. 2015. "Rights Activist Shot Dead After Seminar on Baloch Issue." *Dawn*, 25 April. Accessed December 12, 2016, http://www.dawn.com/news/1178152

Arino, Maria Villellas. 2008. "Nepal: A Gender View of the Armed Conflict and the Peace Process." Working Paper No. 04. Barcelona: Ecole de cultura de pau.

Afghan Women's Network (AWN). 2013. "Afghanistan Monitoring Women's Security in Transition: A Baseline Report." Cordaid.

Baskota, Gautam, and Rita Manchanda. 2001. "Where There Are No Men: Women in the Maoist Insurgency in Nepal." In *Women War and Peace in South Asia*, edited by Rita Manchanda, 214–51, New Delhi. SAGE Publications.

Bell, Christine, and Catherine O'Rourke. 2010. "Peace Agreements or Pieces of Paper? The Impact of UNSC Resolution 1325 on Peace Processes and Peace Agreements." *International Comparative Law Quarterly* 59(4): 941–80.

Bhushan, Bharat. 2015, August 8. "Historic Naga Deal Explained." *Mainstream* LIII (33). Accessed November 10, 2016, http://www.mainstreamweekly.net/article5860.html

Bose, Tapan. 2015, December 26. "Indo-Naga Framework Agreement: Apprehensions and Expectations." *Mainstream* LIV (1). Accessed November 24, 2016, http://www.mainstreamweekly.net/article6157.html

Buchanan, Cate et al. 2012. "From Clause to Effect Gender & Peace Agreements CHD." Accessed November 24, 2016, http://www.hdcentre.org/uploads/tx_news/24ClausereportwebFINAL.pdf

Chaterjee, Partha. 1989. "The Nationalist Resolution of the Women's Question," in *Recasting Women: Essays in Indian Colonial History* edited by Sangari, Kumkum and Sudesh Vai. New Delhi: Kali for Women.

Chautari, Martin. 2013. "The Debilitating Dynamics of Nepal CA 2008–13." Briefing Paper No. 8. Kathmandu. Accessed November 10, 2016, http://www.martinchautari.org.np/files/BriefingPaper8_EngVer.pdf

Cockburn, Cynthia. 1998. *The Space between Us: Negotiating Gender and National Identities in Conflict.* New Delhi: Zed Press.

Coomaraswamy, Radhika, and Dilrukshi Fonseca, ed. 2004. *Peacework.* New Delhi: Kali for Women.

Coomaraswamy, Radhika. 2015. "A Global Study on Implementation of UN SC R 1325: 'Preventing Conflict Transforming Justice Securing the Peace'." New York: UN.

Das, Samir. 2008. "Ethnicity and Democracy Meet When Mothers Protest." In *Women and Peace Politics*, edited by Paula Banerjee. New Delhi: SAGE Publications.

D'Costa, Bina. 2014. "Marginalisation and Impunity: Violence Against Women and Girls in the CHT." Chittagong Hill Tracts Commission. Accessed November 10, 2016, http://www.iwgia.org/iwgia_files_publications_files/0679_CHT_violence_against_omen_Study_2014eb.pdf

Enloe, Cynthia. 1993. *The Morning after Sexual Politics at the End of the Cold War.* Berkley, CA: UCLA Press.

Guhathakurta, Meghna. 2010. "Resistance Politics in the Hills." In *Ashes and Hopes: Chittagong Hill Tracts in the Blind Spot of Bangladeshi Nationalism*, edited by Naeem Mohaiemen, 74–76. Dhaka: Drishtipat Writers' Collective.

Human Rights Watch. 2009. "Pakistan: *Swat* Deal Grave Threat to Rights." Accessed December 19, 2016, http://www.hrw.org/news/2009/04/15/pakistan-swat-deal-grave-threat-rights

———. 2013. "Afghanistan: Urgent Need for Safe Facilities for Female Police." Accessed December 19, 2016, http://www.hrw.org/news/2013/04/25/afghanistan-urgent-need-safe-facilities-female-police

International Crisis Group. 2013. "Women and Conflict in Afghanistan." Asia Report No. 252. Accessed December 19, 2016, http://www.crisisgroup.org/~/media/Files/asia/south-asia/afghanistan/252-women-and-conflict-in-afghanistan.pdf

Judith, Pettigrew, and Sara Shneiderman. 2004, January. "Women and the Maobadi: Ideology and Agency in Nepal's Maoist Movement". *Himal Southasian* 17(1): 19–29.

Karlidag, Melika. 2014. *UN Security Council Resolution 1325 in Afghanistan: Civil Society Monitoring Report 2014.* Kabul: Afghan Women's Network.

Kumar, Krishna. 2001. *Women and Civil War: Impact, Organisation and Action.* Boulder CO: Lynne Reinner Publishers.

Lederach, Paul John. 1999. "The Challenge of 21st Century: Just Peace." In *People Building Peace,* edited by Paul Van Tongern, 27–36. European Centre for Conflict Prevention, Utrecht.

Mac Ginty, R. 2006. *No War, No Peace: The Rejuvenation of Stalled Peace Processes and Peace Accords,* 24. Palgrave MacMillan.

Manchanda, Rita. ed. 2001. Women War and Peace in South Asia, 102–30. New Delhi: SAGE Publications.

———. 2004a. "Maoist Insurgency in Nepal: Radicalising Gendered Narratives." *Cultural Dynamics* 16 (2/3): 237–58.

———. 2004b. *We Do More because We Can: Women in the Naga Peace Process.* Kathmandu: SAFHR Monograph.

Manchanda, Rita, and Tapan Bose. 2015. *Making War Making Peace: Conflict Resolution in South Asia,* 142–70. New Delhi: SAGE Publications.

Martin, Ian. 2007. "Implementing Commitments to Women's Equal Participation." Cited in Falch, Ashild (2010). Women's Political Participation and Influence in Post-Conflict Burundi and Nepal PRIO PAPER. Accessed December 19, 2016, http://un.org.np/unmin-archive/?d=activities&p=activity_detail&aid=50

Mazurana, Dyan. 2010. "Understanding the Gendered Legacies of Armed Conflict: Women's Rights and Lives during Armed Conflict and Transition." Periods and Governance Paper IDRC/DFID. Accessed November 12, 2016, https://idl-bnc.idrc.ca/dspace/bitstream/10625/43897/1/130394.pdf

Mehrotra, Deepti. 2009. *Burning Bright: Irom Sharmila and the Struggle for Peace in Manipur.* New Delhi: Penguin.

Meintjes, Shiela, Anu Pillay, Meredith Turshen, 2002. "There Is No Aftermath for Women," in *The Aftermath,* pp. 3–17. London: Zed Press.

Ministry of Women Affairs. 2008. "National Action Plan for the Women of Afghanistan, 2008–2018." Accessed November, 10, 2016, http://mowa.gov.af/Content/files/TABLE%20OF%20CONTENTS.pdf

Ogura, Kiyoko. 2009. "A Chapamaar's Peace." *Himal Southasian.* Kathmandu. Accessed November, 10, 2016, www.himalmag.com/component/authors/articles/Kiyoko-Ogura.html

Onesto, Li. 2005. *Dispatches from the People's War in Nepal.* London: Pluto Press.

Paffenholz, Thania, Potter Prentice, and Cate Buchanan. 2015, May. "Fresh Insights on the Quantity and Quality of Women's Participation in Peace Processes." Policy Brief. Geneva: CMI.

Rajasingham, Darini. 2001. "Ambivalent Empowerment: The Tragedy of Tamil Women in Conflict." In *Women, War and Peace in South Asia: Beyond Victimhood to Agency* edited by Rita Manchanda. New Delhi: SAGE.

Rana, Kalpana. 2012, May 29. "We Were not Consulted When Citizenship and the Electoral System Were Decided." International IDEA. Accessed July 28, 2012, http://www.idea.int/asia_pacific/nepal/interview-with-kalpana-rana-nepal.cfm

Roy, Esha. 2012. "The Election No One Watches." *Indian Express,* 15 January. Accessed December 19, 2016, http://indianexpress.com/article/news-archive/web/the-electionno-one-watches/

Saferworld. 2010. "Security in South Asia, 'Common Ground.' Gendered Assessment of the Needs and Concerns of Maoist Army Combatants for Rehabilitation and Integration: A Report'." Accessed November 10, 2016, http://www.saferworld. org.uk/downloads/pubdocs/Common%20ground_%20LR.pdf

Suan, H.K.K. 2013. "Adding Fuel to Fire." *The Hindu*, August 9.

UN Secretary General Report on Women Peace and Security (UN SG Report on WPS). 2015.Report No. S/2015/716. Accessed December 19, 2016, http://www. securitycouncilreport.org/un-documents/search.php?IncludeBlogs=10&limit=1 5&tag=%22Security%20Council%20Resolutions%22+AND+%22Women%20 Peace%20and%20Security%22&ctype=Women,%20Peace%20and%20 Security&rtype=Security%20Council%20Resolutions&cbtype=women-peace-and-security

UN Women. 2015. *Guidebook on CEDAW GR no 30 and UNSC Resolutions on WPS*. New York. Accessed December 19, 2016, UN Women, New York, http://www. unwomen.org/en/digital-library/publications/2015/8/guidebook-cedawgeneral recommendation30-womenpeacesecurity

WRN (Women's Regional Network). 2013. *Surviving War & Transition in Afghanistan*. Kabul: Community Conversations.

———. 2014. *Unequal Citizens: Women's Narratives of Resistance Militarisation Corruption and Security*. Delhi: Community Conversations.

Yami, Hisila (Comrade Parvati). 2006. *People's War and Women's Liberation in Nepal*. Raipur, Chhattisgarh: Purvaiya Prakashan.

———. 2003. "Women's Perspectives in the Maoist Movement," in *The People's War in Nepal* edited by Arjun Karki and David Seddon, pp. 165–82. Delhi: Adroit Publications.

Participant Analysis
and
Field Notes

3
Herstory: Women and Peace Movements in South Asia

*Roshmi Goswami, Kumudini Samuel, and Nighat Said Khan**

South Asia's Feminist Peace Politics

Following the adoption of UN Security Council Resolution 1325, the promotion of women's participation in all aspects of peacebuilding, including peace negotiations and mediation, is strategically recognized as a key issue in successful peace processes and peacebuilding. Also established is the evidence that the exclusion of women and the lack of gender expertise in negotiations lead to irreversible setbacks for women's rights, leaving crucial issues, such as women's engagement in post-conflict governance and women's access to economic opportunity, justice, and reparations, neglected in peace accords. In the global arena, UN agencies within the UN Inter-Agency Standing Committee on Women, Peace and Security and, in particular, UN Women, have been important in supporting efforts of women's movements to engender the peace and security agenda.

*The authors gratefully acknowledge Hameeda Hossains' contributions on Bangladesh.

Women's actions for equitable and just peace, however, did not start in the international arena. Women's local experiences, grassroots- and community-based peace activism and organic autonomous women's movements are precursors to UNSCR 1325 and the associated cluster of seven WPS resolutions. Indeed, UNSCR 1325 is based primarily on the experiences of women living and working in diverse conflict contexts, particularly in the global south. However, international initiatives including that of UN Women tend to overlook the tremendous contributions of women peace activists of the global south and the expertise that exists therein. This is particularly true of South Asia where there are vibrant, dynamic, and holistic women-led peace and conflict transformation networks and initiatives that go far beyond 1325's prescriptive National Action Plans checklist. These were initiated decades before the UN addressed this important aspect of conflict and peace.

This chapter is neither exhaustive nor strictly chronological and attempts briefly to draw attention to the critical contribution of South Asia's women peace activists by walking with some of the key figures as they recall "moments" and "memories" in the making of "herstory" in national, regional, and international forums. It argues that a specific South Asia feminist politics undergirds many women's peace initiatives and intricately connects their peace activism with larger struggles against ethnic, caste, class, and gender oppression. It is the politics that recognizes that women are invariably "caught" in national, religious, ethnic, and communal narratives as signifiers and symbols of identity and "carriers" of "otherness". Women do not only bear the brunt of inter and intrastate conflicts as victims of direct violence and the indirect consequences of wars, conflicts, and violence but conversely are also active in keeping together the fabric of war-torn societies and do critical work to transform conflict and ensure sustainable and just peace. This chapter seeks to highlight the existence of a South Asia women's peace movement and examines the significance of cross-border solidarities in building peace within and across borders.

While UN Women and other partners of the UN family have focused their energies on the mandates of the Women Peace and Security (WPS) resolutions, South Asian feminists and women's peace activists have looked beyond the technicalities of these resolutions and persisted in raising political and structural questions. At issue was not the mere getting of more women and expertise at the table but about questioning: What is it that women are negotiating or mediating for? What is on the table during peace talks and who determines what should be on the peace table? What do or should women bring to the peace table? What can be compromised and how can women's rights and entitlements not be traded away?

The specificity of a South Asian approach was evident at the regional "Open Day" by the UN Women's South Asia Regional Office on WPS in New Delhi in 2011 when women peace activists from South Asia emphasized the need to challenge peacebuilding as an apolitical engagement and to use peacebuilding as a transformative agenda that questions both the patriarchal nature of states and the patriarchal and neoliberal development paradigms set in motion in post-conflict reconstruction. There were evidence-based warnings from Afghanistan, echoed by feminists from Bangladesh, India, Nepal, Pakistan, and Sri Lanka about the kinds of alliances women become part of in a post-war period and that it is essential to ensure that women are not co-opted by the very same patriarchal processes they otherwise challenged. In Kathmandu, in April 2014, at the Regional Consultation for the Global Study on UNSCR 1325 organized by the Asia-Pacific Women's Alliance on Peace and Security (APWAPS), South Asian voices were raised against militarization of the WPS agenda, that is, making "war safer for women," and instrumentalizing women to counter-violent extremism.

Born out of close linkages to social movements and national politics, and propelled by regional geo politics, South Asia women's peace movements have been vibrant and sharply political, underpinned by complex and sophisticated feminist thinking and ideology. Above all, women's peace activism questions and denounces hostilities among the member states and the militaristic approach to governance in South Asia. As Menon (2004) noted, "A positive outcome of the failure of states across the South Asia region to reach politically negotiated and peaceful resolution of their conflicts has been the emergence of a range of collectivities involved in peace activism—the most vibrant being the women's peace networks.".

The feminist understanding of women and peace, that is, "if women have a distinctive angle in peace it is not due to their being more 'nurturing' but more to do perhaps with knowing oppression"

(Cockburn 1998), resonates in the South Asian context, given the region's deep gender inequalities and subjugation of women. In other words, because women are historically excluded from the structures of power in both the public and private spheres and have *lived experiences* of extreme subjugation, they have a greater stake in working for peace and justice in which they envisage or aspire toward a change in the status quo. This necessarily entails keeping inclusive and participatory democracy alive, for women realize that it is only through democracy and social justice that they will realize their aspirations (Menon 2004). At the core of South Asian women's peace activism in the earlier period was a strong critique of unequal structures of power and a recognition and respect for differences and diversity. It challenged national narratives and identities and forged common struggles across borders.

From the Local to the Regional: Building South Asia Solidarities

Although South Asian women's peace movements significantly came together in the 1980s, the individual journeys and the internalization of a South Asian identity of some kind predate that period and laid the ground for the richness and dynamism of the movements that followed. For instance, in pre-Independence Sri Lanka, women particularly associated with international left politics were engaged in anti-war activism in colonial Ceylon (post-Independence Sri Lanka) from the 1930s. They opposed the jingoistic militarism of Poppy Day, commemorating the end of World War I, through the radical *Suriya Mal* campaign of 1933–36 that provided a rallying point for anti-imperialist youth groups. Subsequently, women associated with left-oriented organizations were active across ethnic divides in Ceylon's struggle toward independence.

It is noteworthy that the struggle for independence in the subcontinent produced many linkages across land and sea borders and saw the involvement of women in common political movements and assertions of the time. For instance, in 1941, the *Lanka Samasamajists* in exile in India became part of the newly founded Bolshevik–Leninist Party of India (BLPI) in opposition to Indian Stalinist Communists who supported the war. Vivienne Goonawardene, a member of BLPI, cut her political teeth in India's struggle for independence. In recognition of her role, she was invited to the Quit India 50th anniversary celebrations in 1991.

In 1947, even as governments and militaries celebrated the formation of the two independent states of India and Pakistan, unprecedented communal violence between Hindus, Muslims, and Sikhs destroyed the social fabric. It was women, who, to a large extent, grappled with the consequences of this mayhem. They took on individual responsibility for providing shelter and services for many women survivors of sexual and other forms of physical and mental violence, who arrived from across the new borders. In East Pakistan, there were community organizations, such as women's *shamitis* formed across the religious divide, in which Hindu and Muslim women worked together to protect and support each other. The poet and civil society activist Sufia Kamal, who crossed over from Kolkata to Dhaka, joined hands with Congress party activist and anti-communal violence campaigner Leela Nag in Kolkata to protect vulnerable women in their respective cities and promote communal harmony. At the same time, both in East and West Pakistan and in India, it was women and women's organizations that attended to women refugees and survivors who had been displaced, abducted, or just abandoned. Politically affiliated organizations, such as the All India Democratic Women's Association and the Democratic Women's Association in Pakistan, spoke up for peace between India and Pakistan.

In Sri Lanka, several peace initiatives date from the 1970s. At the official state level, Sri Lankan Prime Minister Sirimavo Bandaranaike proposed making the Indian Ocean a Zone of Peace at the summit of the Non-Aligned Movement in Lusaka in reaction to the US–UK decision to transform the island of Diego Garcia into a nuclear base. (In 1971, the UN General Assembly adopted the Sri Lanka proposed resolution on the Indian Ocean as a Zone of Peace.) At the civil society level, the 1970s saw progressive women belonging to the Sri Lankan Left active in international solidarity efforts for liberation struggles across the world, and linking up with Afro-Asian peace networks. Women like Kusala Abhayawardhana, social activist and later *Lanka Samasamaj* party member, joined a peace march originating in Sweden to persuade heads of state and foreign ministers to agree to disarmament. She was active in the Women's International League for Peace and Freedom (WILPF). In Colombo, she commemorated the anniversary of Hiroshima and Nagasaki through WILPF.

The "Liberation Struggle" in East Pakistan motivated women in South Asia to come out in support. Sri Lankan women formed a solidarity grouping, Friends of East Pakistan, and opposed the Sri Lankan government's grant of re-fuelling facilities to West Pakistani planes en route East Pakistan. Sri Lanka's canonical third world feminism scholar and activist Kumari Jayawardena was in the forefront on these protests. In West Pakistan, any opposition to the military action in what was then East Pakistan was suppressed. However, the left-oriented Democratic Women's Association led by Tahira Mazhar Ali organized several public protests against the military's suppression of democratic rights in East Pakistan. Pakistan's feminist intellectual and left political activist Nighat Khan joined in these protests. In India, political and humanitarian activist Mohini Giri worked with refugees from East Pakistan and later with Indian war widows after India got involved in the "war of liberation" in East Pakistan.

The first UN World Conference on Women (WCW) held in Mexico led to a global recognition that women has been left out of development process and several initiatives were taken at the national, regional, and international levels to support women's groups and networks. In 1977 at an Asia Pacific meeting organized by the UN in Iran, a trans-regional autonomous solidarity network, the Pacific and Asian Women's Forum (PAWF) was formed with feminist academic and left activist Kumari Jayawardena from Sri Lanka and the creative gender equality rights feminist Kamla Bhasin from India. Both Kumari and Kamla were closely associated with the struggles for social and economic justice in their countries as well as globally.

In Lahore, Nighat Khan, a founder of Women's Action Forum (WAF), who has intellectually mentored a generation of politicized women in Pakistan through the ASR Resource Centre and the Institute of Women's Studies, Lahore, initiated her series of personal "people-to-people" journeys to India in 1979. PAWF got transformed into the South Asian Women's Forum (SAWF) with three of Sri Lanka's leading feminists Kumudini Samuel, Sunila Abeysekera and Sepali Kottigoda coordinating it from Colombo. It needs emphasizing that these women, in the forefront of cross-border solidarity and common struggles built on a huge effulgence of women peace activism in their respective countries while subscribing to a strong internationalism evidenced in their speaking out against Apartheid in South Africa, nuclear testing in the Pacific, and so forth. It is also important to highlight that both PAWF and SAWF were autonomous, non-funded networks, dependent only on the political commitment of those involved.

Pakistan was then under a military government from 1977 until 1988. General Zia ul Haq justified the military dictatorship on the grounds that he had to "Islamize" Pakistan. Military power with religious sanction was a formidable oppressive force and exceedingly dangerous to challenge. The linchpin of the Islamization process was a retrogressive interpretation of Islamic laws. Women and religious minorities bore the brunt of this "Islamization." Women decided to fight back. In 1981, WAF was formed to challenge both militarization and Islamization especially as they affected women. WAF broke the overall silence when it demonstrated against the government in 1983 in Lahore. WAF, a non-funded organization, continues to struggle against militarization and Islamization, and works for peace and human and women's rights.

In India, the path breaking "Towards Equality" Report on the Status of Women in India (1975), steered by scholar feminist Vina Mazumdar, unsettled social complacencies and propelled the next round of feminist activism of campaigns against dowry deaths, custodial rapes, and intersectional discrimination—being poor, minority/Dalit, and a woman. It was a period of intense social ferment especially in the wake of the declaration of "Emergency" and suspension of fundamental rights (1975–77). It triggered massive pro-democracy and social justice protests. India's vibrant women's movements of the 1980s were an integral part of these larger social struggles for equality and justice.

In Sri Lanka, the 1980s saw an increasingly militarist and extremely repressive response to the ethnic conflict in the Tamil majority North and the insurgency in the South, resulting in women's organizations shifting focus from "practical" gender concerns to "strategic" gender interests and challenging unequal relations of gender, ethnicity, and class. This period saw the emergence of Mother' Fronts demanding justice for the involuntarily disappeared. In 1984, a broad-based alliance across ethnic communities "Women for Peace" called for negotiations between the state and the Tamil militant groups. As Sunila Abeysekara, who mentored a generation of not only Sri Lankan feminists but also many in South Asia, explained, "Women for Peace epitomized the role women play in creating space for a conversation between Sinhala, Muslims, and Tamil women during the conflict."

The fact that so many of the "mentors" in the South Asia peace movement—Kumari, Sunila, Kumudini, Nighat, Kamla, Hameeda Hossain—and most of those involved in this in the earlier decade had a Left orientation and were politicized in the struggles for democratic rights has meant that they brought politics into women's organizing. Consequently, the hallmark of women's activism spanning from the mid-1970s to the mid-1990s was that their peace activism was linked to the struggles of other oppressed groups. For instance, in Sri Lanka, it meant supporting peasants fighting against land grabs by sugar multinationals, women workers in the Free Trade Zone struggling for the right to organize and women workers in the plantations demanding equal wages for equal work. Women's activism, therefore, straddled the movements for democracy, civil rights, interracial justice, and social justice in Sri Lanka.

In engaging with the "Woman Question," the focus was on the root causes of women's oppression and subordination, the dual and sometimes triple burden of women, the different strands within feminist discourse, and how women's emancipation could be achieved. A common thread could be perceived across South Asia in the nature and content of activism within autonomous women's groups as links began to be made between groups such as Saheli, Vimochana, Stree Shakti Sangathana, and Bombay Women's Centre in India; Naripokko and Women for Women in Bangladesh; Women's Action Forum, ASR Resource Centre, Simorgh, and Shirkat Gah in Pakistan; and the Women and Media Collective (WMC) and multiple autonomous women's groups in Sri Lanka.

As many founder members of these autonomous feminist groups came from a tradition of left activism, they knew that the women's question was not a priority for the left political parties that were extremely patriarchal in structure and ethos. Consequently, these progressive women's groups developed an agenda for their activism, often drawing from each other. They were clear that the women's movement must be autonomous of both the state and of party politics. The month-long South Asian Women's Studies course organized by Kamla Bhasin in Bangladesh in 1986 and the regional dialogue on "Women and Law" organized by Sri Lankan lawyer and human rights activist Radhika Coomaraswamy, then Director of the International Centre for Ethnic Studies in Colombo, provided important opportunities for women to collectively understand the multiplicity of inter and intrastate conflicts and the connectivity with patriarchy. These women continue to form the core of a feminist and politically active regional women's peace movement in South Asia.

As these regional interactions became more intensive, so did their intellectual understanding of a regional feminism as articulated in the South Asian Feminist Declaration (Bangalore 1989). The consciousness of the South Asia solidarity was translated into action in 1989 when the LTTE assassinated human rights defender Rajani Thiranagama in Jaffna, Sri Lanka. On the 60th day commemoration protest against her slaying, a number of feminist friends from India and Pakistan were present in Jaffna, despite the threats from LTTE and Indian Peace Keeping Forces.

Working Together Regionally: South Asia Mentors

What brought many of these initiatives together was the sustained mobilization engendered around the UN World Conferences on Women, from 1975 to 1995, and their reviews. At the time of the First UN WCW in Mexico City 1975 (declared International Women's Year), the International Socialist Women's Convention in East Berlin was organized by the Socialist bloc in October 1975. South Asian feminists were active participants. The Communist Party of India (Marxist) followed it by organizing a regional conference in Trivandrum. However, women living in conflict situations did not claim attention nationally or internationally till a decade later. At the Third UN World Conference in Nairobi in 1985, for the first time, delegates discussed women's participation in safeguarding world peace, averting nuclear catastrophe, halting the arms race and complete disarmament, and linked peace with development.

The South Asian women peace movement gained further momentum during the international campaign on "Women's rights are human rights" in the lead up to the UN Human Rights Conference in Vienna in 1993. It was this activism from the local to the global that brought about international acknowledgement that women's rights were human rights and importantly focused global attention for the first time on violence against women. Equally significant was women's collective activism in the run up to the Fourth UN World Conference in Beijing in 1995. Women in the region made several efforts to influence United Nations to address the problems of patriarchy, political economy, and militarization in a regional as opposed to a national perspective. The national coordinators of the Beijing process from Bangladesh, India, Pakistan, Nepal, and Sri Lanka worked closely on the regional perspective. Within their countries, they initiated processes to draw in women from the margins. For the first time, there was attention to the narratives and experiences of "conflict" areas such as the North East and Kashmir in India; Baluchistan and Kashmir in Pakistan; the Chittagong Hills Tract in Bangladesh; the Tamil struggles in Sri Lanka; and the war in Afghanistan.

In India, of particular note was the formation of the North East Network (NEN) under the leadership of social activists Monisha Behal and Roshmi Goswami who came from this highly militarized and marginalized border region scarred by multiple and protracted insurgencies. They brought into the Indian women's movement a deep and nuanced understanding of the impact of protracted conflict on the lives of women and the multiethnic dynamics of conflicts in the Northeast. A strong solidarity developed between Northeast India and Sri Lanka around this time. A workshop organized by NEN at the NGO Forum in Huairou at the Beijing Conference on women and armed conflict was conceptualized in collaboration with Sunila Abeysekera. NEN's work on women's rights and armed conflict was informed by the sophisticated feminist politics and human rights understanding of the more experienced Sri Lankan women.

Sunila Abeysekera remained a guide and mentor till her death in September 2013. She travelled to Northeast India several times to facilitate different initiatives, including a workshop on Women and Peace-building (with Kamla Bhasin) to prepare the Naga women to participate in the Naga Peace talks. A milestone in NEN's work on women's human rights and conflict transformation was achieved when Sunila Abeysekera and Shanthi Dairiam of the International Women's Rights Action Watch Asia Pacific conceptualized and facilitated a five-day historic conference on "Women's Rights Are Human Rights" in Shillong in 1997.

Again, in keeping with her politics and commitment of reaching out to women in the margins in conflict affected regions during the

Maoist conflict in Nepal, Sunila Abeysekera and Indian legal scholar and women's rights activist Kalpana Kannabiran worked closely with Nepali human rights defender and former National Human Rights Commissioner Renu Rajbhandari to train grassroots women, including Maoist women, to document cases of sexual and gender-based violence in the conflict affected districts of Nepal. The findings were used for advocacy at the UN Human Rights Council.

Kamla Bhasin, whose regional activism personifies a South Asian feminist identity and South Asia solidarity, as a culmination of her regional initiatives, launched Sangat—a South Asian feminist network—in 2002. Sangat focused on deepening peace and friendship within and between countries as essential for development and democracy in the region. In 2013, Sangat, in collaboration with Peace Women Across the Globe, organized a three-week long multitrack training on women and peace mediation, drawing women from 12 countries of South, South East, and the Middle East Asia with the intention of creating a cadre of peace activists.

Pursuing Accountability: Taking Responsibility for War Crimes

The Vienna and Beijing Conferences gave greater visibility to the questions of accountability for human rights violations and crimes of war against women. The Bangladesh 1971 war experience of mass scale sexual violence played an important role in the provenance of the global discourse on sexual violence in conflict. Bangladesh women's participation in the Gender Caucus for the International Criminal Court was a cumulative outcome of an accountability process that South Asian women wanted in the region. In Bangladesh, during the nine months of the 1971 Liberation War women suffered brutal forms of violence, physical, sexual, and psychological. (They also became peacekeepers, sheltering freedom fighters, carrying messages, and hiding arms.) After the war, women's groups worked with the survivors of violence and demanded that sexual violence be recognized by the state and women who suffered violence be given a space to share their experiences.

Bangladesh government had responded by providing shelter and economic rehabilitation to the women but there was silence on the issue of rape, thus the social stigma remained. Worse, the women who had conceived because of rape by the Pakistani soldiers or local collaborators were made to undergo abortions and give up their babies for adoption. Two women members of Parliament persuaded the prime minister to recognize the women survivors of rape as *Birangona* (brave heroines), but the name came to mean fallen women.

In a parallel process to restore their dignity, women's groups came together to create a space for women survivors to talk of their experiences of violence and their strategies for survival. Women also reached out in solidarity from across the borders. In 1984, when Pakistan socialist feminist Nighat Khan came to Dhaka for a meeting, she openly stated, "The government of Pakistan must apologize and the apology is not just saying sorry, it is much more than that."

In 1973, Bangladesh had enacted a law for the trial of war crimes that included rape. This preceded the incorporation of rape in the International Criminal Court statute. For over four decades, the struggle for justice for war crimes, particularly for sexual crimes, was sustained through documenting oral histories of women such as *Ami Birangona Bolchi* collection. In 1992–93 a Peoples' Tribunal on crimes against humanity was convened in Dhaka by two important cultural icons and political activists, Sufia Kamal and Jahanara Imam. However, before the three women survivors could testify, the government clamped down on the proceedings and started sedition trials against the organizers. The struggle for accountability for war crimes, including sexual violence, continued. In 2010, the government initiated the war crimes tribunal. Prosecutions are ongoing.

Bangladesh Liberation war was the test case of South Asian solidarities, that is, pressuring respective governments to acknowledge accountability. Nighat Khan through ASR, a socialist feminist organization based in Lahore, persisted in trying to get the Pakistani government to acknowledge the role of the military and the government in violently suppressing the democratic aspirations of the people of East Pakistan and culpability in the genocide of 1971. Chapter 8 of the Beijing Platform for Action (BPFA) on "Women and Armed Conflict" provided an entry point to women's groups to push respective governments to address this "area of concern." Moreover, with Benazir Bhutto as Pakistan's Prime Minister at the time of Beijing Conference, there was greater attention on the gender equality agenda in Pakistan.

Significantly, at the UN Preparatory meeting of the 4th WCW in New York in March 1995, leader of the Pakistani Delegation, Salma Waheed, Secretary in the Women's Ministry, conceded that the Pakistani statement needed the input of NGOs and invited the feminist activist Kumudini Samuel from Sri Lanka to attend the ASR Resource Centre "negotiations" on drafting the official statement. The Pakistani UN Mission acknowledged, "Pakistan can't be separate from South Asia." This allusion was important since the main "negotiation" was on the "sensitive" issue of 1971 and the call to take responsibility for crimes against humanity "even in retrospect" that was included in the Pakistan National Report presented in Beijing. Subsequently in 1996, Pakistan's WAF made a public apology on "its own behalf" to the women of Bangladesh for the 1971 crimes.

Although states participating in the UNIFEM intergovernmental South Asia regional meeting "Commemorating Beijing" in September 1996 ignored the BPFA's chapter on Women in Conflict Situations, Tahira Mazhar Ali, the Chairperson of Pakistan's National Consultative Committee, highlighted this omission, especially in the context of the impact of regional conflicts on development and women. An intergovernmental "SAARC Women for Peace" platform was proposed by Pakistan and a parallel "NGO SAARC Women for Peace." However, the dismissal of the Benazir Bhutto government took the momentum out of the Pakistan-backed proposal. Nonetheless, Sunila and Kumudini from Sri Lanka, Nighat from Pakistan, and several others from Sri Lanka kept up the momentum for a SAARC NGO Women and Peace forum. They held two meetings in Colombo in 1997 and 1998 and, later that year, organized a meeting in Nepal attended by Sunila (Sri Lanka), Nighat (Pakistan), Hameeda (Bangladesh), Ruth Manorama (India), and Amjana Shakya (Nepal) and floated a South Asian Women's Institute for Peace Studies (SAWIPS). Although SAWIPS proved unsustainable, its module on women and peace was integrated into the 3-month Certificate Course at ASR Institute of Women's Studies, Lahore. The IWSL had started conducting structured courses in 1998 and had a South Asian focus, South Asian students and faculty.

In Delhi, women formed an informal group for women and peace in the wake of the Kargil war that brought two nuclear-armed neighbors to the brink of interstate war. They organized a seminar on "Women's Vision: A Culture of Peace" in August 1999. The Gandhian, Nirmala Deshpande, Mohini Giri, and Syeda Hameed called for demilitarization and denuclearization on Hiroshima Day, 6 August 1999. They proposed to form a South Asian initiative to be called the Women's Initiatives for Peace in South Asia (WIPSA). SAWIPS and WIPSA members met in regional conference of NGO-SAARC Women for Peace in Dhaka in 1999 supported by UNIFEM and agreed that there was a need for three interlinked and parallel processes—SAWIPS, WIPSA, and a South Asian Women for Peace (SAWP). It was agreed that WIPSA would organize a day of joint peace action on the borders between Bangladesh, India, and Pakistan in December 1999. However, this was stymied by deteriorating Indo-Pak relations.

However, the sense of commitment of the region's women peace activists and groups to challenge their respective state's militarization and repression at home as well as taking responsibility for the destabilizing consequences for the region remained an abiding concern. Cross-border advocacy against militarization and human rights violations continues to motivate women's solidarities. For instance, in 2008, at a People's SAARC mobilization in Colombo on the theme of Food Security and Peace, women's groups from the region used the opportunity, led by WMC, to organize a creative disruption on the street to call for a peaceful solution to Sri Lanka's ethnic conflict.

Border Crossings and Joint Activism

Easing of tension in South Asia's dominant conflict axis, the India–Pakistan relationship, provided an incentive to formalize the many ad hoc cross-border interactions that were sustained during difficult periods and to widen and deepen women peace missions across national borders. Indian members of WIPSA, using the newly opened bus service from Delhi to Lahore, took the initiative to go to Pakistan in 2000. In Pakistan, ASR hosted a 45-member Indian women's peace mission in coordination with NGOs and media groups, including

Pakistan—India Forum for Peace and Democracy (PIPFPD) and Human Rights Commission of Pakistan. The next month, 86 Pakistani women travelled to India. Exchanges between women academics and university students followed. WIPSA, India chapter, later registered itself as a national organization and expanded its peace missions to Bangladesh and Nepal.

Mobilization around the Beijing PFA five-year review process provided a further opportunity to intensify and consolidate regional interactions. A regional conference by SAWP was convened to focus on the implementation of the Armed Conflict chapter of the Beijing PFA. It built on the advocacy work of national women's organizations, such as WMC (Colombo) and the ASR Resource Centre (Lahore), to raise the issue of women conflict and peace at the national, regional, and international levels, including the United Nations. The campaign intensified at the Beijing +5 Review meeting in New York in June 2000 when the Secretary General of the UN Security Council acknowledged the gravity of the issue.

Sri Lanka in many respects was the trailblazer in intellectually defining and mobilizing around women war and peace, but importantly regional and international solidarities were crucial for strategic leverage in getting women and gender concerns included in the peace process of 2002–05. At an international women's consultation organized by Radhika Comaraswamy at ICES, a memorandum was drafted calling for a gender-sensitive framework for peacemaking that protected human rights and respected humanitarian norms. It took note of reports of child conscription; the high security zones in the North and East, and non-inclusion of the concerns of local communities, including Muslims in the negotiations.

The Memorandum reflected the concerns of women from many different locations and countries ranging from East Timor to South Africa, Bosnia, Palestine, India, Northern Ireland, and Cambodia and from the International Criminal Court and the Ad Hoc Tribunals for the former Yugoslavia and Rwanda. It represented the scope within feminist politics for strategic and political alliances across difference in a terrain of transversal solidarities (Yuval-Davis 1997).

However, as the plenary talks in Sri Lanka progressed, women's concerns continued to be marginalized in the formal process. To strengthen the lobby for women's representation, Kumudini Samuel strategized to organize a women's fact-finding mission of local and international activists to the conflict affected districts as a critical first step to get women represented at the peace negotiations. Its report and recommendations were used for advocacy with peace negotiators at the third round of peace talks in 2002. The result was the appointment of the subcommittee on gender issues to advice the plenary of the peace talks on the inclusion of women and gender concerns in the peace process.

Positional Difference on UNSCR 1325

Several activities in the NGO Forum of the UN Beijing +5 Review in New York in 2000 focused on women and conflict. Some of the debates were contentious. Northern NGOs, particularly WILPF and Women Waging Peace Network, were pushing for the UN Security Council to pass a resolution on women and conflict so as to give weight to the demand that countries in conflict prioritize attention to the impact of conflict on women and women's inclusion in conflict resolution. Those involved in these debates from the global south were reluctant to support a process whereby some countries would be singled out and insisted that any agreement of the UN should be applicable to all member nations. Nighat Khan, supported by Kumudini Samuel of the WMC, advocated focusing on the UN General Assembly to move toward a convention not only in the interests of a larger ownership of the issue but also to incorporate a mechanism that ensured regular reporting. It could involve incorporating a section in CEDAW based on the chapter of "Women and Armed Conflict" in BPFA (1995). "The UN Security Council," Nighat Khan argued, "had an unfortunate history of 'punishing' the underdog and for military interventions."

However, these points were lost in the general momentum for immediate "action." The Presidency of the UN Security Council at that point was Bangladesh and, given Bangladesh's own experience of crimes against humanity and sexual violence against women in 1971, the role of the Bangladesh Representative to the UN was significant in getting the UN Security Council Resolution to adopt 1325 on 31 October 2000. In some ways, this was a spurious victory since almost immediately the US Secretary of State, Madeleine Albright, dismissed the resolution as a "Halloween joke." Notwithstanding ambiguity around the UNSCR 1325, the role South Asian women played on foregrounding the WPS agenda should not be underestimated.

Subsequently, South Asia women activists took the position that while endorsing the principles of UNSCR 1325 they would continue to work on and within the PFA chapter on "Women and Armed Conflict." They also took the position to further intensify an understanding of CEDAW, its binding nature on state parties, its wider principles within a human rights framework and make it applicable to conflict and peace. This was partly a result of their understanding of the politics of the Security Council because regional and national imperatives demanded a more politically sensitive and flexible framework, especially since many conflicts in the South Asian region had dimensions and nuances that resisted categorization as "conflicts."

The high profile activism at the international level was grounded in an expanding network of local, national, and regional initiatives. Meenakshi Gopinath, in the vanguard of gendering the security discourse and expanding the dialogic space across borders, launched Women in Security, Conflict Management and Peace (WISCOMP) in 1999. WISCOMP seeks to enhance the role of women as peace-builders, negotiators, and agents of non-violent social change. From her privileged position as the Principal of a prestigious women's college, Meenakshi positioned WISCOMP as a highly influential forum for nurturing the diverse perspectives and capacities of women in the region.

Parallel were the processes, such as South Asia CEDAW, monitoring network with partners working on areas of their expertise. NEN, a network partner, focused on women in armed conflict situations for the CEDAW shadow report when the Indian government presented its official report to the CEDAW committee in January 2000. Similar country chapters were written by the Forum for Women, Law and Development (FWLD) Nepal, WMC Sri Lanka. Using CEDAW, the Women's Human Rights Charter, as a framework for conflict and peacebuilding bridged the gap and the tension between the two streams—women's human rights and women, peace, and security. In the work of UN agencies, including UN Women, these remain unbridgeable streams.

South Asia women's groups shadow reports to the CEDAW Committee contributed in a significant way to the global advocacy for a general recommendation (GR) on women in armed conflict to be included in CEDAW. South Asian organizations, such as WMC (Colombo), organized influential consultations and collaborated in making representations before the CEDAW drafting committee working on the GR on an open day of discussion at United Nations and a consultation for the Asia Pacific region in Bangkok 2012. CEDAW GR 30 was adopted in October 2013, and its significance for South Asia is that it goes beyond the limited conventional definition of armed conflict under humanitarian law and includes subnational conflicts, ethnic and communal conflicts, war against terrorism, foreign occupation, low-intensity protracted conflicts, and so on. In addition, it gives a critical spin to the state accountability by clarifying territorial and extraterritorial jurisdiction, obligations of international aid agencies as well as peacekeeping forces and calls for regulations against non-state actors, including national and multinational corporations. With this expansion and critical depth of analysis, GR 30 is a game changer in the field of conflict transformation and peacebuilding.

Building a South Asia Women and Peace Solidarity

Challenging militarization and promoting just and peaceful resolution of conflicts has been a key commitment of several regional peace networks and alliances where women also play leadership roles. However, with the exception of the South Asia Forum for Human Rights (SAFHR), they do not address the specificities of the impact of conflict and war on women nor call for the active participation of women in peace processes. PIPFPD, Peoples' SAARC, South Asians for Human Rights, South Asian Free Media Association, Pakistan Peace Coalition, and some other key national peace networks subsume women under a homogenous "peace movement" with the exception of the Pakistan-based People's Peace Alliance on Women and Peace. SAFHR stands out for its rigorous academic and conceptual parameters under the leadership of its research director, Rita Manchanda, and has included consistently and systematically women, conflict, and peace in its seminal research, teaching, and advocacy.

In the area of feminist research on women and conflict and foregrounding women's voices, the contributions of Ritu Menon and Urvashi Butalia have been pathbreaking. Through the first feminist publishing house, Kali for Women, and subsequently through Women Unlimited and Zubaan, they have built a South Asian women's solidarity of research on WPS. Moreover, Urvashi's documentation of the voices of Kashmiri women and stories of partition, Ritu's account of partition and analysis of peacemaking in the region are among the finest in South Asian literature and have ushered in a huge outcrop of research on WPS. To the list should be added the work of gendering nation, nationalism, and war in the writings of Amena Mohsin (Bangladesh) and Neloufer de Mel (Sri Lanka), among others including the authors of this chapter.

International donor dynamics, including UN agencies, can and have been a source of support in facilitating South Asia solidarities in building a transformative gender empowering peace as indicated above in this chapter. However, there is also a need for caution about the distorting consequences of the play of donor/UN dynamics. This was evidenced in the strong support for the Afghanistan–Pakistan (Af-Pak) initiative of the Obama regime by UN agencies, including UN Women. Pakistan human rights and peace activist Nighat Khan, in particular, warned against the limitations of this kind of bilateral peacebuilding that ignores the geo-politics of the region and the complicating dynamics of the interests of other bigger actors, more precisely India.

Post UNSCR 1325

Since the passing of the UNSCR 1325, there has been a plethora of agencies, networks, and projects on the implementation of this resolution. To a large extent, these networks have been initiated by groups in the United States of America and Europe and by donor agencies that primarily focused on "setting" up networks and groups in the Global South. During the initial years post SCR 1325, the interest was on Africa but, since 2005, UN Agencies, the donor community and "first world" women's peace networks (many of them formed after the passing of the SCR 1325) turned their interest to Asia. This was due in part since women and peace became a part of the donor checklist for funding projects and the annual assessments of 1325 by the United Nations.

It is important to highlight the distinction between the earlier organic, spontaneous and autonomous South Asian women's peace movement, and the activities and networks formed after 2000 framed as the latter are on projects, agendas, timeframes, and connected to each other as a result of initiatives taken elsewhere. Most of these project-based, and often single issue, networks not only lack a holistic political understanding of intra and interstate conflicts but also take their own projects and activities as a starting point rather than building on what has been a dynamic women's peace movement in South Asia that built itself on sharp analysis of the state, militarization, war, conflicts, patriarchy, heteronormativity, and feminism. They do not reflect an integral aspect of feminist collaboration that would sustain its momentum even if the network or project ceases to exist. The political understanding and the affective and deep friendships of the earlier periods continue. While there are exceptions to this trend and many of the feminists involved in the earlier decades are part of some of these new initiatives to a large extent, their own "herstory" has been subsumed by the immediacy of project- or program-based activism.

More positive, in terms of donor/UN dynamics, was the support for an initiative on peacebuilding in the region that would build upon the experience and expertise and under the leadership of South Asian peace activists. The idea took shape at a meeting between Nighat Khan, Roshmi Goswami, and Anne Marie Goetz—the Senior Advisor on WPS of UN Women in New York in 2010. It was concretized when Roshmi Goswami joined UN Women South Asia office to lead their regional program on WPS. An expert group consisting of Bandana Rana and Sapana Malla Pradhan (Nepal), Rita Manchanda and Anuradha Chenoy (India), Saba Gul Khattak and Nighat Khan (Pakistan), Sima Samar (Afghanistan), Amena Mohsin and Hameeda Hossain (Bangladesh), and Kumudini Samuel and Sunila Abeysekera (Sri Lanka) was formed to conceptualize and lead the regional program on WPS in South Asia. UN Women would play a facilitating role. The expert group's first initiative was a regional conference on the "Changing Dynamics of Peace building in South Asia: Recasting Women's Agency and Transformative Strategies" in Kathmandu in 2013.

This pioneering attempt of actualizing UNSCR's core message of recognizing and valuing women's contribution to peacebuilding by having women peace activists take the driving seat and a UN agency the back seat proved short lived. Various factors, including lack of funds, internal contradictions, dynamics and power struggles within UN Women, and throttling norms and systems, ensured a quiet death of this innovative initiative. Nevertheless, outside UN Women the existing solidarity amongst different members of the group is triggering off a new cycle of peace activism and women's human rights work in the region.

Bibliography

Convention on the Elimination of All Forms of Discrimination against Women. Accessed December 10, 2017, http://www.ohchr.org/EN/ProfessionalInterest/Pages/CEDAW.aspx

Cockburn, Cynthia. 1998. *The Space Between Us: Negotiating Gender and National Identities in Conflict*. London: Zed Books.

General Recommendation No. 30. 2013. CEDAW. Accessed December 10, 2017, http://www.ohchr.org/Documents/HRBodies/CEDAW/GComments/CEDAW.C.CG.30.pdf

Goswami, Roshmi. Speech for *The Gokarna Dialogue Meeting March 2012: Women at the Peace Table–Asia Pacific*. The Centre for Humanitarian Dialogue.

Manchanda, Rita. (ed) 2001. *Women War and Peace in South Asia: Beyond Victimhood to Agency*, New Delhi: SAGE Publications.

Menon, Ritu. 2004. "Doing Peace." In *Peace Work*, edited by Radhika and Coomaraswamy Dilrukshi Fonseka. New Delhi: Women Unlimited.

Samuel, Kumudini. 2011. "Women in the Sri Lankan Peace Process: Included but Unequal." In *Rethinking Transitions, Equality and Social Justice in Societies Emerging from Conflict*, edited by Gaby Oré Aguilar and Felipe Gómez Isa. Belgium: Intersentia.

———. 2009. *The Centrality of Gender in Securing Peace: The Case of Sri Lanka*. New Delhi: WISCOMP.

———. 2006. *Acknowledging a Hidden History: Women's Activism for Peace in Sri Lanka 1982–2002*. Colombo: Social Scientists Association.

Yuval-Davis, Nira. 1997. *Gender and Nation*. London, UK: SAGE Publishers.

4

Building Transversal Solidarities: Women's Search for Peace in Sri Lanka

Kumudini Samuel

In May 2009, the Sri Lankan State defeated the Liberation Tigers of Tamil Eelam in a brutal battle that lasted eight months and waged amidst a captive civilian population trapped in a zone of war. This unilateral military victory reinforced authoritarian rule and blatantly promoted majoritarian triumphalism. It privileged state-centered security and sought to negate minority identities based on race, religion, language, or political ideology. The president set the tone declaring in parliament on May 2009 that, "There are no minorities in this country; after the conclusion of the war all Sri Lankans are divided into two main categories—patriots and traitors." This in effect foreclosed all political space for negotiation and precluded any inclusive discussion on what the post-war order should be. It paved the way for state-centric economic development, rife with corruption, with no regard to consultation with the periphery and often at the expense of accountability and rights. It ignored the need for reconciliation and conflict resolution and moved instead to silence dissenting voice and opinion that sought to question the regime and its acts of commission or omission. Therefore, even as the regime insisted that peace has been won, it expected all citizens to accept restrictions on rights, freedoms, and liberty in the name of securing the nation and the state.

A Change of Regime and the Hope for Democracy

Despite authoritarian rule and the stranglehold on dissent exercised by the Mahinda Rajapaksa regime, an early call for presidential elections in January 2015 served as the impetus to catalyze a broad spectrum of forces ranging from civil society to cross-party political elites, into a rainbow coalition that made possible democratic regime change based on a platform of good governance, anti-corruption, opposition to dynastic politics, and constitutional reform. As the compulsion of regime change necessitated unity among a range of strange bed-fellows, it came at the cost of silence on the national question and a political solution to the ethnic conflict which found no place among the promises of the 100 day platform for change. The new government of President Maithripala Sirisena and Prime Minister Ranil Wickremesinghe consolidated their alliance with a victory in the Parliamentary elections of August 2015. A government made up of a coalition of different understandings of politics has now begun a process of constitution-making and commenced work on transitional justice, central to democracy, national unity, and reconciliation.

Civil society and women have been able to utilize the political space opening up to ensure that marginalized groups, including women, have greater political voice and representation in nation building than before. These gains were achieved through a concerted civil society engagement to ensure democratic regime change so as to open up the possibility of a process of political negotiation for state reform, political restructuring, and anticipated social transformation. This chapter discusses the engagement of autonomous women's organizations with peacebuilding and peacemaking through the years of war and in its aftermath, particularly their initiatives in coalition building across ethnic identities and regional belongings.

Cross-ethnic Connections

In the early years of the armed conflict between 1970 and 1980, forging links among ethnic communities antagonistic to each other was the central activity of peacebuilding. In the late 1970s, the newly emerging autonomous women's groups were largely organized along ethnic lines and their membership was aligned with the one or the other ethnic community. Some were multiethnic in nature while others were based regionally and organized along ethnic belongings. The strong feminist ethos which underpinned the formation of such organizations, however, militated against any communal motivation. By the 1980s, alliance building around national issues allowed for the recognition of difference while retaining a commitment to broader unity around commonalities and political practice. Therefore a politically significant feminist alliance emerging in this period—the Women's Action Committee (WAC)[1]—was able to critically discuss Sinhala nationalist representation of Sri Lanka as the home of a homogenous Aryan Sinhala race that was also the custodian of Buddhism. Women who gave leadership to the WAC were associated with Left or progressive social movements of the 1970s and early 1980s. As women engaged in what they termed as the "critical struggle for women's liberation," WAC espoused a feminist ideology which identified patriarchy as a system of social oppression within capitalism. Members of the WAC linked their feminist politics to the emerging identity-based ethnic politics and the oppression of minorities.

In the early 1980s following the ethnic pogrom of July 1983, WAC responded to Sinhala nationalism at different levels. It demanded redress of minority grievances; emphasized equal rights and opportunity for Tamils of the hill country; criticized state sponsored colonization in the Eastern Province and advocated language rights. WAC agitated for the repeal of the Prevention of Terrorism Act and Emergency Regulations, and condemned the violations of the armed forces and police, including sexual violence against Tamil women. Among its constituencies at the community level, WAC discussed the emergence of Sinhala nationalism, the need to address the root causes of the ethnic conflict and the importance of a politically negotiated solution.

In solidarity with the newly formed Jaffna Mothers Front, WAC echoed the demand of the northern women that "Rape of Women Should Stop." In an open letter to President Jayewardene in December 1984, the WAC linked the State's use of sexualized violence with militarism in the pursuit of a military solution to the ethnic conflict. It warned that "more and more men from the south would become pawns in the war machine." It called upon all parties to the conflict to resume negotiations "with a commitment to bring about a just solution to the conflict." In what became WAC's campaign leaflet, it urged "Women of the South, (to) support the struggle of women in the North against injustice and repression, for peace and freedom!" (WAC leaflet, n.d.).[2]

The word "peace" did not enter the political lexicon of Sri Lankan feminists nor form a part of their activism till 1984 when a Women's Committee for Peace was established and petitioned the State for a peacefully negotiated settlement to Sri Lanka's ethnic conflict. Commencing with one hundred signatures of leading women academics, politicians, professionals, artistes, and activists from all ethnic communities, the signature campaign was subsequently taken island wide. Initiated by a group of feminists from the south of the country, this effort crystallized in the formation of the broad multiethnic coalition—Women for Peace in 1984 (Jayawardena 1985; Samuel 2001).

With increasing militarization, state repression, and intensified ethnic conflict, WAC was confronted with the exigencies of responding to immediate violence and violations by the state as well as Tamil militancy. It had little time to reflect on how women were being defined and constructed by nationalist ideologies as the guardians of "cultural" boundaries. Debates about women as central markers of identity—of the nation, community, ethnic, or religious group—were to surface later in the 1980s in Sri Lankan feminist writings. However, discussions within southern women's forums such as WAC and Women for Peace paid little attention to the rise of Tamil nationalism and its corresponding use of symbols and myth.

Critical debate on nationalism and the women's question emerged in Tamil society, particularly in Jaffna, through the work of Tamil feminists in groupings such as the Women's Study Circle, Jaffna and later the Poorani Women's Collective. In the context of increasing militarism and attendant violence against women including sexual violence by the armed forces, feminists in Jaffna began to contest the patriarchal aspects of Tamil cultural ideology "through a new understanding of sexual violence against women" (Maunaguru 1995: 166). In the north as in the south, rape was publicly hidden and not part of social debate. However, in the context of an ethnic war and an enemy state represented by a hostile military, the rape of Tamil women at the hands of the armed forces became a political concern of Tamil nationalism as a manifestation of racial violence. Tamil feminist activists linked rape to gender and power, as well as the general level of violence directed against women. Paralleling these debates, the WAC too contextualized rape in the context of increasing violence against women and militarization and rejected patriarchal constructs and definitions of rape.

Autonomous Women's Organizing Among Tamil Women in the North

Autonomous women mobilizing within the context of the emergent Tamil militant movement, first found expression in the formation of the Jaffna Mothers Front in 1984. Responding to a mass round up of young men in Jaffna, women who were concerned about their children, irrespective of their political persuasions or affiliations, spontaneously mobilized to form the Mothers Front. Nirmala Balarathnam who closely identified with the left political party, LSSP, assumed its official leadership, and women activists spanning feminists to those from the women's wings of the Tamil militant groups, made up its constituency. The Mothers Front, through public agitation, successfully negotiated the release of youth detained in the round up, protested against custodial rape, state-imposed goods embargos, and the establishment of "no go" or security zones along the coast (Samuel 2006).

The leadership of the Mothers Front had to define for itself an identity that was different from the individual political identities of the women who mobilized within its ranks. It coalesced around the notion of social motherhood which was articulated in terms of moral responsibility (Maunaguru 1995). It emerged as a mode of legitimate struggle in a period and context where conventional forms of male resistance and dissent were dangerous and difficult to organize. The women invoked "motherhood" as a protection against reprisals as much as they used it as a moral duty to safeguard the lives of their children (de Alwis 1998). The social construct of motherhood also influenced their struggle to take on peaceful and nonviolent forms and enabled them to build solidarity with women's organizations in the south.

Significantly, in the early years, the Mothers Front articulated its political positions and determined its interventions independent of the militant groups, including the LTTE, which was consolidating its authoritarian control of the Tamil struggle in the northern and eastern districts. However, the Mothers Front's unproblematic appropriation of the social construct of motherhood did not challenge the position and status of women in Tamil society and did not create for itself an empowered and alternative political identity or existence (de Mel 2001). Therefore, when the LTTE chose to appropriate its activism to suit its political expediencies in the late 1980s, the women had no independent fallback position other than the essentialist role of mother, which buttressed the moral rather than political justification for its work (Samuel 2003). "Nevertheless, this construction of 'motherhood'— appealing for peace represents an important moment of protest which contradicted the [Nationalist] image of the mother calling for war" (Maunaguru 1995: 168).

Further, the feminist politics of the 1980s enabled the WAC and Women for Peace to build a "terrain of solidarities" across multiple identities and different ethnic belongings. This was made possible precisely because the WAC, Women for Peace and the feminists within the Mothers Front and the Women's Study Circle in Jaffna based their politics on a commitment to eradicate the ideology of patriarchal power domination permeating identities such as sex, gender, ethnicity, class, and political affiliation.

The Formal Peace Process

Through the 1980s and 1990s, peace was a concept that was linked to the demand for a negotiated political solution to the ethnic conflict. As the war intensified, a year before the ceasefire agreement of 2002, a reflection of women's aspirations for peace was to manifest itself across the country in many independent and dispersed initiatives on International Women's Day. The Polonnaruwa District Committee made up of women from all ethnic communities, living in villages that marked the border of the conflict ridden Northeastern Province marched across the town calling for an end to the war; women from the People's Peace Front handed over a petition calling for a halt to the war to all political parties; the All Ceylon Women's Trade Union Forum organized a candlelight march in Colombo; the Kurunegala District Women's Committee spearheaded by the Women's Development Foundation marched through Kurunegala town brandishing pots and pans, linking the cost of war to rising food prices; Kantha Shakthi organized a seminar in Balangoda focusing on issues of peace and poverty; the Women's Development Centre organized a Kantha Mela in Kandy; the Uva Community Development Centre, Badulla, brought together Sinhala, Tamil and Muslim women highlighting the need to build respect for the concept of a plural and multiethnic Sri Lanka, in the wake of the prison massacre at Bindunuwewa in the Uva Province; the Jana Sansadaya brought together thousands of women, including a large number of women from "Rana Viru" (military war hero) families in a demonstration for peace from the Southern Province. In speech after speech across the country women made clear their desire for an end to the war (Samuel 2006).

As the year progressed, negotiations commenced between the government and the LTTE leading to the ceasefire agreement of February 2002 and subsequent peace talks. Ten months after the Ceasefire Agreement and four months after the formal peace talks commenced, it was agreed that a women's committee be established to "explore the effective inclusion of gender concerns in the peace process." Established as the Sub-committee for Gender Issues (SGI) and comprising of ten women nominated by the government and the LTTE, it was the first effort by the Sri Lankan government and the LTTE to recognize the involvement of women in peacebuilding and peacemaking. The committee used gender as a conceptual frame for its work and focused broadly on sustaining the peace process; resettlement; personal security and safety; infrastructure and services; livelihood and employment; political representation and decision-making; and reconciliation (SGI Press Release 6/3/2003, www.peaceinsrilanka.org).

The experience of the SGI showed that by recognizing women militants as active political agents, there was a possibility of an engaged feminist discussion and a sharing of feminist resources with militant women (Emmanuel 2006). Logically, the process could enable women combatants to engage with and shape peace processes beyond the narrow conceptions of territory and power sharing. Such mechanisms allowed for the possibility of opening up formal spaces within peace processes to critically challenge dominant patriarchal and masculinist nationalist discourses from within. Unfortunately, the peace talks of 2002/2003 were short lived and the SGI could not continue its work autonomously once the LTTE withdrew unilaterally from the peace process (Samuel 2011).

Coalition Building in the Aftermath of War

In the aftermath of the war and in the site of political exclusion, women, particularly Tamil and Muslim women continued to be marginalized, discriminated, and disempowered as normative frames bound by patriarchy overlooked the particular gendered reality of war, on women. Their experience clearly had produced "different meanings based on gender, sexuality and race/ethnicity as well as local and cultural circumstances" (Petchesky and Laurie 2007: 16).

The security regime—its laws, policies, and practices—had a particular gendered impact on women in the Tamil community. Women had to deal with the continued detention of family members or the disappearance of loved ones who had "surrendered" to the military at the end of the war. They had to deal with the social and political implications of family members, former combatants, who were in "rehabilitation centers" or those who were attempting to reintegrate with communities post-rehabilitation and live a "normal" life. Many women continued to search for the missing and the disappeared, struggling with the tremendous burden of loss suffered in the final battles of 2008/09 during which an estimated 40,000 civilians died under siege in the battlefields.

In the midst of these everyday realities, the question of sexual violence in wartime, a silent and invisible reality that women dealt with mostly in private, gained political currency and international attention with the publication of the OHCHR Investigation on Sri Lanka (OISL), in 2014. The findings of the OISL report related to a range of violations committed by both the Sri Lankan armed forces and the LTTE during the 2008/09 war. The nature of the final battle in Vanni; the horrendous human rights violations that took place in the course of the military victory and the continued realities of life under a heavily militarized and securitized state, provided the impetus for women to break the barriers of ethnic isolation and begin a journey toward post-war recovery and survival. Women's groups, particularly in the north and east of the country had to deal with securing effective and appropriate humanitarian assistance for the thousands displaced by the war and virtually incarcerated in camps for the displaced. They had to seek human rights protection as well as guarantees of safety and security for civilians living in the former war affected areas. At the same time, women's groups were also concerned with how to begin a discussion on a political settlement that would meet the democratic aspirations of minority ethnic communities to live in equality and free of discrimination.

The nature of the war's ending, continued militarization, and the absence of a political solution impelled women again to engage in collective dialogue; to device a kind of "border crossing" across various "conflict lines." And so, four women's organizations—Women and Media Collective, Viluthu, Women's Development Centre and the Association of War Affected Women—took the lead to organize a cross-cultural women's consultation, in the north central town of Giritale, (the Giritale Consultation), bringing together 80 women activists from all districts island wide. Working through the challenges of security, language, and religious barriers, a safe space was created for dialogue among women from different ethnic and religious identities, geographic locations and class and political belongings. As noted in the report of the consultation, it was held "...in the midst of a host of very complex factors including a difficult political environment, problems of travel and communication and anxieties relating to the safety and security of the participants" (Women and Media Collective 2011: 8).

It was commendable that the women chose to come, and a majority of the participants were Tamil speaking and from war affected districts. Some of the women were feminists and human rights activists of long standing; others were new to women's issues and coming into public activism after long years of war. The space allowed women to speak of the ravages of war so that their stories could be heard, and they could in the process be helped to recover. The need to campaign for the removal of high-security zones and for the restoration of civilian administration was foremost among concerns expressed by Tamil women. For those whose lives had forever been transformed by war, their first concern was how to live in safety and security and free from fear. Security and peace was envisioned in terms of secure livelihoods and sufficient incomes; adequate housing; access to decent health services and education; freedom from poverty and a chance to rebuild their lives and futures.

In the discussions, women framed their aspirations in terms of Constitutional and international law guarantees of equality and nondiscrimination of both minority and women's rights. This was seen as the only means of preventing a return to war in the future. These discussions presaged women's active intervention in the constitution-making and transitional justice processes of early 2016, where women frame the political need of power sharing between the center and the periphery in terms of fundamental rights guarantees, voicing a strong articulation of equal rights that spanned civil and political rights protections as well as socioeconomic and cultural rights commitments.

The Giritale Consultation captured an important moment in women's activism in Sri Lanka. It came at a time when women's organizing was marked predominantly by ethnic belongings and women's politics was often expressed in ethnocentric and exclusionary ways. At Giritale, the discussions were by no means easy and a consensus on how to strategize toward demilitarizing the north and east remained elusive. The Giritale report notes,

> Some of the women's groups felt very strongly that there should be a campaign calling for the removal of army camps from the north and east. Others argued that there was still a question of maintaining security in the war affected areas and that there should be a campaign to ensure that the military adhered to human rights standards and practices. This was not an issue on which consensus could be reached. (Women and Media Collective 2011: 10)

Importantly, the Giritale Consultation created the space for the emergence of transversal solidarities where there was an understanding that "notions of difference should encompass, rather than replace, notions of equality" (Yuval Davis 1999: 2) as conceptualized by Nira Yuval Davis in her theorizing on "transversal politics."

Coalition Building

For much of the war-years, except for exceptional campaigns such as—the call for expediting justice for the rape and murder of Krishanthi

Kumarasamy; the call for formal peace negotiations and the inclusion of women in the peace process and the response to the Asian Tsunami of 2004—women's groups dealing with the conflict worked on regionally specific concerns. In the final years of the war and its aftermath, women activists from the north and east began to mobilize on the issue of violence against women. The Giritale Consultation also consolidated emerging solidarities among women who shared a common belonging to a region directly affected by war—the north and east of the country.

During the years of war, the Mannar Women's Development Federation (MWDF) emerged out of conversations between Tamil and Muslim women in the district of Mannar seeking ways to address the contentious issue of displacement. In addressing the rising incidence of violence against women, they strategically focused on economic empowerment. Their work led them to challenge both State structures and the LTTE on questions of political violence and child recruitment. This more politicized work led to the creation of the Mannar Women for Human Rights and Democracy (MWHRD), which addressed war related sexual violence against women. MWDF provided support in coping with the horrendous fall out of the final battle in Vanni and the incarceration of civilians in Manik Farm, helping to reunite families and dealing with post-war detentions (Thangaraja 2014). MWDF reached out to former women cadres of the LTTE who were returning to ostracization in their villages. MWDF built relationships across ethnic, religious, caste, and class barriers and helped women deal with the issue of returning Muslims and the tensions over resources and land.

MWDF worked with women who were hitherto isolated by virtue of their location in the former LTTE controlled areas, and strengthened the activism of two of the main organizations located in these areas—the Mahashakti and Yugashakthi women's federations. It facilitated the formation of the Mullaitivu Women's Development and Rehabilitation Federation. The solidarity and connections built, provided the impetus for the first ever interethnic northern women's collective, the Tamil Muslim Women's Network (2010), which bridged the ethnic divide in the region. This work paved the way for the formation of a broad women's coalition across the north and east of the country and in the district of Puttalam called the Women's Action Network (WAN).

In the east, in 1996, the Suriya Women's Development Centre (SWDC) established the Eastern Women's NGO Forum bringing together women's groups, working mostly with poor and low income communities and marginalized women such as war widows, in three eastern districts affected by the conflict. One of the key campaigns of the Forum was, the "clothes as witness to violence" project which brought the hidden issues of domestic violence and sexual violence against women, into the public domain. Bolstered by the wider network established in the aftermath of the Asian Tsunami (2004), the Women's Coalition for Disaster Management (WCDM), joint campaigns around violence against women were initiated. A critical component of the work of women's organizations associated with the WCDM and in particular SWDC is a critique of the gendered nature of the political economy of conflict and violence. Whereas WCDM is making policy interventions on the economic repercussions of conflict particularly in the context of post-war recovery and development, SWDC's work is focused on the care economy and the economic cost of war.

In the formation of these alliances and coalitions, it is possible to discern a transversal politics based on a "conceptual—and political—differentiation between positioning, identity and values" (Yuval Davis 1999: 2). In WCDM and WAN are women who are positioned very differently in relation to class, caste, religion, ethnicity, marital status, educational attainments, cultural practices, age etc., who nevertheless identify themselves as belonging to a collectivity—of women directly affected by the conflict and the aftermath of war in the north east of Sri Lanka, who can work toward a common agenda of social transformation and social justice (Yuval Davis 1999). As Thangaraja notes, "In Sri Lanka, women's bodies are constantly ethnicized, and ethnicity has been the primary framework within which most struggles have functioned" (2014: 91). Networks such as WAC in the 1980s and later formations such as WCDM and WAN, have tried in myriad ways to use the feminist framing of the personal as the political, to breakdown ethnic polarization at the microlevel and build a terrain of transversal solidarities that can create a pathway for the future.

The Engagement with Constitution-making

Other locations of common political strategizing which are forging an ideological alliance among women's organizations dealing with conflict resolution include the important exercise of making common representations before the Public Representations Committee on Constitutional Reform. These transversal dialogues have provided the opportunity for decentering the hegemony of the south and creating the space for a much broader and inclusive dialogue across regions between feminists and other activists. The emerging transversal politics of peacebuilding among women in Sri Lanka is manifest in the dialogues and cooperation taking place among women irrespective of identity politics in the context of constitution-making and the search for transitional justice.

Following regime change, in August 2015 the new government embarked on a process of constitution drafting and transitional justice. The sharing of state power is at the heart of constitution-making and this requires state restructuring. Also crucial is strong fundamental rights chapter, an equality clause and scope for judicial review to challenge existing discriminatory laws. In 2016, the government embarked on a wide consultation process through the establishment of a Public Representations Committee on Constitutional Reform. Women's organizations from across the country mobilized to make individual and collective representations to the Committee at national and district levels. For instance, Women and Media Collective conducted a series of consultations in 22 districts to ensure that women's groups prepared substantive submissions and engaged with the process.

Women advocated for a strong and inclusive-equality clause, including protection for persons with diverse sexual identity and orientation and critically called for the inclusion of socioeconomic rights in the Fundamental Rights chapter. They called for specific recognition of the inherent and individual dignity, autonomy, and personhood of every person. Women's right to life, bodily integrity, and protection from violence without reservation, women said, should be specifically recognized.

As the report of the Public Representations Committee noted, "Women's representations covered all areas of the Constitution" and in general "women from all parts of the country called for the recognition of Sri Lanka as a plural, multi-cultural and multi-religious country" (Report on Public Representations on Constitutional Reform, May 2016, Public Representations Committee, Colombo, available at http://www. yourconstitution.lk/PRCRpt/PRC_english_report-A4.pdf). Women also "argued for the democratization of the polity, peace, reconciliation, nondiscrimination, equality including equality of opportunity" (115). In addition, women made a strong call for affirmative action to redress historic discrimination in the area of political representation. These representations ensured that the PRC recommend that the Bill of Rights should include a special section on Fundamental Rights for Women. Also included in the recommendations was the establishment of an independent Women's Commission and the use of gender neutral language in the Constitution. The Constitution is now being drafted by a series of subcommittees of the Constitutional Assembly, and women across ethnic groups and from different regions of the country are working with other civil society organizations to ensure the Constitution includes their demands.

Interestingly, a representative of the PRC indicated that while male representations were more concerned with state reform and the devolution of power, women's representations focused on who would wield power and how power would be exercised. Attention was directed to social justice concerns, personal and economic security, including rights to land and employment, health, education, and environmental justice.

The Engagement with Transitional Justice

Transitional justice process is another area in which women across ethnic groups are working together. A Consultative Task Force (CTF) has been appointed by the prime minister to seek public representations on potential mechanisms for truth seeking, justice, reparations, and nonrecurrence. The CTF is headed by a woman and at least a third of its members are women. In the Zonal Task Forces constituted to hear submissions across all districts include as members, many women activists—for women who have been working around conflict and conflict resolution, transitional justice is a critical concern. For them, transitional justice includes restorative justice as well as redistributive justice stemming from a deep concern to seek redressal for civil and political rights harms, but also socioeconomic rights harms. As the discussions on the transitional justice process continue among women of different ethnic belongings, there is the possibility for a future imagining of coalitions among women where women's social and political location could be a resource for the construction of a feminist perspective on social reality, on which feminist political struggles for transformative change can be grounded (Hartsock 2003).

Conclusion

The emerging practice of "transversal politics" among women in Sri Lanka is a "a mode of coalition politics in which the differential positionings of the individuals and collectives involved will be recognized, as well as the value systems which underlie their struggles" (Yuval Davis 1997: 25, quoted in Cockburn 2015).[3] In this process there is also a discernible "model of feminist politics, which takes account of national as well as other forms of difference among women, without falling into the trap of identity politics" (Cockburn 2015: 5). The basis for such feminist politics is grounded on "knowledge acquired by dialogue carried out by people who are differentially positioned." In moving forward, transversal politics could well be "the political guidelines for all political activism, whether at the grassroots level or in state and supra-state power centres" (Cockburn 2015: 92).

The activism around constitution-making and transitional justice may well be the watershed, following which women will confront their choices of privileging a homogenizing ethnic identity over other identities and move to a transformative peace. The new political alliances that were built and consolidated in 2015 with the change of government are now being propelled toward the search for a just and sustainable peace. This climate of inclusivity has opened up space in small but incremental ways for women to search for common values on which difference, especially ethnic difference, can be transcended. As Cynthia Cockburn notes with regard to the Women's Support Network in Belfast, Northern Ireland, carefully established shared values such as justice, nonviolence, and equality, constituted the basis to overcome difference since wrongs had to be admitted; injustice suffered by all sides in the conflict recognized and thereby obstacles to peace removed (Cockburn 2015).

In other words, the feminism of transversal politics is able to take into account the multiple differences among and between women themselves, and allow for both the acknowledgment of difference as well as the building of strategic and political alliances across difference in a terrain of transversal solidarities.

Notes

1. Due to exigencies of space, I only discuss a selected number of women's alliances/coalitions in this article.
2. WAC leaflet. n.d. Feminist Trends in the Women's Action Committee, 1982–90. University of Colombo (2006).
3. Transversal Politics: A Practice of Peace (Peace in Progress No. 22 February 2015. Accessed December 19, 2016, http://www.icip-perlapau.cat/numero22/articles_centrals/article_central_1

Bibliography

De Alwis, Malathi. 1998. "Motherhood as a Space of Protest: Women's Political Participation in Contemporary Sri Lanka," in *Appropriating Gender: Women's Activism and the Politicization of Religion in South Asia,* edited by Patricia Jeffrey and Amrita Basu. London/New York: Routledge.

De Mel, Neloufer. 2001. *Women and the Nation's Narrative Gender and Nationalism in Twentieth Century Sri Lanka.* Colombo: Social Scientists Association.

Emmanuel, Sarala. 2006. *Dealing with Women's Militancy: An Analysis of Feminist Discourses from Sri Lanka.* Social Policy Analysis & Research Centre, University of Colombo, Colombo.

Hartsock, Nancy. 2003. "The Feminist Standpoint: Toward a Specifically Feminist Historical Materialism," *in Feminist Theory Reader,* edited by Carole R. McCann and Kim Seung-Kyung. *New York*: Routledge. Originally published in *Money, Sex and Power.* Longman Press, 1983.

Jayawardena, Kumari. 1985. "Some Aspects of Feminist Consciousness in the Decade 1975–1985," in *UN Decade for Women: Progress and Achievements of Women in Sri Lanka.* Colombo: CENWOR.

Maunaguru, Sitralega. 1995. "Gendering Tamil Nationalism: The Construction of 'Woman' in Projects of Protest and Control," in *Unmaking the Nation: The Politics of Identity and History in Modern Sri Lanka,* edited by Pradeep Jeganathan and Qadri Ismail. Colombo: Social Scientists' Association.

Petchesky, Rosalind P., and Melissa Laurie. 2007. *Gender, Health and Human Rights in Sites of Political Exclusion.* Women and Gender Equity Knowledge Network, WHO.

Samuel, Kumudini. 2001. "Gender Difference in Conflict Resolution the Case of Sri Lanka," in *Gender Peace and Conflict*, edited by Inger Skjelsbaek and Dan Smith. London: SAGE Publications.

———. 2003. "Women's Activism, Motherhood and the State in the Context of Sri Lanka's Ethnic Conflict," in *Feminists under Fire: Exchanges Across War Zones*, edited by Wenona Giles, et al. Toronto: Between the Lines Press.

———. 2006. *A Hidden History: Women's Activism for Peace in Sri Lanka 1982–2002*. Colombo: Social Scientists' Association.

———. 2011. "Women in the Sri Lankan Peace Process: Included but Unequal," in *Rethinking Transitions, Equality and Social Justice in Societies Emerging from Conflict*, edited by Gaby Oré Aguilar and Felipe Gómez Isa. Antwerp, Portland: Intersentia, Cambridge.

Thangaraja, Priya. 2014. "Forging Feminist Alliances: A Front Line Struggle of War Affected Northern Women," in *Our Struggles, Our Stories* edited by Shreen Abdul Saroor, 67–94. Colombo: Women's Action Network.

Women and Media Collective. 2011. "Women's Cross Cultural Consultation: Giritale, Sri Lanka, July 2010." Accessed December 1, 2016, https://www.scribd.com/doc/104857219/Women-s-Cross-Cultural-Consultation-Giritale-Sri-LankaYuval Davis, Nira. 1997. *Gender and Nation*. London: SAGE Publications.

———. 1999. "What Is 'Transversal Politics'?" *Soundings*, 12(Summer): 94–98.

PART II

MILITARIZATION AND VIOLENT PEACE

5
Militarization Values, Attitudes, and Practices in South Asia

Anuradha Chenoy

Militarism is the ideology that endorses military values in civilian interaction and easily intersects with other ideologies, value systems, relations, structures, and practices. The interwoven triad of militarization, masculinity, and patriarchy profoundly influence state–society relations in the South Asian countries even as they connect with global capitalism. Militarization occurs wherever power is primarily backed by the reservoir of force in both material manifestation and ideology. It is a national–state building exercise that is heightened with the political economy of war, force, security, and control.

National security conceptions and aggressive nationalism provide militarism legitimacy and manufactures consent, making it both a state and society process that is located in social, political, and economic institutions. It is practiced by formal as well as informal groups in society which act as vigilante forces. It is voiced from the media which privileges militarist values over democratic ones. Militarization is known to be the most active process during conflicts; however, it is also part of transitional and post-conflict society processes and can develop in any society where there is a rise of majoritarian nationalism that is not curbed by state forces.

Feminists have repeatedly shown that militarization constructs a particularly aggressive and homogenized form of masculinity that connects it to force and power. Such a concept of power spills over into public spaces and impacts social relations. In the process of militarization, women are easily slotted in unequal, traditional, and sexualized roles. As a consequence, women are the first to lose their rights and autonomy and have to wage struggles to gain what men get naturally by way of rights, while boys/men learn to accept power and control as an entitlement over women. Women who challenge and dissent are targeted. Moreover, as neoliberalization seeks women as consumers and part of surplus workforce, women are also co-opted into masculine ideologies and co-opted into the lower category of security forces. New forms of militarization are readapted to the needs of the nation/state that is in perpetual transition. In an atmosphere where the security threat to the nation has become the justification for taking away fundamental freedoms, women lose these freedoms in different ways than men.

In this paper, we examine in a contemporary and comparative frame some of the values, practices, and sites of South Asian militarization. We argue that (a) militarization is evident at different sites, from the borders to everyday common places, during conflict and post-conflict situations; (b) it co-exists with procedural, formal democratic institutions (c) supports and intersects with all sorts of fundamentalisms; (d) it is intimately connected to the military–industrial surveillance complexes that form the political economy of militarization; (e) the practice of militarization can be challenged by people's movements and feminist ideas; (f) in contemporary times, the "deep state" reinforces militarization and masculinity by constantly reconceptualizing and co-opting gender relations, and (g) representatives of extremist ideologies work as vigilante forces in society to reinforce sectarian and militarized ideas.

The state can be demilitarized through popular pressure and by changing institutional practices that challenge fundamentalisms, xenophobic nationalism, privileged class/caste, and patriarchal ideologies. Demilitarization is necessary to end violence against women and create genuine democratic practices. I concur with the argument that militarized politics is the new kind of war under globalization. Nordstorm and Martin (1992: 14) argue that focusing on conventional war is a mistake and it is necessary to understand the patterns of nonconventional war, domination, and repression that characterize political violence in the world today. It is therefore important to understand defense and security as part of "normal" politics of how states maintain themselves as for example "patrolling borders at home, and disciplining claims to sovereign authority and national identity within" (Walker 1993: 151–52). We believe that South Asia can be seen within this frame because conflict and post-conflict situations have a spectrum of continuum that we will explain below.

Characterization and Specificities

Militarization intersects conflict and post-conflict transitional sites in South Asia, with its long histories of internal "disturbances." For example, in the north of Sri Lanka, the Chittagong Hill Tracts in Bangladesh, the Naga Hills, and Kashmir Valley (officially not recognized in India as conflict areas), the northwest regions of Pakistan and the minority regions of north Myanmar. In some cases they have become post-conflict areas, in other cases they are seen as "disturbed areas" and protracted low intensity conflict areas. In a sense, conflict and post-conflict situations here merged because conflicts have transformed not into peace with justice, where root causes have been addressed, but into internal domination by victorious elites linked to the state and where relations are often mediated by security agencies. This heavy securitization is felt differently by women who are at risk of being sexualized subjects and targets of control.

Women in South Asia feel the gendered impact because women continue to face insecurity, more so when armed men increase in their surroundings. As reported by the Women's Regional Network on Afghanistan, far from women's rights making progress in such militarized contexts, their greater sense of insecurity was a likely cause of their decline. "People follow us with their eyes when we leave our home" (WRN 2013). So women who go into public spaces are viewed as "outsiders" and made to feel alien and as the "other." Once they are marked as "outsider," domestic and social violence against them can increase.

In South Asia, women's insecurity rises in relation to different contexts that include the following.

International Militarized Geopolitics: International geopolitics continues from past colonialisms to current political economy and geostrategies of great power hegemony. It is manifested in the extended (world) "war against terrorism" centered in Pakistan and Afghanistan, and in regime changes in several West Asian countries. This influences the politics of South Asia as a whole, because of the geostrategic and socioeconomic linkages between these countries. India's great power ambitions and new strategic alliances and military pacts have led to increased military expenditure. Pakistan's alliance with the US, its frontline status for US military operations and its own ambitions of achieving strategic depth through its border with Afghanistan have increased the role of the military. China's increasing economic and great power interest, as well as the increased interest of other countries like Russia, EU, Israel (and others as arms sellers), brings geopolitics and power rivalries into all of South Asia.

Militarized Boundaries: South Asian states' boundaries are highly militarized and range across land, sea, air space, and now cyberspace. Singularly, the states of the region—especially India–Pakistan and India–China, have failed to resolve cross-border conflicts through sustained negotiations. The interesting exception is the India–Nepal open border and the free access it affords to citizens of both countries. The recent Land Boundary Agreement between India and Bangladesh confirms a border between the two and creates new citizens of people whose identity as citizens had been questioned by both states before this agreement. This is again a positive indication that borders can be demilitarized if there is political will. Many borders between India and Myanmar remain fuzzy and undefined but have not been sites of conflict.

Military's Direct Capture of State Power: This is evidenced in Pakistan, Bangladesh, Myanmar, and the Maldives' contemporary history of military coups. The military continues to wield great influence over civil policies in several South Asian States. In Myanmar, the military continues to wield excessive power over formal and informal civil and society institutions. Sri Lanka is gradually demilitarizing after its 2015 presidential elections. Pakistan's military exercises control over internal security and foreign policy. Direct and indirect military intervention in civilian affairs militarizes institutions and policy choices and impacts women and society.

Military's Takeover of Development Roles: The military has been expanding its engagement in state reconstruction in both conflict and post-conflict situations. It has been given power over civil and governance structures and enjoys impunity through special laws in some regions of the otherwise democratic countries of South Asia. The military has been used in post-conflict reconstruction in many regions of transition like the Northern and Eastern provinces of Sri Lanka, in North West Pakistan, in Myanmar and so on. In India, it has projected a development role as part of "civic action" aimed at the counter insurgency objective of "winning hearts and minds" in conflict affected areas. In all these regions the military occupies large swathes of land, develops business and personal interests, and becomes an interest group with a long-term stake in low intensity conflict. The clearest site of militarization is when there is an overwhelming physical presence of the military as part of ruling regimes and elites.

A Dominant Militarized National Identity: This has occurred when the notion of military power becomes central to the notion of national identity. The majority community has a bigger presence in the military and some of the smaller minorities have little say in military policy as is evident in the region. These notions are influencing policies, budgets, and foreign and domestic policies. Conflict zones are ideal sites for militarization since they are characterized by extreme binaries between state militaries and violent nonstate oppositions. The paradigm of "with us or against us" gets imposed where the middle ground of debate, discussion, moderation, and toleration is absent and purposely delegitimized.

Securitized Zones and a Spreading Security Apparatus: Their spread has increased the power and control of the military over individual lives, impacting men and women differently. Many of these security apparatuses have got entrenched in response to threats from violent/terrorist groups. In some instances, the nature of the conflict has changed from one between insurgent group and the state to another between communities. For example, after the Indian state's peace negotiations with one group—the NSCN (IM), the conflict between the hill tribes and the ethnic Meitei community in the Manipur Valley has increased. Similarly, tensions between ethnic communities in Myanmar and the Chittagong Hill Tracts in Bangladesh have increased. The reasons cited are conflict over land and resources. South Asian states have not dismantled these over-securitized zones, even after threats have declined and peace agreements been signed.

Securitized Thinking: It is based on threat perceptions in conflict and post-conflict situations remaining high and continuing to create a panoply of counter fears. Securitized thinking is an extension of militarism that constructs stereotypical gender roles, and women are pigeon holed into motherhood and national roles. They are the first to lose their autonomy and rights in the name of family, community, and nation so as to be protected by male and patriarchal statehood.

Militarized Oppression and Peoples' Resistance: Peoples' struggles and opposition to militarization is evident in movements against land acquisition for corporate agriculture, manufacturing, mining, against nuclear plants and defense industries, all of which face oppression and securitized/militarist responses from the states and corporate interests. For example, sedition charges were leveled against the leaders of movement against the Kudankulam nuclear plant in Tamil Nadu, India.

Levels and manifestations of militarization vary greatly between states and within states, and between political parties and formations. In South Asia, Pakistan has undergone many decades of military rule. Bangladesh had an interregnum of military rule. In Nepal, the military has a privileged role in successive ruling hierarchies. In Sri Lanka, the military played an important role in the civil war that lasted for 23 years and has an exalted position in society in the aftermath. India has democratic rule and structures (except for the brief period of internal emergency 1976), and a healthy civil–military balance, except in regions of conflict and insurgency where the military influences policies even as elected regimes are in power. In regions of extreme left-wing insurgency, there is the use of force by both the state and the insurgents.

Most often, the militarized regions within democracies are the territories of an ethnic/minority or subnational group that has demanded rights and autonomy. For example, Jammu and Kashmir and the North East states in India; the North and East in Sri Lanka; Balochistan and the Federally Administered Areas of Pakistan; the Chittagong Hill Tracts in Bangladesh—all are regions where tribes and minority communities live. The South Asian states have tried to integrate these regions into the "mainstream," producing movements of resistance. State policy often combines multiple methods that include democratic means like elections, development, as well as the use of force. Militarism fits in well with uneven and quasi-democratic structures. In the case of Sri Lanka, a majoritarian nationalism promoted post-conflict militarism. There was a period of saturated presence of the security forces and was characterized by bias and violence against women. Laws that strengthen military operations in civilian areas continue to be used to bolster the military.

Regimes and powerful executives who take the decision for going to war, especially when they have been effective in curbing insurgencies, have often continued with authoritarian policies after the war — as in Sri Lanka, thus producing new forms of authoritarianism. Also, in spite of several peace agreements between the government and secessionist groups in India's North East, laws that give impunity to the military have not been repealed. Women are excluded from peace negotiations and do not have a say in the peace agreement or in the post-conflict state reconstruction. Women and civil society stakeholders remain at the periphery. The experience of women in conflict areas confirms their marginalization from peacebuilding roles.

Women have to renegotiate their lives during conflict and negotiate with militarized men in post-conflict situations. Even while post-war situations are characterized by the very large presence of women headed households, rehabilitation is rarely gendered and priority is given to men, resulting in the experience of rehabilitation being very different for men and women.

Women in all these regions feel the impact of militarization differently because, the more the military, paradoxically, the less the security. Judge Najla Ayubi (2013) pithily stated: "In Afghanistan, increase in security forces does not mean increase in women's security." In fact women feel they need security from the military and have reason to fear the men in uniform. Men in uniform in these securitized zones see themselves as extensions of the power and masculinity of the state, asserting their privilege over "the other," both men and women. Women become gendered targets. Ordinary men have to protect "their" women from the military and they do so by confining women's movements. The multiple incidents of rapes in all these high-security areas by men in uniform need to be seen in the context of state sanctioned impunity for the security forces. Reports have shown that rape and gendered harassment has been used to undermine the honor of a community that is identified as opposing the state and nationalism. Also, violence is used to keep women "in their place," and make them behave.

Nonstate actors position their militant action as representative of an ethnic or minority community, resulting in the community as a whole being targeted as anti-national and isolated, despite the fact that in most cases, ordinary people support a negotiated solution as opposed to armed conflict. In such binary situations, noncombatants from both sides are targeted as collateral damage and suffer collective punishment. Women are co-opted as human shields, combatants, and cadre by nonstate subnationalist movements and militia. A large number of women have constituted the cadre base of the LTTE, the Maoists in Nepal and India and in the Northeast. The documentation of women's experience in these movements has shown how patriarchal norms dominated their roles, even though they had believed that joining the armed movements would empower them.

In binary militarized situations, civilians in the region—whether agriculturalists, professionals and in business or the media are vulnerable to being used and abused by different armed actors. In particular, human rights defenders are targets as they report on rights violations. An important shift in militarization, pointed out by Kaldor, is the elimination of the distinction between war and human rights abuse (Kaldor 2001: 8). Militarized regimes and militia use the methods of enforced disappearance, fake encounter killing and false charges against dissenters, to enforce their power and order. Women dissenters are targeted in gendered ways, with the intention of destroying their reputation. They are called national security risks, and open to attack, that are often led by chauvinist aggressive nationalist social forces.

In South Asia, human rights defenders have been attacked in a variety of ways—from Asma Jehangir who warned that the Pakistan security establishment planned to attack her; Sunila Abeysekera and Nimalka Fernando who were threatened during the civil war in Sri Lanka, to the torture and attacks on Soni Sori who was labeled a Maoist terrorist and Teesta Setalvad who was labeled a national security risk. Hina Jilani emphasized at a South Asia conference of women in Kathmandu (UN Women 2013) that 45,000 people have been killed in Pakistan because of terrorism, and human rights defenders were easy targets. The point that Jilani makes is that in negotiations with the Taliban, women's security is not raised and women's rights are compromised. She argues that "it appears as though the first point of compromise will be women's security. The capacity of states to control has been built but not the capacity of the state to protect." Militarized, national security states view dissent especially from women, as unacceptable.

Conflict and post-conflict zones have their specificities, but there are similarities. Surveillance on individuals and groups increases. There is mystification about who and how many are killed, raped, abducted, or missing. There is an atmosphere of fear, shadowy politics and rumor as to the perpetrators, with multiple actors—state and nonstate, blaming the other. Women are subjects of this fear, and guarded and kept away from public spaces and thus disempowered.

Militarization, Violence, and Women

The military in states-in-conflict argues that cases of rape are "isolated incidents" or "aberrations" (emphasis added). However, even a single rape serves to cause fear and insecurity and to collectively oppress women and curtail their freedoms. Rape is used to enforce sanctions on women's mobility and choices. Women's groups have been active in South Asia in opposing rape and in asking for better laws and higher conviction rates of rapists. The Indian Supreme Court stated on August 26, 2013 that the conviction rate of rapists is appallingly low and that rape victims do not get community support. The Justice Verma Committee Report' recommended changes in the Armed Forces Special Powers Act in relation to charges of rape. The government did not accept that recommendation, although sections of the Report were used to amend the Criminal Procedure Act.

The threat of violence against women is used to deter them from public and political activities. The use of the weapon of rape to dishonor women, looms as a perpetual threat. It should be no surprise that a study by an NGO on men's use of violence against women in the Asia and Pacific region revealed that from 10 to 62 percent of men interviewed reported perpetrating some form of rape against a woman in their lifetime. Half of the men who reported having raped a woman did so for the first time when they were teenagers. Rape of an intimate partner was more common than nonpartner in most cases. Rape was most commonly motivated by sexual entitlement. The majority of men who perpetrated rape did not experience any legal consequence (P4P 2013). In South Asia, violence against women is rampant, starting with the bias against the girl child to domestic violence in the household that upholds patriarchy. WHO statistics that are commonly cited show that in many of the South Asian states 70 percent of women have faced domestic violence at least once or twice in their homes. Our argument is that women's common experience of patriarchal violence is reinforced in militarized societies and demilitarization is linked to the empowerment of women.

History has revealed that violence against women is an integral part of war and militarization. UN Human Rights High Commissioner Mary Robinson has shown that the high incidence of rape during wars may be explained in part by the failure, until recently, of international lawmakers to deconstruct the role of rape and sexual assault during armed conflicts and the failure to recognize, identify, and prosecute them as violent crimes (Robinson 2010). Since the state needs force and the power to destroy, the state requires "masculine toughness." Connell (1995) has argued that all acts of violence are deeply embedded in power inequalities and ideologies of male supremacy.

A question often arises: should state violence and nonstate militant violence be equated? State violence needs to be exposed because it is the responsibility of the state to protect all citizens, and use the law and constitutional methods in relation to those who dissent and even commit crimes involving violent action. It is also the responsibility of the state to protect other citizens who might come in the way of becoming collateral damage in exchanges between state and nonstate militia. But crimes and illegalities committed by the state, and impunity given by the state to its own actors who commit purposeful crimes is condemnable, unjustifiable, and abuse of human rights. All such acts by state officials must be tried in a court of law.

At the same time, political violence committed by nonstate actors under the cover of acting against state repression and retaliation, or in pursuit of political aspirations like terrorist activities, are criminal activities and cannot be justified except in cases of extreme state or imperialist oppression (like the Vietnam war). These violent acts cannot be justified or given any real and meaningful religious sanction. They should also be held accountable and punished for their crimes. Justifying one form of violence or privileging another is accepting and justifying militarization.

In recent times, peace activists have argued that the use of drones can be justified to kill dangerous militia. But while the nonstate militia is criminal, the state is not. If the state is allowed to carry out extrajudicial murder, it would lead to a lawless society by the defenders of laws, and there would be no system of justice left. Extrajudicial murder cannot be justified in the name of war or the state.

Political Economy of Militarization

The foundation of militarism is the $85.3 billion global arms industry of which the US accounts for the largest share of weapons export of $66.3 billion in 2011 (*New York Times* 2012). America's closest competitor is Russia, with $4.8 billion in sales in 2011. India is one of the biggest arms importers, and is in a drive to modernize its military. South Asian economies can be considered militarized in ways different from the western arms producing economies. The government of Pakistan spends seven times more on its military than on schooling. There are five million children who should be in school but are not, and two-thirds of them are girls. And girls like Malala Yousafzai have been targeted, by fundamentalists at large, for wanting to go to school.

South Asian economies are based on high-defense expenditures. In Sri Lanka, defense expenditure increased after the civil war was over; India proposes to spend US$10 billion on defense from 2010–20; Bangladesh has just signed a $10 million defense and nuclear deal with Russia. Despite high GDP growth in India averaging 6 percent every year since the 1980s, Sen and Dreze argue that "There is probably no other example in the history of world development of an economy growing so fast for so long with such limited results in terms of broad-based social progress" (2013). The low HDI index in all of South Asia must surely be correlated to the steep rising curve of military expenditure, just as the low gender development index is linked to the ideological mix of militarism–patriarchy.

Each government in South Asia justifies the sustained increase in defense expenditure and claims national security as the reason for the negligible rise in social sector spending and public expenditure. Women are more affected than men when public expenditures are cut. And poor and lower class women are the worst affected by these polices, as they cut back on their own basic necessities so that their children get fed and educated and the family has adequate shelter. All gender development indices of South Asia show the relative differences in women's health, literacy, and access to basic services which remain lower than those of men. Amartya Sen has argued that national security and human security need to co-exist and that both are important for human development and peace.

Militarization of Development

Militaries in South Asia are making use of soldiers in development works in the areas of conflict and post-conflict reconstruction. One example is in north Sri Lanka, where the military has expanded its presence in development and reconstruction activities. Ranjany Chandrasegaram, a Sri Lankan social activist stated that although the Lessons Learnt and Reconciliation Commission (LLRC) recommended a reduction in the military, "the state in the north and the east has moved them (military) deeper into the villages, and huge headquarters are being built inside these villages and military personnel being appointed civil administrators" (UN Women 2013).

There are an estimated 80,000 widows after this civil war, but the resources are controlled by the military and the military has displaced women's daily economic activities by taking over small-scale activities such as gardening, small factories, sanitation, and health workers. As a consequence, Chandrasegaram argues, "Women are unable to rebuild their lives because of this mass take over by the military. You can see that women are facing mental and emotional trauma, and they are affected health wise also as they are unable to build secure livelihoods." The military in Sri Lanka's north has become the employer of women. This would make the women serve the very military that is charged with human rights abuses of their own community, and often their own relatives. In Kashmir and in India's North East, the military is engaged in development activities hat embeds them into civil spaces and allows them greater control over women in issues like employment. In Manipur, the Assam Rifles organizes meetings with the Meitei mothers' groups on issues of drugs, development, sanitation, etc. Interestingly, this was welcomed by the Meira Paibis (Meitei, Manipuri women's groups) but seen with distrust by the Naga women, creating further rifts between the two communities.

When the military takes up development activities which are essentially civilian activities, the spaces for women decrease, as they get boxed into the lowest status within military hierarchies. Chandrasegaram has shown that in Sri Lanka, women's groups working in the north and east had to get permission from the military to engage in certain kinds of activity. So, even the Social Affairs Ministry came under the Ministry of Defense. Furthermore, conflict and post-conflict spaces see an increase in surveillance and gendered and ethnic marking, with the result that the security gaze is almost perpetually monitoring daily life. In circumstances where women require the military's permission to work in a particular area or task, women's choice gets restricted by the constant fear of being watched. In such circumstances women have either to work with the military or starve or face other kinds of consequences. So as Chandrasegaram says, there is really no choice even though they say they choose to do these things, it is actually a coercive and constructed choice.

Sri Lanka experienced military expansion during war time but did not cut back its military expenditure with peace. According to the feminist scholar Neloufer de Mel, five years after the war ended an estimated 75 percent of the military is stationed in the north and east resulting in a military–civilian ratio of 1:5, perhaps the highest in South Asia. "The government has turned the military into a soft power," she said, speaking at a South Asia Conference. The army runs businesses in Colombo, including hospitality; they are in the education sector where they run orientation courses for students in military orientation without academic consultation. Many civilian posts are occupied by the military in post-war Sri Lanka (UN Women 2013).

The common experience of South Asia has been that the involvement of the military in civilian areas allows the military to gather intelligence against civilians and intimidate them. This activity supports the surveillance–national security state that protects the state and controls the people.

Militarization and Fundamentalism

Right wing fundamentalism is a close partner of militarism. Fundamentalism is the politicized interpretation of religious sanction where violent intolerance of the other is justified. South Asian states are ridden with different religious fundamentalisms that have intermittently led to intercommunity or communal clashes. In all of these, the community leaders with extreme right wing inclination have used the threat of the dishonor of "their women—wives, daughters, mothers" as the main pretext to use violence against the other. During this violence, the women of the "other" community are targets of sexual violence and abuse.

This pattern can be observed in all recent riot cases in which sexual violence and harassment became male entitlements. This binary perspective of women—ours to protect: theirs to prey upon—has been part of the public discourse in South Asia at the start of communal riots and to incite violence between communities. In the region of Muzaffarnagar, Uttar Pradesh, in September 2013, rumors of a youth from one community, allegedly sexually harassing (termed "eve teasing") a girl from another community led to the retaliatory killing of three young men from the two opposing (Muslim and Hindu Jat) communities. This incident triggered riots where almost 500 people including women and children were killed, women sexually abused and 50,000 people displaced. In this region just before these riots, caste— *khap panchayats* had been held, some in the name of protecting "*ma–bahu–beti*" or mother–daughter–daughter-in-law. In other words, protection and honor of women folk of specific castes were fore grounded. In most sectarian and intercommunity violence all over South Asia, women have been marked for gendered violence, particularly rape. In most of these riots, victims did not get protection from state agencies.

Fundamentalism is committed to confining women to traditional roles, enforcing law-based segregation, veiling women, and denying them the autonomy of choice. In such cases fundamental rights are gendered. Women who resist are subject to punishment ranging from social isolation, harassment and rape, to death. Fundamentalists use the idea of protecting women and sanction violence against them, if "their" women are violated by the other. In some instances, the state in South Asian countries has protected fundamentalist men who are charged with provoking terror in other countries. For example, there is Hafiz Saeed, head of the banned Jamaat-ud-Dawah, said to be a front of the Lashkar-e-Taiba, accused of masterminding terrorist attacks (e.g., Red Fort, India 2000), and with a US$10 million bounty on his head. He roams freely in Pakistan, calling for Jihad on India in front of huge audiences in Pakistan.

The opposition to militarized fundamentalism is a secularization of public spaces where women have the right to move freely, be educated, and exercise choice. Demilitarization of international, regional, and local spaces is intimately linked to ending violence against women.

Culture, Glamor, and Militarization

There is the glamor aspect of militarism expressed in films from Hollywood to Bollywood and other South Asian local cinema that filters to television, visual media, and video games. There is, for example, much reverence for men in uniform, who are seen as the "brave hearts" in service of the nation. Several Indian TV channels equate nationalism primarily with men in uniform. Bob Garfield (2012) wrote in *The Guardian* that the worship of the uniform serves the interest of the government. Heroes win the sympathy of people at the expense of reason and ultimately their own dignity. Thus, honoring somebody's sacrifice in this way is abusing them again because they are being used as trump cards to silence doubts. The use of soldiers to serve the interests of the powerful is cannon fodder. State nationalists cannot resist such glamorization.

Nations and subnationalist movements develop cults of heroism around men and women who fight for the protection of the nation. More skeptical analysis which questions the policies of war is equated with critiquing heroes and martyrs, and seen as a betrayal of the nation. Thus war politics is a mixture distilled from the manipulation of the emotion of loss, protection, and security. It is possible to honor and respect "loss" without iconizing war, and the policies that make war. Feminists have shown that such glorification inevitably leads to degrading women and militates against the very idea of demilitarization (De Mel 2007 and Enloe 2000). Such reverence allows for cover ups of defense deals, and reinforces support for laws that give impunity to army men when they commit human rights violations in areas of armed conflict. Reverence of the military uniform downgrades professions linked to human security and the service done by school teachers, health workers, sanitation workers and so on.

Militarization and Democracy

Democracy in South Asia co-exists with authoritarian tendencies and militarization. The increase in militarization is matched with a simultaneous decline in democratic institutions, freedom, and the rights of citizens. Nationalism and patriotism can be used to justify and legitimize militarization, just as national security can be used to legitimize egregious actions of a ruling regime, including contra-constitutional excesses such as programs of targeted assassination. Zwick's assumption that militarization as an aspect of state building is not an abstraction but an active process that reinforces existing structures, especially those of inequalities within society, can be validated from examples in South Asia (Zwick 1984: 124). State institutions display their biases when it comes to women's issues and national security.

Feminists have repeatedly shown that the militarized lens casts women in primarily traditional roles of motherhood, nurturing, and in relation to their sexuality. In recent times, in reaction to the women's movements and the rhetoric of women's inclusion, the military lens has widened to co-opt women as combatants, in keeping with new push button technologies. As new high technologies like drones and surveillance are incorporated to tackle essentially civil conflicts, South Asian states are making attempts to co-opt women into the military services. So, while the gendered image of woman was one of being weak and therefore in need of protection by the macho male, that image is being challenged as more women are being inducted into the security services and public spaces.

However, as the increase of women in military service in the US has shown, women face sexual abuse and rape from within the military itself, given the sexist training, the innate masculinity and patriarchy that cannot be ripped out of the military's cultural ethos. So the belief that more women in the military could make it more sensitive to women is empirically unsubstantiated. Women are now welcome to join militaries and militias in order to protect other weaker women and some weak men and children (all often clubbed together). In India, for example, the government is very proud of its women police contingents in UN peace keeping roles. In South Asia, armies continue to be dominated by men, and the policies and the decision-making are primarily by the male.

Women's induction into the militaries has not altered the character, attitude, or values of the military or militarization. Though South Asia contributes the largest contingents for UN Peacekeeping operations, these troops come from the same cadre that is active in controlling ethnic communities and borders and have been charged with human rights abuses. Militaries in South Asia, as elsewhere, have incorporated a short module on gender issues in training programs as a concession to the international women's movement and Security Council Resolution 1325. The normative pressure ensuing from the cluster of SCR on Women Peace and Security should be used to make national military forces and international peace keepers more gender sensitive.

It is not just threats but even threat perceptions that lead to an increase in security and militarization. For example, even though small secessionist movements all over South Asia are no match for the highly armed South Asian states, they are still perceived as major internal threats. Women and motherhood are symbols of the nation and so women's bodies get embedded in the politics of constructing and destroying the nonnationalist "other," as an assertion of power.

Militarization of the state is manifest where political parties have armed wings; militarized cadre and governments not only allow militias to exist but covertly use informal militias in disturbed areas. In many South Asian democracies, militarism occurs wherever there is the state of exception, that is, the civil constitution is in abeyance and fundamental rights stand suspended because of the state of emergency and emergency laws that accord extraordinary powers to the security forces. Because of their long duration, such laws give the security forces extraordinary powers and influence to say "No" when any elected representatives asks for the removal of such provisions. For instance, in the midst of a growing public demand to withdraw or review AFSPA, India's Finance Minister Chidambaram stated that the government could not amend the law because there was "no consensus" between it and the armed forces (*The Hindu* 2013). The state of exception is part of the militarization process, whereby it normalizes it into everyday practice.

These laws violate the constitution, but are still upheld by autonomous judiciaries (India SC: NPMHR vs GOI 1997). In the midst of a sociolegal culture of impunity, state institutions like the national and state human rights commissions delay justice and compensations. Moreover, the mandate of these officially constituted human rights commissions does not extend over national security domain. All South Asian states have their versions of the Armed Forces Special Powers Act (AFSPA) and other draconian laws. Civil society groups in all South Asia have shown how these have been used to abduct men, silence women, harass families, give impunity to the violators, and deny justice to victims and their families. The traumatic effect on women and the devastating impact of women's bodies becoming the embodiment of honor is well-documented.

Democratic institutions can have militarized responses, especially on national security issues. As the military expands its role in conflict and post-conflict areas, it erodes the roles of other state institutions, like the local self-government bodies, the judicial institutions, and civil administration. Women have to negotiate with state institutions all the time and have a different relation with the state from men, especially when in times of conflict, women's bodies are part of the negotiation.

In Sri Lanka—even as the civil war between the Sri Lankan forces and the LTTE ended in 2009, with the victory of the Sri Lankan forces leaving in its wake thousands killed, women raped, and livelihood and lives destroyed—militarization and the enhanced national security that was built up systematically during the war, continues. The UN Human Rights Council adopted a resolution condemning war crimes by the Sri Lankan army as well as by the LTTE and called for accountability. President Mahinda Rajapaksa dismissed all demands for international investigations but acquiesced in setting up a national process, the Lessons Learned and Reconciliation Commission (LLRC), which cleared the army and restricted blame to aberrations. Importantly, the refusal to dismantle militarized national security state is impacting democratic structures. Meanwhile, the Sri Lankan Government's selective memorializing symbolizes the triumph of the Sinhala majoritarian state.

In South Asia, the sacrosanct institution of the judiciary has periodically favored militarist decisions. For example, in Pakistan, the judiciary has supported the decision of military dictators in the past, but on a significant occasion, the judiciary has taken serious steps to curb the authoritarian powers taken by General Musharraf. However, in other instances it has not upheld the constitution and rule of law when it has come to curbing Islamic judgments that violate fundamental rights. The legacy of military rule has ordained legislation like blasphemy laws, Hudood ordinances, federal Shari'a courts, and laws that discriminate against minorities like the Ahmedias, Christians, and Hindus. All of these laws are harsher on women and have been used to target women and minorities (Human Rights Watch 2013).

In India, human rights activists estimate that there are 60,000 pending cases of habeas corpus petitions (Mathur 2013). Women get targeted by state institutions for being wives of suspected militants and face nonbailable warrants and prison sentences. In Sri Lanka, in 2013, Chief Justice Shirani Bandaranayake was impeached by the Parliament for "professional misconduct." All observers of Sri Lankan politics showed this to be a case where a fair minded judge had paid the price for a series of rulings against the arbitrary acts of the executive and government. The International Commission of Jurists called this impeachment sacrilegious of judicial independence.

Post-war Sri Lanka is a classic example of what John Gillis (1989: 5) points out as essential to the interconnections that make up overall process of militarization in any given society. Even as ethnic minorities and some specific regions are the sites of militarization, these exceptional policies start intersecting with the normalized, everyday governance of society as a whole, first impacting a part and then becoming part of the whole. In post-war Sri Lanka, Tamils are no longer the sole targets of authoritarian rule and militarization. Sri Lankan President

Mahinda Rajapaksa announced in 2011 that the island nation had no minorities, and that all citizens were only Sri Lankans. In 2013, the president created a Ministry of Law and Order under himself and with a retired major general as the secretary. This was in reaction to violent clashes following protests by a local community on the outskirts of Colombo over delays on fixing water contamination. In the clash between the security forces and citizens, three were left dead (*The Hindu* 2013). The surprise electoral defeat of the Rajapaksa regime and a new "national" government in power has raised expectations of the revival of democratic politics and institutions. Whether it will be sufficient to roll back the extent of militarization as a state-society process in Sri Lanka, is highly uncertain.

A Case Study of Intersection

It is important to look at the intersection between the civilian and the institutional dimensions of militarism that help shape gender-specific forms of violence. We examine this with a small case study that reveals that if an issue regarding women or national security is raised, even parliamentary institutions associated with liberal democracy can become the sites for militarization and patriarchy. In the Indian Parliament during a discussion on the Criminal Law (Amendment) Act 2013, the definition of rape was broadened and provisions put in so that women would find it less harrowing to report sexual crimes to the police and get justice. The Bill addressed also "routine violence" of stalking, voyeurism, and sexual harassment. When the matter was taken up in Parliament in March 2013, retrograde ideas on women were on display. Senior Opposition alliance leader Sharad Yadav objected to the criminalization of stalking by saying that stalking and voyeurism is "normal practice" of men and warned that this would make employers wary of hiring women. He said: "Who amongst us [men] have not followed girls?" and further, "So what, we are all men after all!" A Member of Parliament of the Bharatiya Janata Party, Bhola Singh added, that the birth of a daughter was cause for despair in the family and suggested that the primary role of women was to bear children. Former Uttar Pradesh Chief Minister Mulayam Singh Yadav said that the jails would overflow, if men were convicted of stalking and voyeurism. Many parliamentarians feared men would be victimized on this account. The point of highlighting this episode is to show how patriarchy remains embedded in institutions central to state power. It is not surprising that the Indian Parliament has been unable to pass the women's reservation bill.

Demilitarization and Women's Movements

Globally, women's movements have resisted and fought against militarization in their everyday struggles. South Asian women's groups— both those affiliated to political parties and independent groups—have struggled against patriarchal structures, relations, social codes, and norms. Feminists argue that women are not essentially peaceful by nature but are socialized into being so. Research as well experience establishes that women tend to be more peaceful than men because gendered roles of birthing and nurturing inculcates in them nonaggressive tendencies. But recent evidence indicates that women can also be aggressive and violent if socialized as such.

Historically, women have not played major roles in war and militarization, and have been kept unequal. Many women's groups have resisted war and militarism, as well as all forms of fundamentalisms. They have been active in promoting peace between India and Pakistan as well as seeking an apology from the Pakistan army on sexual crimes committed against women during the Bangladesh war of liberation. In Sri Lanka, women have supported real peace and reconciliation between communities by opposing militarization. These efforts need to continue and feminist ideas and theorizing are the instruments for demilitarization.

Conclusion

Militarization entrenches patriarchal practices and values and women have to pay the cost. Since militarization is normalized it has to be challenged at all levels from the local to the regional. Thus women's equality is essential and will help in the demilitarization of society. At the same time, both men and women who work for peace should contest the ideas of patriarchy and militarization. Security Council Resolution 1325, which was passed as a result of the pressure of the international women's movement, asks all states to ensure women's participation in peace processes.

Masculinity, as manifested in the military, is the core of the security establishment and forms part of its basic ideological activity and practice. It is through this that both masculinity and militarization can be transmitted into other aspects of society. Most states believe that militarization serves the interests of the ruling elites. Militarism entwined with masculinity is hegemonic, unless countered by women and peoples' movements and opposed by democratic practices. Women's movements need to deconstruct the impact of militarization on women, and examine how gender stereotypes lead to the continuing subjugation of women in order that male privilege and patriarchy be maintained. This is important because militarism and masculinity intersect, and because the political and public roles are replicated in our private lives.

Many of the challenges facing South Asian women are similar. There are therefore opportunities for collective strategic intervention. These however rest on regional sharing of experience, setting common standards, developing regional indicators, and mechanisms (Stenhammer 2013). However, South Asian states have evolved few formal mechanisms of collaboration on peace and security where women have an equal opportunity to participate. Clearly, women's groups will have to take up this challenge through grassroots and informal linkages as opposed to waiting for their states to take up initiatives.

Demilitarization is a major step to end violence against women. The international women's movement has been mobilizing for the inclusion of women into peace negotiations, disarmament, demobilization, and demilitarization and has succeeded in passing seven Security Council Resolutions on Women Peace and Security toward this goal. For demilitarization, women and peace activists have to see the intersection of working against militarization and working for rights of women and their protection from all forms of violence. Working against militarism calls for nonviolent activism as opposed to violent actions and activism against violent state action.

Bibliography

Asbjorn, Eide, and Marek Thee. 1980. "Militarism and Militarization in Contemporary International Relations," in *Problems of Contemporary Militarism.* London: Croom Helm.

Assam Rifles. "Press Release on Meeting with Meira Paibis." Accessed November 4, 2016, http://kanglaonline.com/2013/04/press-release-from-30-assam-rifle-interaction-with-meira-paibis/

Ayubi, Najla. 2013, November 13. *Talk at The Women's Regional Network Community Conversations.* New Delhi.

Chunakara, Mathew George. *The Militarisation of Politics and Society: South East Asian Experiences.* Hong Kong: Daga Press.

Connell, R. 1995. *Gender and Power.* Cambridge: Polity Press.

Cooke, Miriam. 1996. *Women and the War Story.* Berkley, CA: University of California Press.

Custers, Peter. 2007. *Globalized Militarism.* New Delhi: Tulika Press.

De Mel, Neloufer. 2007. *Militarizing Sri Lanka, Popular Culture, Memory and Narrative in Armed Conflict.* New Delhi: SAGE.

Enloe, Cynthia. 2000. *Maneuvers: The International Politics of Militarizing Women's Lives.* Berkley, CA: University of California Press.

Garfield, Bob. 2012. "Veterans Day and Caution against a Cult of the Military." *The Guardian,* UK edition, 12 November.

Gillis, John. 1989. "Introduction," in *Militarization of the Western World,* edited by John Gillis. New Brunswick: Rutgers University Press.

Human Rights Watch. 2013. *World Report, Pakistan.* Accessed September 21, 2013, http://www.hrw.org/world-report/2013/country-chapters/pakistan

Kaldor, Mary. 2001. *New and Old Wars: Organized Violence in a Global Era.* Cambridge: Polity Press.

Kesic, Vesna. 2000. "From Reverence to Rape: An Anthology of Ethnic and Genderised Violence." In *Frontline Feminisms: Women, War and Resistance,* edited by M.R. Walker and J. Rycenga. New York: Garland Publishing Inc.

Mathur, Shubh. February 2013. "Impunity in India." *Guernica.* Accessed November 4, 2016, http://www.guernicamag.com/features/impunity-in-india/

Nordstorm, Carolyn, and Joann Martin. 1992. "Introduction," in *The Paths to Domination, Resistance and Terror,* edited by Carolyn Nordstorm and Joann Martin. California: University of California Press.

P4P. 2013. "P4P Study on Men's Use of Violence against Women." Accessed January 15, 2015, http://www.partners4prevention.org/un-multi-country-study-launch

Peterson, Spike. 1990. "Security and Sovereign States: What Is at Stake in Taking Feminism Seriously?" in *Gendered States,* edited by S. Peterson. Boulder, CO: Lynne Rienner.

Reardon, Betty A. 1993. *Women and Peace: Feminist Visions of Global Security.* Albany, NY: State University of New York Press.

Robinson, Mary. 2010. "Interview." *International Committee of the Red Cross, Review* 92(877). Accessed November 7, 2016, https://www.icrc.org/eng/assets/files/other/irrc-877-robinson.pdf

Sen, Amartya and Jean Dreze. 2013. *An Uncertain Glory.* London: Allen Lane.

Skanthakumar, Balasingham. 2013. "Authoritarianism and Militarism in Post-War Sri Lanka." Paper presented at the Historical Materialism Conference, JNU, New Delhi.

Steans, Jill. 1998. *Gender and International Relations.* Cambridge: Polity Press.

Stenhammer, Anne F. February 15, 2013. UN Women, South Asia.

UN Women, South Asia. 2013. Paper presented at the Conference on the Changing Dynamics of Peace Building in South Asia. Kathmandu, February.

Walker, R.B.J. 1993. *Inside/Outside: International Relations as Political Theory.* Cambridge: Cambridge University Press.

WRN (Women's Regional Network). 2013. *Surviving War & Transition in Afghanistan.* Kabul: Community Conversations.

Zwick, Jim. 1984. "Militarism and Repression in the Philippines." In *The State as Terrorist: The Dynamics of Governmental Violence and Repression,* edited by M. Stohl and G.A. Lopez. Westport, CT: Greenwood Press.

Participant Analysis
and
Field Notes

6
Gender and Patriarchy in Militarized Kashmir

Anuradha Bhasin Jamwal

Any attempt to locate how women are positioned in the extremely militarized state of Jammu and Kashmir (J&K) would inevitably foreground sexual violence and rape. Kunan Poshpora 1991 and Shopian 2009 are two of the most defining images of women in the Kashmir conflict. On the night of February 22–23, 1991, over 30 women and children were said to have been gang-raped by soldiers of the 5th Rajputana Rifles. On May 30, 2009, two women were found raped and killed in ankle deep water of the Rambiara stream, surrounded by three security camps, in Shopian. These two incidents are etched deeply in the psyche of the people of Kashmir not only for the horrifying reality of the incidents but also for their symbolism of vulnerability of the women in a region regarded as one of the militarized areas of the world. The two incidents—Kunan Poshpora and Shopian, epitomize the shocking cover-up by official investigating agencies which has been characteristic of two decades of insurgency and counter insurgency in J&K.

The armed conflict has its origins in 1947–48 itself when India and Pakistan with their competing claims and occupation of territories, heavily militarized the borders of the two divided parts of the state. However, it is since the 1990s that militarization of the region has become absolute, with army and paramilitaries not only manning the borders but also the interiors, virtually usurping and controlling the lives of the civilians with jackboots and guns, and impacting their lives in a myriad ways.

The security forces including the state police have been accused in thousands of cases of torture, humiliation, encounters, disappearances, molestations, sexual assaults, and other forms of harassment. J&K has a long list of rape victims, none of whom has got justice, denied through botched up investigations, fudged evidence and the culture of impunity sanctioned under special security laws. Equally, nonstate armed combatants, both those fighting the state and those patronized by it, too, have been accused of oppression and human rights violations, including sexual violence.

Women in Conflict Zones: Complex Dichotomies

Women's role and vulnerability goes beyond the simple story of sexual assault, which expectedly stays central to the gendered discourse in view of the shock that such cases inspire in the psyche of the people. But besides the bodily harm that conflicts inflict on women, they are also pushed to the margins, making them invisible in the political, social discourse, and even in the campaign for human rights. This is despite the fact that the human rights front is the one sphere where women continue to play a role campaigning for justice. In the highly militarized space of J&K, gendered stereotypes sanctified by religion, customs, and traditional mores which normally constrain women are further overlaid by the perception of threat in a high-risk environment. It disallows them from participating in the public sphere beyond their routine mundane roles. While political groups across the spectrum including the Kashmiri separatists tend to instrumentalize women as objects of virtue or victimhood to suit their political positions, the culture of militarization and violence has proved fertile ground for regressive and right-wing women groups like Dukhtaran-e-Millat. Such organizations have gained strength from the tendency of the separatist organizations to liberally use religious motifs and rhetoric to build up their constituencies.

It is important to remind that in the early years of militancy, its religiocultural manifestations, such as the imposition of *burqa* did not find popular resonance among Kashmiri women and was to some extent resisted. The peak years of militancy in 1990s, was to witness the increasing adoption of the *burqa* which reinforced women's further marginalization and contributed to the growth in the rate of school drop outs. In recent years, headscarves and *hijabs* again have become popular among the younger generation of women. It is an aspect of their assertion and a symbol of their religious identity, in reaction to what is generally construed as the repressive and contemptuous policies of the Indian government with respect to Kashmir.

In short, the gender narrative in a militarized Kashmir is not a simple story but a complex one as women negotiate their personal and public roles through the various limitations imposed on them. Despite their overall marginalization, some women have successfully gained a foothold in the public arena in political organizations and as civil society activists or unorganized agitationists. In the human rights discourse, women have been at the forefront seeking justice and trying to organize themselves beyond their roles as victims. However, there are few instances in Kashmir of women challenging the masculine context of nationalism and militarism. Certain issues including the limited scope of women's political participation in the separatist conglomerate, that is, only in the mid and lower rungs of the Hurriyat, remains uncontested. So do laws defining the state's "permanent resident" which are ambiguous enough to be discriminatory and challenge the citizenship of women marrying outside the state. Where religion-based demography inspires psychological insecurities, women voluntarily forsake gender concerns.

Women in a militarized conflict are both vulnerable as well as susceptible to the ideological and material dynamics of the situation. This is reflected in their complex and contradictory responses, often marked by paradoxes and dichotomies. Women are exploited by both extremist ideologues as well as security forces; they are easy targets for both sides for co-option as informers and spies. Many of the women suspected to be working for security agencies had their ears and nose brutally chopped off by armed insurgents; there have also been cases of forced marriages with militants and surrendered militants working as renegades at the behest of security agencies. Women's marginalization and extent of suppression can be gauged from the fact that such developments do not figure in the popular discourse on militarization.

Militarization in Kashmir is impacted by the interplay of the Indian and Pakistan armies on both sides of the territory of J&K divided by the disputed Line of Control, their mesh of intelligence agencies, and nonstate actors propelled into action by their competing claims of nationality and territoriality. That complex dynamics in turn has brought into play competing claims of legitimacy to one or the other form of militarization, of which women often become an active part, even as they continue to be the ones disproportionately impacted by the militarized situation. Feminist scholars and media reports have amply highlighted women's role in the Kashmir conflict as victims of sexual abuse, displaced persons, as grieving family members, primary caretakers and as active participants in war and peacemaking.

Increasingly, feminist research on women confronting militarism, extremism, and nationalist conflicts have drawn attention to the complex co-relation between conflict, socioreligious and ethnic identities, and women's agency. While the agency is built mainly around the oppression due to armed conflict, the levels of this activism vary, depending primarily on religious and ethnic lines, and less on the magnitude of conflict and victimization. Activism, mostly low key, is shaped around the masculine notion of nationalism and militarism but the ways in which women respond are diverse. In the Kashmir Valley, while many women exhorted their young boys to cross the border for arms training so as to fight the Indian security agencies, the women of Mandi and Loran in Poonch border district (Jammu) discouraged their boys from picking up the gun. In the late 1990s and beginning of the new millennium, a period that coincided with the disenchantment of Kashmiris with the gun and the beginning of the now stalled peace process between India and Pakistan, women in Kashmir Valley too, began discouraging husbands and sons to do the same.

In the Kashmir story, there were mothers who urged their militant sons to surrender in the vain hope that they would be able to pursue their normal lives, while others such as mother of Javed Andrabi constantly urged her son through her letters to "fight jehad" and "lay down his life" as a suicide bomber. When men become active participants in combat as state sponsored militia in their roles as—surrendered ultras, village defense committee members, spies, informers, and porters—women's varied responses have been conditioned by identity politics, cultural and regional differences, and personal choices. If for Tahira, a half-widow, it became an ordeal keeping her teenage son locked indoors to prevent him from joining the street protests of the summer of 2010 when boys/young men took on security forces with stones; there were other mothers who volunteered to be in the forefront of such protests and act as shields for their sons. Notwithstanding which political structures they endorsed, state or nonstate, many women have played a vital role in acting as human shields to protect the men of the family.

The trajectory of activism is also shaped by the way victimization is experienced, either as an off-shoot of the binary of "us and them" or from within the context of the "honor paradigm" especially in relation to rape and sexual assault. To grapple with the complex role and engagement of women in Kashmir's conflict, it is crucial to understand the specificity of conflict-related sexual violence as against other forms of human rights abuse. It is also equally significant to understand the context of the intricate fabric of religious and ethnic differences within the state of J&K.

Binaries of "Us and Them"

Different communities in J&K position themselves differently in the aftermath of violence, marking a sharp distinction in the boundary between "us" and "them." Nothing illustrates this better than the case of Shehnaz Kouser. She was abducted by militants in the early years of militancy and during her six months in "custody," she was raped, tortured, and drugged, until she began to work for her captors—the militants. Shehnaz was rescued by the police when they captured one of the militants she was with, in all likelihood, with her help. The police handed her over to the Intelligence Bureau (IB) who whisked her off to Delhi. For two years, she not only worked for them but was subjected to the same sexual abuse that the militants had meted out to her. Finally she returned to Jammu and got married. But the nightmare followed her. When her husband got to know that she had been raped by both the militants and the IB men, he abandoned her and their two children.

Interestingly, when she was rescued from the militants, the police, and the Hindu right wing in Jammu region, including the Rashtriya Swayamsevak Sangh (RSS) and the woman's group Nari Jagran Manch, appropriated her case, using her in a propaganda blitz to demonize the militants and show how "Muslim women suffer due to Islam or

Muslims." Later, she was abandoned and fell prey to abuse by the men of the intelligence agencies. Shehnaz's story is a grim reminder of how easily a woman's personal tragedy gets usurped, manipulated, and subverted by political organizations and individuals for their own narrow interests. In the process, the victim's fate is relegated to the background. The collective strength of civil society crumbles as political parties, bureaucrats, and other vested interests project one kind of victimization, thus subjecting women to another kind as well.

Honor Discourse in Rapes

The graph of rapes in Kashmir compared to other rights abuses is very low as most rapes are not reported. Most "rapes" occur in remote areas which have little access to media or human rights groups. But more importantly, survivors do not come forward because of the social stigma, and the "honor" discourse in which rape is constructed. At one level, rape as a violation of a woman's honor and dignity tends to stigmatize the woman and leads to her social ostracism. At another level, it is male honor, hurt and bruised, that tends to take precedence over the violation of the bodily integrity of the woman and her psychosocial suffering. It is significant how the politics of rape and its aftermath ends up doubly disadvantaging the woman. Not only is she deprived of the chance to move on with her life with dignity but also the right to grieve. Victimization becomes existential and eternal, something even glamorized (in contradiction with the syndrome of stigma) as it is used to launch high-profile protests and provide the material for propaganda on human rights abuses. As for the victim, she is forgotten and expected to disappear. By placing rape within this "Honor paradigm," authentic documentation of human rights violations gets hindered and the possibility of building an accurate case for prosecution remains elusive.

In 2003, in the urban hub of Shopian in south Kashmir, some college girls were molested in broad day light by the security forces. The incident sparked huge demonstrations and the police had to shoot to dispel the crowd. As for the victimized girls, they had to confront two hostile fronts—the army as well as their family members who strongly disapproved of their audacity of making it a public issue. Psychological violation begins in the home and the neighborhood of the victim, where the violation of honor takes precedence over their victimization.

In an early and internationally publicized case of the bride who was raped by the state paramilitary BSF soldiers in 1990, journalist cum writer Basharat Peer tracked down Mubina Gani in her south Kashmir village nearly two decades later. Her husband, unlike in most other cases, had not abandoned her. But the couple was ostracized by their relatives and villagers (Peer 2008).

The Shopian rape and murder case (2009) draws attention to the scope and limits of a publicly supported and sustained campaign for justice by the Majlis-e-Mushawarat. But it is important to emphasize that in the Shopian case the rape victims had been killed, making the "honor discourse" irrelevant. Adding to the complexity of the construction of the rape discourse in the militarized context of J&K, is the recent revival by Kashmiri human rights activists of the conflict's best known and most controversial gang rape incident in Konan Poshpora (1993). After two decades, the survivors are back demanding justice (Batool et al. 2016).

Hierarchy of Violations: Rape Versus Disappearances

The campaigns for justice are far weaker in cases of rapes and molestations where a live victim, a woman, is seeking justice for herself. The demand for justice becomes far stronger when it is a case of torture, a custodial killing or an enforced disappearance and women come forward, not just in the traditional role of mothers, daughters, and sisters but they enter the public domain as household heads. This reflects the centrality of the patriarchal ethos which continues to define and limit women's socially acceptable political role as protestors in the public space opened up by conflict. Women enter the political domain only in the category (and hierarchy) of agitationists—on the streets or in a more organized form as members of the Association of Parents of Disappeared Persons (APDP). Women are highly visible in these public protests as they take the lead as mothers, wives, sisters, and daughters.

In the Kashmir valley, in particular, women's presence in the public space has been most conspicuous in the period of internal armed conflict. Scholars have suggested that the political mobilization of women in the conflict actually began with domestic activism, where women, in their day to day lives, were engaged in negotiations of power with security forces for the rescue and safety of their families. However, this role was restricted largely to that of an agitationist against the patriarchal state's failure to fulfil its responsibility as "protector." Complementarily, women supported the armed struggle and willingly sent their sons and brothers to struggle against the Indian oppressors. They peopled the mass fronts against human rights violations acting as human shields for their men, including during crackdowns and searches. Women's political activism was thus limited to the protection of their families and within traditional cultural roles. There was no question of challenging the gender stereotypes of culture and religion or building solidarities on women's issues and activism with other regions of the J&K state.

A somewhat perceptible change occurred during the years of calm between 2000 and 2008 beginning with disenchantment with the gun and a quest for peaceful resolution of the Kashmir dispute. That respite provided an opportunity for quality education, research, academic quest, and interactions beyond the university campuses, enabling a younger generation including women to discover newer idioms of expression through writings, poetry, and art. Post-2008, renewed turmoil changed the narrative of the resistance movement from violence to peaceful agitation. Commonly called the Kashmir Intifada and characterized by street protests and stone-pelting, the conscious shift from gun to agitation inspired the younger generation to take charge. The break from gun culture produced offshoots of creative writing and activism in fields related and unrelated to conflict. However, the continuing graph of human rights violations by security forces kept alive the hold of the extremists on the imagination of the young and pushed some youth toward religious radicalization.

The controversial execution of Afzal Guru, convicted of the attack on the Delhi Parliament in a trial that many questioned and a process that raised many questions, deeply alienated and angered the Kashmiri people. It propelled sections of educated and religiously radicalized youth getting toward the gun culture—the former with the logic that peaceful resistance was impossible and the latter driven by larger pan Islamic goals. The extremely complex and still changing narrative of resistance and the possibility of the contagion of global extremist ideologies so far have made little perceptible change in the way gender issues or women activism are negotiated through Kashmir's militarized space. Such ideologies have placed the subordination of women as an integral part of their agenda. For the present, youth including girls are caught between an increasing quest for knowledge on one side and religious radicalization on the other.

Regional Identity Politics

The levels of women activism, even within the traditional roles inscribed in a patriarchal script vary along the lines of different sociocultural graphs. While the Kashmir Valley witnessed public protests by women against rapes or custodial killings and torture cases, the women in the militancy affected areas of Jammu region are conspicuous by their absence in public mobilizations against human rights violations. This is more so in the border districts of Rajouri–Poonch than in Doda, where cultural and linguistic ties overlap with Kashmir valley.

This invisibility and difficulty in locating women voices along the borders and Line of Control, separating the Indian administered Kashmir from Pakistan administered Kashmir, as well as the abject denial of a potential threat from the army including a sexual threat, stems from many factors. First is the traditional conservative patriarchal culture. Second is the inaccessibility of these areas and the often vast distances between houses in this hilly belt. Third, the army's footprints have been much larger and grounded in these border districts, right from 1947, as the area was witness to a history of rebellions and uprisings for independence. It saw Pakistan-induced militancy operations up until 1965, and to some extent even 1971.

However, there is also a tendency to normalize the heavy militarization through a denial of what may seem abnormal to an outsider. "The army is important for our own safety," many including women would vouch for this, maintaining that Pakistan would devour them if the army were to be removed. Alongside, anecdotes of incidents of army harassment are still commonly in circulation and a little prodding brings back tormenting stories of the army's repression in the 1965 and 1971 wars. But there is a casual but intentional bid to desist from army bashing, unlike in the Kashmir valley.

Nonetheless, the fear that stalks in the wake of the army's manifold presence surfaces during casual conversations. Women talk about fearing the sight of army vehicles, army check points and camps, and being compelled to marry off daughters at ages as early as 13 and 14 years to ensure "their safety and protection." A woman sarpanch living close to the border in Poonch district spoke of the time of peak militancy when she spent sleepless nights sitting in the middle of the room in her mud house with a rifle, to protect herself and her daughters. She spoke of a surrendered ultra who was a terror in their village. Evidently, there is fear of earning the army's wrath, if they speak out. But their silence and hesitation is also because the army is their sole provider for basic needs. The civil administration is completely absent in the villages along the LOC.

Militarizing Women

Though there is no known evidence of women receiving arms training and joining the ranks of militants, the Hill Kaka area in Poonch, where women for the first time were armed as members of the Village Defence Committee is an exception. More common are women supporters of militant outfits who are active in public space, often shielding the men from the ire of the security forces. Also, women are active in the support role of informers and couriers, working both for the militants and the security forces. In the initial years of militancy, every woman in a burqa who visited the camps of security forces, often to seek the whereabouts of their missing or arrested sons and husbands, ran the risk of being branded an agent from both sides. They were looked upon with suspicion even within their own families.

In the post-1996 era, woman informers became more commonplace. The abduction and forced marriages of women are directly or indirectly connected to the growing prevalence of women in role of informers and couriers, which also coincided with corruption and malpractices in the ranks of militant organizations. The Indian agencies added to the confusion with their own sponsored "proxy" organizations of surrendered ultras—*Ikhwaeen*. The more militarized the civilian area became, the more vulnerable women became to entrapment. Many fell desperate prey to the possibility of earning some money in very difficult economic circumstances, Also, their entry into public space brought a sense of liberating power at first, but woman often found themselves doubly trapped, and even more vulnerable as did Shehnaz Kouser, who first worked for the militants and later for the security agencies.

Women sympathizing with militant groups face the ire of the security forces and vice versa. In the summer of 2001, when the army busted a hideout in Hadi Marore of Surankote district and killed the militants in an encounter, they found two women in the hideout, one pregnant with child. The women had been forcibly married by militants. A doctor working in Surankote maintains that during the decade between 1996 and mid-2005, coinciding with the peak militancy period in the region and excessive counter insurgency operations of the Indian security forces, there was an increasingly high graph of medically terminated pregnancies.

One year after the much publicized Hill Kaka Operation of May 2003, in which civilians had enthusiastically participated as part of the counter insurgency network, nine persons of a family including women and children were killed by militants. The incident was preceded by the kidnapping of women folk of the families of militants of the neighboring village by Village Defence Committee members who were part of the Hill Kaka operation. The move was defended by the VDC members as a defensive one, since the women were used as shields to protect their own men. Finally when they let the women go, the militants retaliated by killing the women and children of the VDC members.

Women in the Militarized Pakistan–India Border

Women are the worst sufferers of the psychological and economic impact of the border conflict. They are impacted by physical and psychological insecurity and the constant uncertainty caused by ceasefire violations and consequent displacements, loss of life and livelihood, and dislocation of educational and health facilities. Since 2014, civilians have suffered more casualties in the firefights between Indian and Pakistani forces on the international border with both sides targeting each other's villages rather than security pickets. A defining image of October 2014 shelling is of Surekha Kumari, a 15-year old girl in Chellari village, who lost three members of her family including her mother and grandparents. Her father and two younger brothers were seriously injured. A student of class 10th, she was forced to drop out of school and become a homemaker. Bureaucratic red-tapism further added to her worries of providing for the surviving members of the family and medical treatment as compensatory ex-gratia relief promised to them was not paid even a year after that incident.

In the border areas, the proportion of those rendered handicapped by landmines is very high; the women who take the cattle and sheep for grazing, are often at great risk. In Kerni village in Poonch district, 35 people were maimed by landmines. Half of them are women. India uses light weight plastic MM16 landmines which are targeted to blow off the limbs of the victims. For injuries, the government pays only ₹5,000–₹10,000. Also the Locomotive Disability Act, which can ensure jobs for the physically challenged, is not applicable to J&K.

Displacements, partial or more permanent, is almost a routine feature on the borders and also in the militancy affected areas of the state. Whether it is the border displacements during the Kargil war, the 1990 exodus of Kashmiri Hindus or the uprooting of the people from remote hilly areas of Doda, it has profound gendered implications. Conflict-induced displacement brings in its wake poverty for people who earlier grew enough food on their farms to suffice their needs. Women are obliged to take over the role of managing livelihood for the family while their men slip into acute frustration, depression, and even addiction.

Women as Peacemakers

In the border districts and Kashmir valley, rarely are women visible in the role of peacemakers. However, across the border in the Neelam Valley on the borders in Pakistan administered Kashmir, women who bear the brunt of the daily border firings often to facilitate or check border infiltration, have dared to assert themselves as peace activists. According to a BBC report, women of Neelam Valley have been maintaining massive vigils and protests against the presence of militants there, even at the risk of persecution and the wrath of a section of the Pakistan military apparatus. Their predicament is desperate as they are sandwiched between high inaccessible mountains on one side and the Line of Control with Indian army soldiers having vantage position on the other, making it impossible for them to flee in times of danger. It is a shared plight of people who live on both sides of the divide.

Conclusion

In a militarized region, there is much potential for women to create a constituency of peace by making the necessary transition from victimhood to activism. There are indeed cases of women organizing themselves to raise day to day issues or challenging human rights abuse. However, in proportion to the magnitude of the oppression suffered by the women, when the tradition of patriarchy is reinforced by militarization, this organizational capacity of the women of J&K remains wanting. Whatever little assertive role is played by women as agents of peace often pivots around the question of the safety and security of families; the engendering of their own oppression, which is multilayered, remains virtually absent.

While one finds women agitating against torture, enforced disappearances, and killings of their family members and voluntarily act as human shields to protect men, instances of women playing a more assertive role in seeking justice for sexual violence or for their own economic and social deprivation remain virtually unheard of and unreported. It is still rarer to find men spontaneously and selflessly reacting in the way women do by acting as human shields to save their women from marauding soldiers or nonstate gunmen during crackdowns and raids. Divisive caste, regional and religious identities, and related political and social affiliations further forbid the strengthening of women's solidarities, hampering their capacity to widen their social base. Such solidarities rarely transcend beyond conference rooms and workshops where alliances in search of a common ground form part of the intellectual discourse and peacebuilding strategy. In practice, the expressed solidarities remain limited to certain circles or are too feeble to produce a mass impact with women-centered values of peace and development.

References

Batool, Essar, et al. 2016. *Do You Remember Kunan Poshpora, Zubaan Series of Sexual Violence and Impunity in South Asia.* New Delhi: Zubaan Publishers Pvt Limited.
Peer, Basharat. 2008. *Curfewed Night.* Delhi: Random House India.

7
Risky Subjects: Militarization in Post-war Sri Lanka

Neloufer de Mel

The entrenchment of militarization in Sri Lanka's sociopolitical fabric was one of the most significant outcomes of its ethnic war, fought during 1983–2009 between the Sri Lankan security forces and the Liberation Tigers of Tamil Eelam (LTTE) over a separate Tamil state. Militarization, as the process by which communities not only become reliant on militaries for their security and everyday well-being but also consent to military control of civilian life and spaces, was a precondition of the war (Chenoy 2002, 4; de Mel 2007; Enloe 2000, 3). Its continued role in the management of post-war society made it a vital ally of the early post-war Sri Lankan state. Early post-war militarization did not, however, function in exactly the same way as before. Constituted by both "hard" and "soft" power, it was driven by a new set of security strategies that had also developed in response to the US-led global "war on terror" and "new technologies that inform as well as [supposedly] protect" (Coomaraswamy 2015).

Militarization as hard power was explicit during the Sri Lankan war in the rapid expansion of the military and its battalions, intensified weapons procurement, and the visibly heightened deployment of military personnel at roadside checkpoints, and in cordon and search operations. Post-war, militarization as soft power (characteristic of post-war communities yet to transition to post-conflict ones) allied itself to the post-war developmental state, supplying intelligence and manpower for its developmental projects in the war-affected north and east of the country. In this, the early Sri Lankan post-war state drew directly on international blueprints, advanced from the 1990s onwards, of development as a conflict resolution mechanism. The argument was that if conflicts emerge from uneven development in the first place, post-war developmental drives, led by the State, act as useful strategic tools in counter-insurgency, enabling control and surveillance of hostile territory and populations even as they appear benign and welfarist (Venugopal 2014). The conceptual and strategic link of development to conflict (that also returns the State as a main actor in the economic management of conflict-affected areas), results in a strong bond between the development and military complexes.

Sri Lanka was no exception. The link between developmental actors and the military (reflected in the reassignment of the Urban Development Authority to the Ministry of Defence soon after the war) facilitated economic ventures by the military such as the running of hotels, restaurants, and transport chains on land it occupied in the north. In turn, the military undertook surveillance and supplied intelligence to the State. It ran a parallel administration in the north. Local residents had to seek permission for events, including weddings, from the military. At the same time, the increased use of digital surveillance by the Sri Lankan state signaled a turn to the securitization of Sri Lanka society as a whole, as a way of measuring and managing security "risks." Yet, the heightened presence of CCTV cameras, for instance, in towns such as Kilinochchi (a former stronghold of the LTTE) in which they proliferate even in small roadside cafés, placed populations in the north (mostly Tamils) under particular scrutiny.

Each of these aspects of militarization had an impact on women in specific ways. Militarism, as the Report of the UN Human Rights Commissioner's Investigation on Sri Lanka (OISL) emphasizes, "serves to uphold and perpetuate structural inequalities that in turn operate to disenfranchise women and girls from public goods, entrench exclusion and marginalization and create the ingredients for a broader platform of broader inequalities that increase the potential for violent conflict to occur" (OISL 2015: 207). Exactly how this occurs, the changing forms of militarization in Sri Lanka, and their gendered impact will be the focus of this chapter.

Measuring Militarization

The most overt feature of militarization during the war, was the rapid increase in the size and visible public presence of both the Sri Lankan and LTTE militaries. The LTTE was less successful in this endeavor, eventually resorting to conscription including that of child soldiers, whereas the Sri Lanka government rapidly increased its armed forces in its decisive, final putsch of August 2006 to May 2009, or phase four of the war. The Sri Lanka army alone absorbed 121,141 new recruits during 2006–09 to fight the war (Chandraprema 2012: 390). According to another estimate, by the war's end in May 2009, the army had expanded from 9 divisions to 20; its 44 brigades had grown to 71 and its 149 battalions increased to 284. By early 2009, the navy's strength had also increased to 48,000 and the air force stood at 28,000 (*Economic & Political Weekly* 2012: 34).

Such expansion inevitably led to an exceptionally high force-density, indicative of the civil–military balance that accounts for the ratio of military personnel to civilians stationed in an area. Estimates vary. While some reports, based on information gathered from the Sri Lanka Army website as well as media reports, estimated that after the war ended, there were 15 army battalions stationed in the northern province in addition to two large naval commands and two air force bases, and that the army divisions in the province occupied 8,844 square meters of its land (*Economic & Political Weekly* 2012: 35), others indicate a far higher presence of the army alone in the north: of 152 battalions stationed in areas such as Jaffna and the Vanni (including Kilinochchi and Mullaitivu) although this reduced to 48 after the January 2015 presidential elections and change of government (Ferdinando 2015). Taken as a whole, however, the combined presence of the military, and the civil defense and intelligence services produced, in the early post-war phase, an estimated force-density in the northern province of one security personnel to every five civilians, making it one of the highest in South Asia (*Economic & Political Weekly* 2012: 35–36).

This deployment is exceptionally high in any post-war context and deeply resented by Tamil communities living in the north, who continue to view the Sinhalized Sri Lanka army as adversarial. Faced with national and international demands for the reduction of troop levels, the Sri Lankan government contested these figures, claiming reduction in troop presence. In an interview to a mainstream Sunday newspaper nearly four years after the war ended, the military spokesman cited a reduction in military outposts in Kilinochchi from 400 to 40, and in Jaffna a decrease in troop deployment from 45,000 to 15,000 (Nathaniel 2013). However, in January 2014, President Mahinda Rajapaksa claimed the entire northern province held only 12,000 military personnel. Yet a couple of days later, his secretary his official secretary was found contradicting him in Geneva claiming that army numbers in the north were down by a third, from 120,000 in May 2009 to about 80,000 toward the end of 2013 (*Colombo Telegraph* 2014).[1] The production of varying figures for varying audiences evident here, reflected a politics of contestation that was also a response to the heightened internationalization of Sri Lanka's war and ethnic conflict. At the same time, the go-slow on troop reduction was justified in terms of the national security imperative of having to monitor persisting threats, given the intermittent discoveries of LTTE arms caches and suspicion of an LTTE rump operating in the Vanni and LTTE diaspora (ICG 2014; Nathaniel 2013; Samarasinghe 2013).

Managing Demobilization

The expansion of the Sri Lanka military to fight the war posed significant challenges of demobilization and demilitarization at its end. An enlarged army of men, trained for war, hyper masculinized in ethos, but confined to barracks was perceived as a recipe for disaffection and military coups. The early post-war Sri Lankan government sought to manage its post-war army through a mix of strategies, ideological and utilitarian, including the "export" of military personnel as UN peace keeping forces abroad to reduce troop numbers at home; shielding the military from judicial accountability trials for war crimes; prioritizing reservations for children of the military in government schools; acknowledging soldiers as war-heroes and building martial victory monuments. The government's promotion of the military's participation in development projects, especially in the hospitality, transport, agricultural, security, and construction business was also part of its demobilization strategy.

The early Sri Lankan post-war army thereby not only operated business enterprises but also provided labor for post-war reconstruction and infrastructure projects including walking tracks in Colombo, and the renovation and refurbishment of heritage buildings. The latter set of activities came under the Defence Secretary's vision of a "sanitized, safe, and orderly city" that would become an "Asian hub" and tourist destination (Godamunne 2014). The involvement of the army in such day to day economic activity, particularly in the north, provided it a tremendous vantage point to observe a "hostile" population up close. Through these activities it not only consolidated the territory it regained from the LTTE, but also enhanced its capacity to penetrate deeper into the daily lives of local communities in the guise of a development partner benefitting the residents of the north and east. As a characteristic of soft power, the militarization of development and business thereby served the strategic goal of deep intelligence gathering even as the local residents were reclassified as "beneficiaries." This was entirely within the COIN doctrine of counter-insurgency developed after the Iraq war in which "winning hearts and minds" of the local population became central, enabling militaries, in theory, to base intelligence and practice on local perspectives, demographics, social structures, cultural codes, and habits (Aylwin-Foster 2005: 5). Yet, a military trained to fight does not adjust as easily (particularly soon after a war has "ended") to a COIN campaign's subtler political framework that requires militaries to work toward the political goal of winning over hostile populations (Aylwin-Foster 2005: 9). Even after territory has been conquered or regained, armies continue to be hierarchical, masculinized, and predisposed to offensive operations (Aylwin-Foster 2005: 3). All of this was evident in the early phase of post-war civil–military relations in the Sri Lankan north.

Witness testimony, including the testimony of women before the officially established Lessons Learnt and Reconciliation Commission (LLRC) in 2010, provides evidence of the extent of military incursion into their everyday post-war lives. The LLRC, in its report, refers to the "intrusive presence" of the security forces in the north and east, their use of the private properties of the war-displaced, their displacement of the civilian administration, their entry into business activities, and their institution of military authorizations to regulate civil functions (LLRC 2011: 254, 274, 277). As a precondition for ethnic reconciliation, the LLRC recommended the restoration of civilian administration in the northern province and a commensurate "recession of the military into the background to enable people to return to normal civilian life and enjoy the benefit from peace" (LLRC 2011: 305). While Provincial Council elections were held in 2013 in the north, signaling the return to some semblance of civilian rule, and approximately 3,400 acres of land returned to their rightful owners following the change of government in August 2015, military presence in the region yet remains high, although its form is more discreet. As of March 2016, an estimated 12,750 acres in the north continued to be retained by the military for its camps and installations (ICG 2016: 13).

Gendering "Risk"

Each of the manifestations of militarization identified by the LLRC as a cause for concern—the intense military presence, the military's functioning as a parallel administration, the acquisition of land for military camps, and intelligence gathering—had a bearing on women, particularly those living in the former war zones of the north.

The penetration of the military into villages in the Vanni, either overtly as troops or covertly as intelligence operatives in civilian clothes, enabled surveillance of the mobility, recreational activities, kinship, and social networks of women. This was reflected in how the military questioned women about their movements and their visitors. The military conducted spot checks on their houses, including at night, making women of the very large number of female-headed households particularly vulnerable. At times, the military visited these women's homes, ostensibly to socialize (Minority Rights Group 2013: 8). Tamil women resented such intrusions but felt they had no choice in the matter (MRG 2013).

A study on women's reproductive health in the Vanni noted that, women respondents interviewed for the study were subsequently questioned by the military following the departure of the research team (The Social Architects 2013). Similarly, the UN High Commissioner for Human Rights who had been on an official visit to Sri Lanka in April 2015 noted that human rights defenders who had spoken to her were questioned by the military after her departure. During the course of a research project on post-war justice, an elderly mother residing in a fishing village in Jaffna whose son had been forcibly disappeared and who had testified at the Presidential Commission of Inquiry into Complaints of Abduction and Disappearances (PCICAD, established in 2013) reported a similar incident. On returning from the hearings, she had been visited by personnel from the local army camp to ask what she had stated in her testimony (personal communication 2013).

The consequence of such military interrogation is often the intimidation and silencing of women. As noted in the study on reproductive health, it inhibits women from accessing essential services and information on healthcare, because, once a particular program has been identified and notified by the military as "risky" and "suspect," women fear to participate in it altogether, thereby avoiding important follow-up visits, in this case, to clinics and hospitals (The Social Architects 2013). Other studies, while noting the historical antecedents of witness intimidation that also occurred during inquiries into enforced disappearances in the south of the country relating to the JVP uprising of the late 1980s, also corroborate the widespread use of witness intimidation in the north and east, resulting at times in the real fear of witnesses themselves being abducted (Pinto-Jayawardena 2010: 139).

The necessity, in the northern province, for civilians to obtain authorization from the military to hold meetings as well as social gatherings, and civil functions such as weddings, in effect, established the military as a parallel administration to civilian state institutions (LLRC 2011: 277). Such a parallel dispensation began during the war when military approval had to be obtained for all movement in the war zones, including for purposes of delivering humanitarian assistance to civilians affected by the war. This had permitted the Sri Lanka government of the time to deploy a humanitarian framework to strengthen the militarization of war-affected areas (Sathkunanathan 2010: 34). Post-war, civilians in the north still require the informal consent of the military to go about their daily business. When women are dependent on authorization from the military for their mobility and activities, a gendered power dynamic occurs which places women at risk of coercion, transactional sex, sexual harassment, and in some instances, of sexual violence. A report by the Minority Rights Group drew attention to the overall post-war increase in sexual activity between Tamil women and Sinhalese military personnel, and Tamil women and men who visit the north for business and family visits. Here, the likely inference drawn was that poverty also forced women who were female heads of households into transactional sex or the sex trade. The report stated that even when these relations were consensual, the long-term costs to the women, such as pregnancy without child support and ostracism from their own communities, were immense (MRG 2013: 7–8).

Land acquisition by the military for establishing permanent high-security zones and the commensurate dispossession of people of their property, has also been a major source of insecurity and resentment for women of the north and east. Large numbers of people around the Palaly airport and the Kankesanthurai port in the Jaffna district, Sampur in the Trincomalee district, Ashraf Nagar in the Amparai district and the Mannar islands remain without homes and/or agricultural land on which their livelihoods were based (MRG 2013; Noble 2013). As noted before, an estimated 12,750 acres remains under military use in the north alone as of March 2016, and these land acquisitions have taken place without prior consultation with their owners, or a registry of those displaced, or a comprehensive reparations package that include adequate compensation payments and/or alternative land suitable to those affected. Importantly, no reparations package that specifically addresses the gendered needs of the 58,121 female-headed households in the north, that also takes into account their land rights, is in place (CPA 2016: 21).

The dispossession of property affects both men and women, but displaced women's narratives emphasize that "home" is not simply a territorial space but a "combination of interconnected physical, social, political, historical and psychological [assemblages]" (Hariharathamotharan 2013: 7). The material and affective place of a home is a vital source of security for women. This is the case precisely because women are vulnerable to eviction from their own land or home due to gendered inequalities, customary laws such as *Thesavalamai* under which Tamil women require the written consent of the husband to sell their land, and expulsion by in-laws if husbands have died or been forcibly disappeared in the war. The physical asset of a house also enhances post-war livelihood opportunities for women by facilitating home-based small enterprises such as food processing, sewing, home gardening, horticultural work, or poultry farming. This is especially important for women who have been injured and disabled in the war and whose mobility is restricted, or as heads of households, have children and elders who are dependents. A house also signifies an inheritance resource that can be passed on to children, and if with life interest, is an insurance asset in old age. It is also an asset that can be used as dowry for marriage, and for this reason, women have been heard to demand houses as reparative justice. For poor peasant women in Jaffna, plots of land may have shrunk because of subdivision over the years to family members, or sale to repay debts. But even the smallest plot of land continues to signify security and economic opportunities in an environment where the latter is scarce. A particular cause of grievance for women, therefore, is the military's entry into what were earlier economic activities of women such as the sale of produce from home gardening and the hospitality trade. The army-run hotel in the Kankesanthurai HSZ, on acquired land, is a case in point (Noble 2013).[2] Women have also been left out of consultations and joint ownership of houses in donor driven resettlement schemes for war-affected persons in the north.

Highest "Risk" Group: Ex-LTTE Cadre

Considered the riskiest group from the security state's point of view, is the cohort of ex-LTTE combatants who have been "returned" to society after a legal process or completion of the rehabilitation programs run by the Sri Lanka military. At the end of the war, nearly 13,000 LTTE cadres surrendered to the Sri Lankan army and were taken to 20 camps in the north and east of the country. Eleven thousand six hundred and ninety-six of these rehabilitees were rank and file or "soft elements," some of them from the LTTE's administrative wing. Amongst this cohort were an estimated 2,024 women (Jeyaraj 2010). At the February 2013 UN Human Rights sessions in Geneva, the Sri Lanka government reported that as of January 15, 2013, 11,456 ex-LTTE cadres comprising 9,203 males, and 2,253 women had been "rehabilitated and reintegrated" into society (Samarasinghe 2013). By 2014, practically all the 11,929 former LTTE cadres were said to be reintegrated.

The ex-combatant rehabilitees are under intense surveillance in their hometowns and villages. They had to register with the army, the police, and the *Grama Seva Niladhari*, (GS or village local government official) on their return, and record their presence at their local police station every week in the first six months. Officials at a Divisional Secretariat in the eastern province noted that the GS had to submit a report on each rehabilitee in his/her area once a month, while the National Intelligence Bureau (NIB) filed a quarterly report (personal communication, August 2013). Given this reporting requirement, it is not surprising that women ex-combatants note the frequent visit to their homes of the military for questioning (HHR and WMC 2014). They also report the presence of operatives from various intelligence units, although there is confusion as to whether these personnel are from the Criminal Investigations Department (CID), the Terrorists Investigations Department (TID), or the NIB given that none of them operate with a transparent mandate. The women are also asked to report to military camps where some have been allegedly subjected to sexual harassment and abuse. This process of registering and reporting on ex-combatant rehabilitees identify them "to the community as people who pose a potential threat, not due to their previous perceived or actual involvement with the LTTE, but because they are constantly monitored and their movements restricted by the security forces" (Hattotuwa 2011). Local communities remain afraid, therefore, that if the military move in following any "trouble," the rehabilitees will be the first to be detained, and those who associate with them second (AISLS 2015; Amarasingam 2014). As a result of the suspicion and stigma that surrounded them, women ex-combatant rehabilitees experience rejection from their own communities and note a loss of respect, in contrast to the esteem they enjoyed as LTTE cadre during the war (HHR and WMC 2014; Thamilini 2016).

The intense surveillance of ex-combatant rehabilitees, and the resulting anxiety amongst their families and communities, also negates their livelihood options. Divisional Secretariat officials noted that despite the availability of government facilitated financial packages, including bank loans for self-employment ventures and income generation, most rehabilitees did not avail themselves of these facilities because of the lack of guarantors, as few were willing to come forward to provide surety, fearing military surveillance and reprisal on themselves. Difficulties in accessing financial aid and earning a livelihood had a greater impact on female rather than male rehabilitees. While the men were able to get jobs in the fisheries, agriculture, or carpentry sectors, women were more likely to find lesser paid jobs in textile shops as shop assistants or in garment factories.

Women ex-combatant rehabilitees remain, therefore, economically more vulnerable and at greater risk of being trafficked or sexually abused, as evidenced in reports of their distress and desperation. For instance, the suicide of two female rehabilitees in the Batticaloa district drew attention to their sexual harassment by an armed group over a prolonged period. This was an important reminder of the consequences of not incorporating prior and follow-up programs for families and societies receiving the rehabilitees—including programs to monitor their well-being on their return (Pathmalal 2011). It was also a reminder that many disarmament, demobilization, and reintegration (DDR) programs emphasize security at the expense of a dialog with the community on ex-combatant return, that would be, in effect, a *political* dialog as part of a peace process (Krishnan 2012: 6–7). Particularly vulnerable to social ostracism are disabled women ex-combatants who cannot find employment, are regarded as unsuitable marriage partners, and are rejected as a burden even by their families because of their disability (HHR and WMC 2014).

Militarization: New Pathways

The manifestations of militarization in the north and east impact women living in those regions in specific ways as outlined above, but many of its post-war features are aligned to policy frameworks that will have a long-term impact on the country as a whole. Civilian positions have been militarized, marked by the appointment of retired military personnel as provincial governors and diplomats in Sri Lankan missions abroad. The education sector also came under military purview, marked by the entry of the military into tertiary education. For instance, the Kotelawala Defence Academy has been made into a rapidly expanding university with faculties of medicine, law, and management. Post-war, the military also took over the curriculum design and management of the orientation program for all new undergraduate students until August 2015. Termed the pre-orientation program (POP) or the Leadership Program, it was held at army, air force, and navy base camps. The military and the government implied that as the POP took place prior to the orientations conducted by the universities themselves, it did not interfere with the latter. In practice, however, there was very little time for both and so, POP replaced the previously academic-designed orientations. Instead of intensive courses in English language, IT literacy, and talks by eminent academics and policymakers on society, politics, and culture organized by university academics, the POP program trained new university entrants in "positive attitude development," physical exercise, "how to eat properly," and a militaristic camp life including waking up at 4.00 am.[3]

The military's entry into education and encroachment into civilian administrative positions was justified on grounds of the weakening and even collapse in the north and east of civilian institutions during the war, and the need for efficiency and discipline not only for these provinces but the whole country. Military management was marketed as more efficient and therefore more productive and conducive to post-war entrepreneurship. Yet militaristic discipline and regulation discourage dissent and alternative thought necessary for innovation. The impact of this on Sri Lankan society in the early post-war phase was self-censorship and conformism. The argument that the soldier and entrepreneur share a commonality in their "willingness to take their destiny into their own hands," and that economically advanced countries facilitate "creative soldiers to become entrepreneurs and vice versa" (Rockefeller 2016.),[4] overlooks principles within military training which underscore the *conformity* of the military corps in which individualism and individual destiny hardly have a place. It also ignores and underestimates the resentment felt by civilians (including would-be civilian entrepreneurs in the north, for instance) when the military (with the unassailable advantage of the State behind it) competes with civilians in the economic field. It is in this context that a remarkable coalition of (a) opposition political parties, (b) Tamil and Muslim ethnic minorities together with a minority of the majority Sinhala population, and (c) diverse civil society groups and political parties came together, just six years after the war ended, to oust the Rajapaksa regime that had advocated greater militarization of Sri Lankan society. What seemed like a successful militarization campaign during the war and the early post-war phase thereby held the seeds of its own, albeit gradual, reformulation when a new political regime and paradigm came into being with the election of Maithripala Sirisena as president of Sri Lanka in January 2015.

Smart Militarization

The role of information and digital technology, and public–private partnerships in data surveillance and intelligence gathering which constitute core components of post-9/11 security strategy is strongly advocated by the new Sri Lankan regime. This is evident in the sharing of mobile phone records or personal information databases (meta data) that the private companies own, but share with governments in the interests of national security. In Sri Lanka, the sharing of such databases is legalized through the Prevention of Terrorism Act of 1978 and the Sri Lanka Telecommunication (Amendment) Act No. 27 of 1996. Such laws can be used, without further judicial oversight or parliamentary debate, to block telecommunications, as happened in 2007 when the State-run telecom agency blocked communications in the north and east, or gather smart information for intelligence purposes through registration on websites such as citizens. lk that was run by the Ministry of Defence (Hattotuwa 2016).[5] When registrations for such sites (including through a mobile bus service) take place amongst dissident communities, they both draw upon and reproduce a context of coercion and oppression. Information on patterns of mobility is also enabled by CCTV cameras (mounted at roundabouts in Colombo and other major cities in the south such as Kandy, Galle, Anuradhapura, and Kegalle), ostensibly to detect crime and traffic congestion, while the current government's proposal to make Kandy the first "smart city" in Sri Lanka goes even further to integrate and monitor government services and their consumption, citizen–government relations, and information on the city including property ownership through digital technology (LBO 2015). Biometric IDs that will not only include finger prints and photographs of individual citizens, but also information on family members (solicited voluntarily), that will in turn enable the government to track patterns of purchase, mobility, payment of taxes, and overseas travel, is scheduled for operationalization in mid-2016 (*Sunday Times*, 19 June 2016: 1).

The advantage to governments in deploying such technology to gather "knowledge data" in order to assess risk is precisely this: the method of information gathering is covert and therefore seen as "smart, efficient and side-effects free" (Valverde and Mopas cited in Amoore and Goede 2008: 9). Due to its guise, smart militarization also attracts less criticism than its harder, more overtly militaristic version. Precisely for this reason, in former war zones where COIN campaigns have been unsuccessful for reasons outlined before in this essay, and where human intelligence gathering by militaries has proved costly in political terms, the use of digital technology for information on out-group/ hostile populations has been internationally advocated as advantageous because it distances the military from the latter (Aylwin-Foster 2005: 6).

Digital technology (meta data, biometric data through smart IDs, CCTV) enables placing populations under scrutiny toward social sorting, including ethnic and gendered sorting, and allows for people's mobility and behavioral patterns to be observed, recorded, and "rationalized" for knowledge on the individual, his/her family and community networks (Lyon 2002:3). In military language this is called "Sighting the target" which involves converting the object into a unit of information, as a condition of the violence and control directed toward it. In a country where electoral lists were used to identify Tamil households for violence, as happened in the anti-Tamil pogrom of July 1983, the information gathered through biometric IDs runs the risk of being similarly deployed, but to greater effect because of the extent of information they carry. At the same time, the consent of populations toward technological surveillance is grounded in its duality: its routineness in every capital of the world, our dependence on ICT, and record keeping as constitutive of modernity itself (Lyon 2002:4). Yet, it is also insidious and lacking in transparency when it impinges on civil and political life. It is this dualism that makes smart surveillance, as with militarization, ambiguous: sought after by one section of the population at the expense of the other, founded on exception and exemption (Amoore and de Goede 2008: 8).

The study of contemporary post-war militarization in Sri Lanka calls, therefore, for attention to its varied geographical features and techniques that have adapted global security frameworks to local conditions. As it transitions from a highly militaristic one to a soft and smart one that makes Sri Lankan society appear less militarized, the need is for a feminist perspective on the relationship between surveillance, criminalization, terrorism, and gendered embodiment. Such an approach would highlight gendered forms of looking and the impact of "networks of participatory surveillance" grounded in the "commercial logic of social media" that operates at the expense, for instance, of women who live at their edges, in former war zones, categorized as suspicious and threats to the State (van der Meulen and Heynan 2016). For the women of the north and east, even as the end of the war and the killings come as an immense relief, the continued (dis)guise of the military in their midst means the full promise of peace is yet to be grasped, for they remain "risky subjects" in the eyes of the State. Persuading local populations to support the government through measures such as troop reduction and withdrawal, systematic programs that address grievances such as displacement and dispossession of land, development of jobs and livelihoods, greater political autonomy, an environment free of intimidation and justice for war-crimes have been flagged as the bases for trustbuilding between both civil–military and civilian–state groups (Keenan 2016). The early post-war Sri Lankan government proved unsuccessful at such tasks. After August 2015 and the new "national unity" government, a change in policy toward reconciliation and transitional justice has occurred but not without enormous challenges. Members of the previous regime ideologically sympathetic to Sinhala ethnonationalism continue to be in power because of coalition politics. At the same time, a clear strategy to persuade Sinhala nationalists that accountability and security sector reform would benefit all citizens is lacking, and financial and human resources to implement transitional justice mechanisms to their optimum, remains weak (Keenan 2016). A beleaguered economy with a high-debt burden also runs the risk of provoking social and political unrest in Sri Lanka that could hijack the constitutional reform and justice processes. For all Sri Lankan women, but particularly those residing in the former war zones, each of the above means an inevitable redrawing of the terms and conditions of their citizenship itself.

Notes

1. https://www.colombotelegraph.com/index.php/lalith-meets-navi-briefs-diplomats-in-geneva-ahead-of-unhrc/
2. Noble, Kath. October 2013. "The Jaffna Air". Accessed December 20, 2016, https://kathnoble.wordpress.com/2013/10/
3. See http://www.lankauniversity-news.com/2012/10/leadership-training-for-university.html (Accessed November 7, 2016).
4. "Why the Military is the best Entrepreneurship Training Program in America". Accessed December 12, 2016. http://www.forbes.com/sites/marklrockefeller/2016/08/03/why-the-military-is-the-best-entrepreneurship-training-program-in-america/#43f681b6482b
5. http://www.scidev.net/global/data/opinion/people-behind-big-data.html (accessed December 29, 2016).

Bibliography

Amarasingam, Amarnath. 2014, 20 May. "Life in the Open-air Panopticon: Surveillance and the Social Isolation of Ex-LTTE Combatants in Sri Lanka." *Groundviews*. Accessed January 20, 2015, http://groundviews.org/2014/05/20/life-in-the-open-air-panopticon-surveillance-and-the-social-isolation-of-ex-ltte-combatants-in-sri-lanka/

AISLS (American Institute of Sri Lankan Studies). January 8, 2015. "Anthropologist." Correspondence with the Research Directorate, cited in Refworld. Accessed December 29, 2016, http://www.refworld.org/docid/54f03b7e4.html

Amoore, Louise, and Marieke de Goede. 2008. "Introduction: Governing by Risk in the War on Terror," in *Risk and the War on Terror*, edited by Louise Amoore and Marieke de Goede, 5–20. Abingdon: Routledge.

Aylwin-Foster, Nigel. 2005. "Changing the Army for Counterinsurgency Operations." *Military Review* (November–December): 2–15.

Chandraprema, C.A. 2012. *Gota's War: The Crushing of Tamil Tiger Terrorism in Sri Lanka.* Colombo: Ranjan Wijeratne Foundation.

Chenoy, Anuradha. 2002. *Militarism and Women in South Asia.* Delhi: Kali for Women.

Coomaraswamy, Radhika. 2015. Preventing Conflict, Transforming Justice, Securing the Peace: A Global Study on the Implementation of United Nations Security Council Resolution 1325. New York: United Nations.

CPA (Center for Policy Alternatives). 2016. *Land Occupation in the Northern Province: A Commentary on Ground Realities and Recommendations for Reform.* Colombo: CPA.

de Mel, Neloufer. 2007. *Militarizing Sri Lanka: Memory, Narrative and Popular Culture in the Armed Conflict.* California, London, New Delhi, Singapore: SAGE Publications.

Economic and Political Weekly. 2012, 14 July. "Notes on the Military Presence in Sri Lanka's Northern Province," *Economic and Political Weekly,* XLVII(28): 34–40.

Enloe, Cynthia. 2000. *Maneuvers: The International Politics of Militarizing Women's Lives*, Berkeley, CA: University of California Press.

Ferdinando, Shamindra. February 23, 2015. "26,865 Out of 34,561 Acres Land Held by Army in North and East Released by End of 2013: Military Battalions Deployed in North Reduced by 48 from 152 to 104." *The Island*. Accessed 14 June 2016, http://dbsjeyaraj.com/dbsj/archives/38881

Godamunne, Nayana. 2014. "Development for Whom? Reimagining Urban Development in Colombo, Sri Lanka." *Journal of Urban Regeneration and Renewal* 8(2): 186–92.

Hariharathamotharan, H. 2013. *A Study of Post-war Women in Sri Lanka: Research on War Affected Female Headed Families in the Districts of Jaffna, Vavuniya and Baticoloa*. Colombo: Women and Media Collective.

Hattotuwa, Sanjana. March 17, 2011. "Jaffna and the Vanni Today: The Reality Beneath the Rhetoric." *Groundviews*. Accessed November 7, 2016, http://groundviews.org/2011/03/17/jaffna-and-the-vanni-today-the-reality-beneath-the-rhetoric/

HHR (Home for Human Rights), and WMC (Women and Media Collective). 2014. "Female Ex-combatants of Sri Lanka." Documentary. Accessed November 7, 2016, http://womenclaimingrights.womenandmedia.org/?p=484

ICG. (International Crisis Group). March 25 2014. "The Forever War?: Military Control in Sri Lanka's North." International Crisis Group. Accessed November 7, 2016, http://blog.crisisgroup.org/asia/2014/03/25/the-forever-war-military-control-in-sri-lankas-north/

———. 2016, May 18. "Sri Lanka: Jump Starting the Reform Process." International Crisis Group. Accessed November 7, 2016, http://www.crisisgroup.org/~/media/Files/asia/south-asia/sri-lanka/278-sri-lanka-jumpstarting-the-reform-process.pdf

Jeyaraj, D.B.S. 2010, 30 July. *What Is Happening to the Ex-LTTE Cadre Surrenderees?* Accessed October 18, 2016, http://dbsjeyaraj.com/dbsj/archives/1599

Keenan, Alan, 2016. "Impunity and Justice: Why Human Rights Council Must Stay Engaged in Sri Lanka." Crisis Group. Accessed November 7, 2016, http://blog.crisisgroup.org/asia/2016/06/17/

Krishnan, Sonny Inbaraj. 2012. *The Transition to Civilian Life of Teenage Girls and Young Women Ex-Combatants: A Case Study of Batticoloa*. Colombo: ICES.

LBO. 2015, 9 September. "Is the Smart City Significant for Sri Lanka?" Accessed September 7, 2016, http://www.lankabusinessonline.com/is-the-smart-city-significant-for-sri-lanka/

LLRC (Lessons Learnt and Reconciliation Commission). 2011. *Report of the Commission of Inquiry on Lessons Learnt and Reconciliation*. Accessed November 7, 2016, www.priu.gov.lk/news_update/.../Final_LLRC_Report

Lyon, David. 2002. "Surveillance Studies: Understanding Visibility, Mobility and the Phenetic Fix". *Surveillance and Society* 1(1): 1–7.

MRG (Minority Rights Group). 2013. *Living with Insecurity: Marginalization and Sexual Violence Against Women in North and East Sri Lanka*. London: MRG.

Nathaniel, Camelia. 2013, October 13. "Army Denies Its Presence Is Responsible for Insecurity of Northern Women." *Sunday Leader*.

Pathmalal, Shakya. 2011, December 4. "The Role of Ex-combatants in Reconciliation." *Sunday Leader*. Accessed November 7, 2016, http:/www.thesundayleader.lk/2011/12/04/the-role-of-ex-combatants-in-reconciliation

Pinto-Jayawardena, Kishali. 2010. *Post-war Justice in Sri Lanka: Rule of Law, the Criminal Justice System and Commissions of Inquiry*. Geneva: International Commission of Jurists.

Sathkunanathan, Ambika. 2010. "Protection Is Not a Life Saving Activity: The Politics of Protection in Practice in Sri Lanka." In *Civilian Protection in Sri Lanka Under Threat*, 34–39. Refugee Studies Center Working Paper Series No. 58. Oxford: RSC.

Thamilini. 2016. *Under the Shadow of a Sharp Weapon*. Colombo: Thrikone.

The Social Architects. 2013, October 11. "Above the Law: Violations of Women's Reproductive Rights in Northern Sri Lanka." *Groundview*. Accessed November 7, 2016, http://groundviews.org/2013/10/11/above-the-law-violations-of-womens-reproductive-rights-in-northern-sri-lanka/

van der Meulen, Emily, and Robert Heynan, eds. 2016. *Expanding the Gaze: Gender and the Politics of Surveillance*. Toronto: University of Toronto Press.

Venugopal, Rajesh. 2014. "Post-war Development in Sri Lanka: Three Contrasting Approaches." 13th Annual Symposium on Post-War Development in Asia and Africa sponsored by the Center for Poverty Analysis, Colombo, 1–3 September.

Wickramasekera, Damith. 19 June 2016. "New Biometric IDs within Two Months," *Sunday Times*. Accessed December 20, 2016, http://www.sundaytimes.lk/160619/news/new-biometric-ids-within-two-months-197895.html

8

Violent Peace in the Chittagong Hill Tracts

*Hana Shams Ahmed**

Flawed Peace Accord and Failed Promises

It has been over 18 years since the "Peace" Accord was signed in the Chittagong Hill Tracts (CHT) of Bangladesh to end a two-decade-long armed conflict in the area. The movement for self-determination that began in the 1970s led to militarization of the area along with a demographic engineering project to displace the indigenous population with the majority Bengalis. In the post-Accord situation, the unaddressed question of the Bengali settlers and the continuation of militarization in violation of the Accord have irreversibly changed the ethnic makeup of the area, making the indigenous people of CHT minorities in their own homeland and living in continued fear of attacks. What exists in the CHT is a form of "violent peace" (Chakma and D'Costa 2013). The indigenous activists have stepped up their demand for constitutional rights for the *Jumma* people (collective name for the indigenous people of the CHT). The Bangladesh government has strengthened securitization of the area and surveillance on

---

*The author is coordinator of the International Chittagong Hill Tracts Commission (CHTC), which reports on human rights violations and monitors implementation of the CHT Accord.

indigenous activists. Military action in 2014, resulting in the death of five indigenous activists, threatened to reignite conflict in the Chittagong Hill Tracts (Amnesty International 2015).

Powerful political interests in the CHT are affecting the implementation of the Accord and the resolution of the critical land issues there. There are many stakeholders in the CHT for whom the status quo serves as a perfect breeding ground for exploitation and impunity. Just like in many other places in the world where marginalized indigenous communities live, this area is rich in resources. Consequently, everyone from the military to political groups, private corporations, and powerful elites have a stake in this land. In Bangladesh, the military has never been an institution whose operations were limited to preserving the country's national security. It has always been deeply involved in the state politics and in the economy.

This chapter focuses on the continuation of conflict and militarization in a supposedly "post-conflict" environment in the CHT. It argues that, the protracted presence of the military in CHT after the end of insurgency and the persistence of impunity for human rights violations, including sexual violence has created a permanent situation of insecurity especially for women. The chapter draws attention to the widespread use of sexualized violence for purposes of land grabbing by Bengali settlers, backed by a partisan administration and a complicit military.

In 1997, when the Accord was signed, there was the promise of a transformative politics. The rebels came in hundreds to surrender their arms to Prime Minister Sheikh Hasina, whose government drafted and signed the Executive Accord. The international community lauded the achievement and the UNESCO awarded Prime Minister Sheikh Hasina with the Houphouet–Boigny Peace Prize. The leader of the opposition party, Bangladesh National Party (BNP), Begum Khaleda Zia denounced the Accord for jeopardizing the sovereignty of the country.

Drawn up to bring an end to a conflict situation, the Accord has been a disappointment to Jumma activists as it proved inadequate to address the issue of autonomy of the indigenous people. Moreover, even the issues that the Accord did address did not bring a peaceful solution to the problem in the CHT. This is evident in the continuation of overwhelming presence of military in the area, the continuing attack on Jumma homes, persisting sexual violence and impunity, land grabbing, and the constant struggle between government and indigenous people for constitutional recognition.

The military had entered the CHT with the objective of putting an end to the movement for self-determination through violent means. After the surrender of the indigenous peoples, the military still remains and is now involved in the administration and economy of the CHT. It plays an important role in fueling the divide-and-rule policy for the indigenous political groups and in backing the government's transmigration program which settled 400,000 Bengalis in the CHT during the 1980s. According to the reports of human rights groups, the military has provided tacit, if not overt, support to Bengali settlers who carry out arson attacks, rapes, and human rights violations against the Jumma people in the continuing struggles over land.

Those involved in the negotiations surrounding the CHT Accord spoke about an unwritten understanding with the government that the Bengali settlers would be resettled outside the CHT. The BNP's steadfast opposition and the suspicion surrounding the Accord negotiations made for caution and conservatism. Also, Parbatya Chattagram Jana Samhati Samiti (PCJSS), the political arm of the armed group, the Shanti Bahini, was under pressure from India (patron to the "rebels" and host to CHT refugees) to sign the Accord. Thus, the PCJSS was persuaded to concede that it would be politically too explosive to put down on paper any understanding on the issue of resettling the Bengalis. But unwritten agreements can only go so far. Post-Accord, Bengali settlers have continued to come into the CHT with support of the military. Moreover, within the CHT, settlers' groups are politically organized with members belonging to all national political parties. In fact the national political groups who otherwise are so divided on national political issues seem to work together in resisting the Accord's implementation.

In particular the threat of rape which was used as an instrument during the war, now in the post-conflict situation in CHT continues to be used primarily to control the freedom of movement of indigenous women and through that to control the daily livelihood practices of the indigenous communities. The presence of settlers has had a particularly adverse impact on the lives and livelihoods of indigenous women of the CHT. Indigenous communities, especially in the hills, have very distinct cultural and social differences from the majority Bengali communities. The clothing and lifestyle of indigenous women sets them apart. Most indigenous women wear a blouse and a wraparound sarong-like cloth. Although, within indigenous families, patriarchy is very much present, especially regarding land inheritance rights, women of the indigenous communities are economically productive, and play a significant livelihood role in *jhum* (slash and burn) cultivation, and the sale of produce in local markets. However, with the arrival of the military and the settlers, there have been constraints on women's freedom of movement in public spaces and changes in the clothing of indigenous women.

Struggle for Autonomy and Militarization of CHT

The formation of Bangladesh was based on Bengali nationalism, and after independence in 1971, the ruling elites of Bangladesh tried to maintain the "nation-state" paradigm (Chakma 2010b). Sheikh Mujib—who led the movement for independence—kept Bengali nationalism as one of the pillars of the constitution. Article 3 of the Constitution declared Bangla as the state language, and Article 6 stated that the citizens of Bangladesh were to be known as Bengalis. Four decades later, Sheikh Hasina's government reinforced that congruence between Bengali nation and state in the 15th amendment to the constitution in 2011. Article 6 (2) states: "The people of Bangladesh shall be known as Bangalees as a nation, and the citizens of Bangladesh shall be known as Bangladeshis." Article 6(2) directly denies the indigenous peoples as citizens of the country and Article 23A categorizes and alienates indigenous people from Bengalis and makes them second-class citizens of the country. In addition, the Government has categorically denied the existence of indigenous people in the country, although the term had been used previously by the same government and also mentioned in various national laws.

The nationalist goal of assimilation and the indigenous peoples' struggle for autonomy had led to the insurgent movement of the Jumma people. The Shanti Bahini (peace force), the armed wing of the Jumma regional political party, the PCJSS, led the two-decade-long armed struggle against the Bangladesh military. The military used brutal force and carried out torture, massacres, rape, and forced evictions, making the Jummas internally displaced and forced thousands to take refuge in India. During the insurgency, the military carried out at least 11 massacres in villages all across the CHT, which some authors have described as a slow motion process of ethnocide (Chakma 2010b). The Bengali elites viewed the armed rebellion as a threat to the national security and territorial integrity of the state. Ironically, a similar marginalization had confronted the Bengalis in East Pakistan and led to the struggle for autonomy, the "Liberation War" and the emergence of Bangladesh. However, when the tables were turned, the Bengalis supported the military's violent suppression of the CHT peoples struggle for autonomy. As historian Mark Levene wrote, "a new state founded in 1971 out of an extremely bloody secession from Pakistan, Bangladesh has always been considered in the camp of the 'victims' not the 'perpetrators'" (Levene 1999).

In the CHT, three military cantonments were set up along with numerous temporary camps. Approximately, one-third of Bangladesh's military personnel were deployed in an area which makes up 10 percent of land mass of the country. At the time of President H M Ershad's military dictatorship, an estimated 115,000 military personnel were deployed in the CHT, resulting in the ratio of one soldier for five Jumma persons (Levene 1999).

Poor, landless Bengali settlers were brought in to act as human shields for the military, as part of the counter insurgency strategy. Under *Operation Pacification*, nearly 400,000 settlers were brought in and provided food rations to induce them to stay. More than two decades later, food rations are still being provided. It was also under military patronage that the CHT underwent considerable Islamization through proselytization, forced marriages, setting up of mosques and madrassas, and renaming of villages with Muslim names. The forced marriage of indigenous women to Bengalis was used as a strategy to change the demography of the CHT, and created anxieties about religious and ethnic identity (D'Costa 2014).

Normalization of Militarization

The CHT Accord had provided for the dismantling of all temporary military camps in the area. No meaningful steps have been taken in these last 18 years toward that. Militarization is perpetuated through guises such as the presence of an executive order known as Operation *Uttoron* (Upliftment). The military's transmigration policy during insurgency time has now turned into a spontaneous ethnic displacement strategy during "peace" time. Also new political dynamics have emerged in the post-conflict situation, bringing in restrictions on movement and monitoring of activities in the CHT. The Director General of Forces Intelligence (DGFI) keeps a close watch on NGOs, activists, and journalists who work on Jumma people's rights issues. Even the few NGOs that work on violence against indigenous women have to avoid using a rights-based language in their mandate, as application for registration has to be approved by the NGO bureau and is subject to scrutiny by the military intelligence agencies. Issues related to indigenous people's rights are viewed as national security issues.

Also, restrictions are imposed on the entry of "outsiders" into the CHT and indigenous people are forbidden to speak to foreigners without supervision (Amnesty International 2015). In the last year, three foreigners have been evicted from the CHT for being closely linked with Jumma activists. On April 23, 2015, the Home Ministry issued a circular imposing discriminatory and unconstitutional restrictions on the indigenous communities of CHT.

The military works closely with the district administration. In most cases, they hand down verbal directives to the district administration, which then hands them out in written form. For instance, government officials were instructed not to allow the celebration of World Indigenous Peoples' Day. The military's close association with the administration enables them to profit from the vast expanse of natural resources available in the CHT—including the setting up of tourist resorts in the most mountainous region of Bandarban, land grabbing and leasing to private corporations, illegal logging and so on.

The CHT shows a continuum of conflict and post-conflict militarization. Democratic concerns require that the continuing presence of the military "post-conflict" be justified within a sovereignty imperative. The nationalist psyche of the majority (Bengalis) accepts this rationale. Moreover, the military intervenes to control public opinion through media. It is quite standard for military officials to appear on TV talk shows and write opinion articles in leading newspapers on what should be the political strategy toward the indigenous communities.

Post-Accord Sexualized Violence and Impunity

On September 11, 2013, an 11-year-old indigenous *Chakma* girl was raped by a Bengali settler in Rangamati district of the CHT of Bangladesh. The Union Parishad (local self-governing bodies) member tried to persuade the girl's parents and the indigenous community leaders to come to a compromise on monetary terms. The girl's father insisted on filing a case at the police station. The magistrate of Rangamati recorded the girl's statement under Section 164, but her parents were not allowed to be present. Instead, a Chakma male, a stranger to the girl, was appointed as an interpreter for taking her statement, translating Chakma to Bangla for the magistrate.

During insurgency, the military had carried out mass rapes and massacres with total impunity in the CHT. The Hill Women's Federation (HWF) was formed to address the rape and harassment of women by the military. The 1997 Peace Accord did not address the issue of rape by the military and other security forces, and there was no compensation for rape victims. The unresolved abduction case of Jumma woman activist Kalpana Chakma (June 1996) is symbolic of the impunity enjoyed by the military in the CHT. Although Kalpana was (allegedly) abducted by military officer Lt. Ferdous and two Village Defence Party members in the presence of her family members, three consecutive investigations failed to put him down as a suspect and take him in for questioning. The DGFI colluded with the military's media misinformation tactics—insinuating she had eloped with an army officer or that she had run off to India, and then announcing a reward to anyone who could locate her.

The protracted presence of military in the CHT even after the end of insurgency has created a permanent insecurity situation, especially for women. According to a recent study of marginalization and impunity in the CHT (D'Costa 2014: 7):

> Impunity has been the single most important factor contributing to increased incidents of sexual and gender based violence (SGBV) in the CHT. The biases of the administrative, political and judicial systems prevent access to equality and justice by Indigenous Peoples and minorities.

As a result, indigenous communities, particularly women and girls, have continued to be victims of atrocities including kidnapping, rape, and torture, as well as domestic violence. Land grabs contribute to an increase in the rate of gender-based violence, as women dispossessed of their land become dependent on their male relatives and thus more vulnerable to violence and sexual abuse. Women's organizations such as the Khagrapur Mahila Kalyan Samity (KMKS) in Khagrachari, Ananya Kallayan Sangathon (AKS) in Bandarban and networks such as Bangladesh Indigenous Women's Network (BIWN) have highlighted that even after the signing of the "Peace" Accord, human rights abuses, in particular SGBV by the law enforcement personnel and illegal Bengali settlers continue to take place regularly in the CHT with impunity (D'Costa 2014).

Post-Accord, most rapes in the CHT are carried out by settlers instead of military personnel. SGBV is used to intimidate indigenous peoples to sell their land at bargain prices. The presence of the military gives settlers a sense of security in the form of impunity for sexual violence against indigenous women. Some arrests of rape suspects have been made but it requires human rights activists to maintain constant vigilance on each case to get cases to move in the court. D'Costa's study draws attention to the pressure on medical doctors in the CHT to falsify medical examination of rape complainants. "Each of the rape incidents that takes place in the hills receives negative medical report: *Rape did not take place* (emphasis added)." To investigate, Bina D'Costa spoke to an NGO worker who quoted a doctor admitting that

> doctors are instructed from the high corridors of administration (over the phone as well as via their representatives) not to produce positive medical reports, as soon as the news of a rape incident arrives. The relation between Bengalis and Indigenous people would deteriorate, they are told as a reason. (D'Costa 2014: 33)

Violence, particularly sexual violence has become disturbingly routine. According to the Kapaeeng Foundation, between January 2007 and October 2012, there were 160 incidents of VAW against indigenous women and girls, 96 percent of these cases were of sexual violence. In none of these reported cases were the perpetrators prosecuted through formal justice system. In 2014 alone, 117 indigenous women faced physical and sexual abuse, 57 percent of these being children. During the first few weeks of 2015, at least three confirmed rapes were reported within sight of military checkpoints, so placed to provide security. These are the reported incidents; the actual number is likely to be much higher (Amnesty International 2015).

Invisiblizing Women in the CHT Peace Process

The Jana Samhati Samiti (JSS) signed the CHT Accord with the Awami League Government in 1997. The Shanti Bahini surrendered their arms and were absorbed in government posts. Not everyone within the indigenous communities supported the Accord. Disaffection resulted in formation of the United People's Democratic Front (UPDF), which asserted that the Accord did not give them regional autonomy, the core objective of the armed struggle. The Hill Women's Federation (HWF) also split into two, and the two HWF groups continue to operate separately in their designated areas. Significantly, in both *Pahari* political groups, men continue to dominate and provide patronage to the women in their groups.

This is in spite of the fact that in the CHT struggle for self-determination, a lot of women participated directly and indirectly. During the insurgency, some women took up arms while many other women took on the "male" role of head of the family, as the men of the family were away in the forest, either as part of the armed resistance or fleeing from military crackdown. Their writings document their struggle for survival, particularly how they reworked their traditional roles in the private sphere and in how they dealt with crises in the public sphere (Guhathakurta 2004). Indigenous women spontaneously joined the Jumma women's resistance movements because they considered that to be a survival strategy.

Importantly, one of the reasons for the split in the HWF and the emergence of the anti-Accord group within HWF was that the indigenous women were not involved in peace negotiations, and their contribution to the struggle was not acknowledged. Their absence in peace talks meant that the issue of justice for Pahari women was never addressed. There was no mention of the sexualized violence faced by women at the hands of the military, let alone provision made for a redress mechanism. There was no attention to confronting the unwritten military policy of forcibly marrying indigenous women with the purpose of proselytization.

In the post-Accord situation, proselytization through forced marriages by settlers continues, the objective being, land-grabbing. In terms of land inheritance, most indigenous cultures are patriarchal in structure except for the *Marma* under the *Bohmong* circle, where women inherit land. Even among the Marma, women do not inherit an equal share of the property relative to their male counterparts. Equal inheritance might be open to some Chakma women, but not by default and only with the familial consent or when explicitly mentioned in a will.

Indigenous women are underrepresented in the traditional and primarily hereditary institutions of circle chiefs (*rajas*), headmen, and village chiefs (*karbari*). A two-tier system of indigenous courts of headmen and chiefs exercise judicial authority in the CHT, especially over personal or family law matters. While the most serious criminal offenses are not adjudicated through the indigenous courts, some of the common issues of dispute that are resolved concern—fathers seeking recovery of daughters (often minors) who have eloped, complaints of domestic violence or desertion by men, and women seeking divorce or child custody. Based upon local customs and processes, the focus is often on reconciliation and mediation (D'Costa 2014). Women's vulnerability is intersectionally compounded by their lack of any significant influence in decision-making. As a result, the CHT's context of militarization and transmigration programs (illegally settling Bengalis) have created extreme vulnerability and poverty for the Indigenous Peoples, and have deeply affected indigenous women and girls' safety and security in the CHT.

Lesser Citizens

The nationalist–assimilationist policy of the Bangladeshi nation-state has turned indigenous people of Bangladesh, and specifically those in the CHT, into lesser citizens of the country. The state successfully propagated this sentiment into the general population, to manufacture public opinion for a national security discourse around the issue, leading to normalization of military presence and immunity and impunity to perpetrators of violence in the CHT. While the government applauded itself on signing of the Peace Accord, it has failed to effect the removal of temporary military camps in the area, in order to normalize civilian life there.

The military and, increasingly now, the Border Guards influence the everyday lives of the common people and politics of the CHT, producing more resentment and alienation, especially in the face of continuing violation of human rights of the indigenous people. Stung by international criticism about the military's persisting presence, more Border Guards are being deployed in the name of stronger borders. It stokes popular nationalist sentiment on the one hand and facilitates grabbing more Jumma lands on the other.

Bibliography

Amnesty International. 2015. "Hidden Bangladesh: Violence and Brutality in the Chittagong Hill Tracts." London. Accessed 7 November 2016, http://www.amnesty.org.uk/groups/wirksworth-and-district/hidden-bangladesh-violence-and-brutality-chittagong-hill-tracts

Chakma, Bhumitra. March 20, 2010a. "Structural Roots of Violence in the Chittagong Hill Tracts." *Economic & Political Weekly* XLV(12): 19–21. Accessed November 7, 2016, http://www.epw.in/journal/2010/12/commentary/structural-roots-violence-chittagong-hill-tracts.html

————. 2010b, July 5. "The Post-colonial State and Minorities: Ethnocide in the Chittagong Hill Tracts, Bangladesh." *Commonwealth & Comparative Politics*, 48(3), pp. 281–300.

Chakma, K., and B. D'Costa. 2013. "The Chittagong Hill Tracts: Diminishing Violence or Violent Peace," in *Diminishing Conflicts in Asia and the Pacific*, edited by Edward Aspinall, Robin Jeffrey and Anthony J. Regan. Abingdon and New York: Routledge, Taylor & Francis Group.

CHTC (CHT Commission). 2013, 7 July. "CHTC Deeply Concerned with Increasing Violence in the Chittagong Hill Tracts." Press statement, CHT. Accessed December 19, 2016, http://www.chtcommission.org/backend/product_picture/515doc.pdf

D'Costa, Bina. 2014. "Marginalisation and Impunity: Violence against Women and Girls in the CHT." Report by the CHT Commission, International Work Group for Indigenous Affairs, Bangladesh Indigenous Women's Network. Accessed on December 19, 2016, http://chtcommission.org/CHT_violence_against_women_Study_2014.pdf

Guhathakurta, Meghna. 2004. *The Chittagong Hill Tracts (CHT) Accord and After: Gendered Dimensions of Peace*. United Nations Research Institute for Social Development (UNRISD), Geneva, Switzerland.

Levene, M.1999. "The Chittagong Hill Tracts: A Case Study in the Political Economy of 'Creeping' Genocide." *Third World Quarterly*, 20(2): 339–69.

Yasmin, L. 2013, July 10–14. "Constructing Indigenous Identity." Unpublished paper presented at the Politics of Indigenous Identity: National and International Perspectives. International Political Science Association, Macquarie University, Sydney, Australia.

9
Failed Peace and Security Strategies in Afghanistan's Transition

Huma Safi

Confronting Greater Insecurities

Afghanistan is a nation confronting a long and deeply complex conflict that has destroyed human lives, displaced millions, ruined its vital infrastructure, and devastated its society. Moreover, internationally driven strategies to bring "peace" and security in Afghanistan have not worked, and many political leaders and policy analysts within and outside Afghanistan contend that they have resulted in greater insecurities. This chapter, in essaying a gender security audit of the Afghan Transition, shares that perspective and argues that policy choices made by the international community and the Afghan government have failed to achieve the principal goals of building peace. Insurgency rages, grievances growing, and insecurity is everywhere.

The challenges and pressures facing the Afghan government and the international community today are stronger than those which motivated the initial military intervention to force Al-Qaeda and the Taliban to abandon their activities. In particular, the human rights situation in Afghanistan is in crisis. Human rights are being violently violated not only by insurgents, but also by the government and their sponsored armed groups, and that too in the presence of the major world powers—the leaders of stable democracies and the champions of human rights.

This is in a context in which strategies to bring peace and security have resulted in the resurgence of the Taliban and the proliferation of irresponsible armed groups affiliated to warlords and jihadi parties, many of whom enjoy the overt and covert support of government agencies and sections of the international community. At the very beginning, a crucial policy error was made by recognizing and legitimizing the informal power of warlords. The international community helped these warlords—the violators of human rights—consolidate their political and economic power. The international community turned a blind eye to their past crimes and continued to support them despite reports of continuing human rights crimes. The international community's emphasis has always been on military solutions, the consequences of which has been more violence, increase in human rights violations and uncertainty about the future. They have persistently deemphasized investing in the civilian sector, for instance, in creating a professional bureaucracy and institutions of governance.

The dominant paradigm of "NATO vs Taliban" has been replaced by multiple overlapping conflicts both between and within Afghan groups—a development that has increased the vulnerability of civilians, especially women facing increased criminality and less-controlled violence. The expanding capability and will demonstrated by the Afghan National Security Forces (ANSF) and armed opposition groups, has resulted in 2014–15 seeing the highest levels of violent activity on record, and thus a corresponding increase in humanitarian vulnerabilities—not only in terms of collateral involvement in political violence, but also actions specifically aimed to shape the humanitarian space (INSO 2015). Women have been in the forefront in this development space, especially as development workers. This further exacerbates the social consequences of the militarization of humanitarian and development assistance that has produced greater vulnerabilities for aid and development workers and undermined legitimacy.

The Transition

The year 2014 was a watershed year for Afghanistan. The transition process was completed by 2014, and the International Security Assistance Force (ISAF) turned over the responsibility for the security of Afghanistan to the ANSF, for the first time since the Taliban regime was toppled in 2001. ISAF left Afghanistan confronting not only security challenges, but also weak governance, runaway corruption, and a continuing culture of impunity. On January 1, 2014 the Resolute Support Mission (RSM) started to advise and train ANSF to take over complete control (Chala 2015). More recently, the American president has announced that some 10,000 US troops will remain to assist Afghan forces in combating the resurgent Taliban's offensive and takeover of territory.

In 2014, the United Nations Assistance Mission in Afghanistan (UNAMA) recorded the highest number of civilian casualties in any given year since UNAMA began documenting civilian casualties in 2009. With 3,699 civilians killed and 6,849 civilians injured in 2014, Afghanistan saw a 22 percent increase in civilian casualties over 2013 (Chala 2015). Afghan women and girls have been the main target of the criminalized violence of multiple armed actors. Routinely, they are victims of rape, abduction, forced marriage, and slave labor. Insurgents also threaten many women activists in sociopolitical life. The list of women assassinated in public office is lengthening—from women police officers to councilors and ministers, for example, Angiza Shinwari, Head of Department of Women Affairs in Flagman province and Jude Fahima, member of provincial council in Nangarhar. Women remain vulnerable targets and no meaningful effort is made to provide security to working women.

The legal framework creates equal rights for men and women, and protection against violence against women. But laws need to be implemented. Many victims have no access to the help they need, although some NGOs are providing protection services to women survivors. Most incidents go unpunished and many remain unreported. In many cases, elders and warlords or insurgents offer local solutions.

NATO has completed its mission; but, what is it that the US troops withdrawing from Afghanistan leave behind—a weak and highly corrupt state, warlords and human rights violators in power? What kind of society have the champions of empowering women, left behind for the women of Afghanistan? We women of Afghanistan are very concerned about all the political games and compromises that are being done under the guise of peacemaking in Afghanistan.[1] In 2014, Equality for Peace and Democracy conducted focus group discussion with 500 women rights activists in different region of Afghanistan; women expressed their concerns about all political games and compromises that are being done under the guise of peace-making in (Afghanistan Equality for Peace and Democracy 2014). The possibility of meaningful participation by women in the proposed peace process was jeopardized by the fact that there were only nine women in the 70-member High Peace Council (HPC) in Kabul, the Afghan body, created in 2010 to ensure reintegration of Taliban and other anti-government elements into society, and in hopes of finding a peace resolution. There are women in the peace committee in the provinces, but their presence is largely symbolic. Women are not part of important meeting with Taliban representatives. Afghan women worry that such peace initiatives would only add to the miseries of Afghan women and girls (Afghanistan Equality for Peace and Democracy, 2014).

Security means providing a stable environment where everyone is able to live and work free of any fear. Instead, gross human rights violations go unpunished and protected by networks formally empowered by the Afghan government and international community. These abuses continue in the so called post-conflict situations and the perpetrators are the very forces who were involved in the conflict for many years. A survey by the "New Afghan Women's Association" based on 2,000 questionnaires showed that "35 percent of respondents identified the perpetrators of sexual violence as influential people, armed commanders and illegal armed individuals" (UN Security Council: SG Conflict Related Sexual Violence 2015, 33, S/2015/203, p.4).[2]

Afghan Local Police: Exacerbating Insecurity

Millions of dollars were spent in Afghanistan on the process of Disarmament, Demobilization and Reintegration (DDR), and Disbandment of Illegal Armed Groups (DIAG), to disarm the militia and the former Mujahideen. A decade later, the government, as part of the transition, initiated a new program to arm them once again under a new guise, the Afghan Local Police (ALP). The Ministry of Interior established the ALP by presidential decree on August 16, 2011, at the request of the International Security Assistance Force (ISAF) with the support of US. According to the US military and the Afghan government, the ALP was rolled out across the country to defend rural communities in areas where there is limited presence of the Afghan National Army (ANA) and the police. It was conceived as an interim measure till such time as the national forces strengthened their capabilities. The official target was to hire 10,000 men for the ALP force. The US Congress approved funding for 30,000. In 2013, it was announced that the ALP force would be expanded to 45,000 with funding guaranteed by the Pentagon until 2018. As of December 1, 2014, some 27,837 men had been recruited to the ALP 2018 (Pessin 2010; Goodhand and Hakimi 2014: 14–15).

The ALP has been accused of committing human rights violations mostly in the north and northeast of the country. According to interviews conducted by the Afghanistan Independent Human Rights Commission (AIHRC) of people and local government officials in the provinces and districts, the ALP is accused of sexual harassment, beatings, murder, robbery, abduction, banditry, and extortion including forcing people to pay *ushr* tax and poll tax. Most of these violations have taken place in areas where former local commanders, Taliban members, and individuals with criminal records have been recruited within the ALP force (AIHRC, 2012, p. 6). Specific violations apart, the ALP has not been able to win public support and deliver satisfaction, due to lack of sensitivity about maintaining an ethnic and tribal balance in the composition of the force. Also, high-illiteracy rates within the force, above 90 percent, and lack of awareness about laws and human rights values have further aggravated the vulnerability of policed population, especially women.

Such short-term military solutions as the creation of an inadequately trained and poorly vetted local police force, and the misguided policy of not alienating the warlords and maintaining good economic and political relation with them, has resulted in rearming the very groups that were disarmed under DDR. It has provided an opportunity for the insurgents to infiltrate and act from within the Afghan security forces.

Such policies have enabled them to tighten their power vertically and horizontally, thus entrenching their impunity.

A report by Human Rights Watch, "Just Don't Call It a Militia," on the impact of these officially sponsored militias and local police, highlighted the growing militarization and the deteriorating security situation for women. It emphasized,

> US and ISAF military forces in Afghanistan have compounded this unpalatable choice (impunity) since they entered Afghanistan in 2001 by elevating abusive armed groups in security partnerships or giving them lucrative contracts in logistics or reconstruction. International forces can appear to be blind about these relationships. In other cases they are in active collusion, even as they talk about their fight against the bad guys. (HRW 2011)

It quotes an international official admitting that "ALP is the exit strategy." (HRW 2011)

Afghanistan office of the NGO Safety Organisation referring to the ALP in its Quarterly Data report (ANSO 2012) warns that "their impact is not always a positive one, as illustrated by cases of local resistance to their deployment, generally because of poorly defined control mechanisms and the disruptive effect they have on existing power dynamics." Particularly in the northeast region of Afghanistan, these ALP are the Talib at night and government forces by day. They identify themselves as ALP, when they commit crimes against civilians and particularly women. The government authority claims they are not ALP, but irresponsible armed groups. "If they are ALP they should be held accountable and controlled by the National police. If they are not ALP then why are they armed?" protest women's groups.

Militarization of Aid

Deteriorating security conditions, rampant corruption, and increased involvement of the military in the humanitarian and development spheres are seen to be at the root of many of the problems facing the country. A large part of the problem of militarization of aid is that assistance is used to leverage military and political objectives. International troops have undertaken humanitarian and development projects in the communities in which they are deployed, as an integral part of a campaign to "win the hearts and minds" of the local population. Its strategic aim is to subdue the insurgency. The majority of the large donor countries, including the UK, US, Canada, and Germany have provided a large part of their humanitarian and development assistance through their military contingents. Even smaller donor countries such as New Zealand use their troops to deliver their humanitarian and development aid commitments.

Provincial Reconstruction Teams (PRTs), the main vehicle through which international military forces and their diplomatic bosses implement aid and development projects, have been criticized by the World Bank for operating outside the purview of the Afghan government. According to 2010–11 fiscal year statistics, 88 percent of development assistance was provided through an "external budget," with implementing partners operating outside the remit of government, and only 12 percent through the "core budget" of the state coffers. (Oxfam 2010) In other words, donors fund a parallel system of support through their militaries that bypass official government systems of oversight.

This has meant that the delivery of humanitarian aid and development assistance in Afghanistan mostly comes in the form of camouflage, and is thus nontransparent and nonaccountable. Not only are such forms of assistance used to leverage political and military purposes, but militarization of aid has contributed to an increase in rampant corruption in the country. Furthermore, it has serious gender consequences at the community level, women are the front line development aid workers in communities, and they have been targeted by insurgent for being associated with foreign troops.

Far too much aid is focused on "quick fixes" and band-aid approaches, rather than on what could produce positive and lasting results for Afghans over the long term. As political pressures rise to "show results" in troop contributing countries, more and more assistance gets channeled through military actors to "win hearts and minds;" while efforts to address the underlying causes of poverty and repair the destruction wrought by three decades of conflict and disorder, was sidelined.

Development projects implemented with military money or through military-dominated structures are aimed at achieving fast results but are poorly designed, inappropriate, and do not have sufficient community involvement to make them sustainable. Military involvement in humanitarian and development activities also puts Afghan lives at risk, as these projects quickly become targeted by anti-government elements.

For instance, the US military in an attempt to win the hearts and minds of the local population in Afghanistan, reasoned that it must demonstrate the concrete benefits of collaborating with Americans in the fight against Al-Qaeda and the Taliban. They used soldiers and other military personnel to build schools and bridges with mixed results. Humanitarian principles are derived from the laws of war. These principles include, among others, *humanity* (aid must save lives and alleviate suffering), *impartiality* (aid is based solely on need), and *independence* (aid is not suborned to political or military objectives). These are not abstract, do-good notions. They are born out of conflict, and there are hard-headed reasons as to why the laws of war provide for humanitarian assistance. Adhering to these tenets assures that the primary interest of aid workers in war-torn communities is helping civilians survive with dignity. As a result, humanitarian organizations are granted access and the aid workers are assured safety. They may even mediate with armed opposition groups on the aid organizations' behalf. This is how relief agencies should operate in violent places, including Afghanistan.

However, as the Afghanistan NGO Safety Organisation observed, aid agencies in Afghanistan were generally attacked as they were perceived as intrinsic to the military and the political objectives of the coalition forces. Aid organizations have appealed to the US administration to take note of this dangerous conflation. On March 11, 2009, NGOs wrote to then Secretary of State Hillary Clinton, noting that "In Afghanistan's cultural and political environment, it is difficult for military actors to achieve sufficient levels of community ownership and trust which are vital for aid effectiveness." Some of the same NGOs in April wrote to heads of NATO countries, including President Barack Obama, urging them not to use military forces for "relief or development activities to attempt to win people's hearts and minds for tactical, counter-insurgency or other military objectives."

On the eve of the London Conference on Afghanistan (2010), NGOs again appealed to donor countries against the dangers of militarized aid in Afghanistan:

As eight non-governmental organizations, working in Afghanistan for up to fifty years and currently serving over 5 million Afghans across the country, we are deeply concerned about the harmful effects of this increasingly militarized aid strategy. As leaders from 70 nations gather in London to debate the future of Afghanistan, we urge them to re-evaluate this approach to development and reconstruction. (Oxfam 2010)

In short, aid organizations want the military to specialize in what it does well—enhancing security—and leave the humanitarian work to civilian groups. Few in the military have experience in the delicate fields of development and post-conflict reconstruction. The military has only weak links to the communities where they try to work. Their language experts are few and spread thinly, and because the military thinks tactically, not in terms of development, consequently their projects tend to be less effective on the ground.

Put simply, the long-term goals of aid work differ drastically from the short-term goals of counter-insurgency. While NGOs might strive to lift literacy rates by boosting enrolment at school, the military might build an impressive classroom in the name of "winning hearts and minds" but leave no teachers behind to staff it.

Taking Responsibility

Poverty, unemployment, and weak, corrupt government are important drivers of conflict. Ultimately, these factors must be effectively addressed if there is to be any sustainable improvement in security, and a lasting peace for Afghans.

The Transition was premised on the assumption that the ANSF was ready to serve the country, with an existing pool of qualified people and financial support provided by international military forces (IMF). But the overall security conditions are rapidly deteriorating with increasing attacks on civilians and greater restrictions on civil society, particularly on women. Taliban are more powerful now, and ISS presence in some provinces of the country is emerging as a major concern. The international community needs to pay attention to security in Afghanistan, and live up to its commitment to help the government of Afghanistan bring sustainable peace and security. Women are concerned that there is minimal, if any, attention being paid to ensuring the promises on rule of law, access to justice, governance, and active participation of women in peace process and security.

The Women of Afghanistan support Afghan National Security Forces (ANSF), but they need to be better trained and supplied As a woman from the province of Kunduz before the recent Taliban offensive said, *"We count on them. If they become strong we can live in peace. We are afraid of illegal armed militias, and the Taliban."* (WRN 2014)

Notes

1. Peace and Security in Afghanistan: Looking Back to Move Forward. Accessed December 19, 2016, http://www.epd-afg.org/wp-content/uploads/2014/03/WPS-paper.pdf
2. United Nations, Security Council, Conflict-related Sexual Violence Report of the Secretary-General, S/2015/203, https://unama.unmissions.org/sites/default/files/wps-sg_report_crsv_-march_2015_0.pd

Bibliography

Afghanistan Independent Human Rights Commission (AIHRC). 2012. "From Arbaki to Local Police." Accessed December 19, 2016, http://www.aihrc.org.af/en/research-reports/1073/index.html

ANSO. 2012. ANSO Quarterly Data Report (Q. 1), Afghanistan NGO Safety Office. Accessed December 19, 2016, http://reliefweb.int/report/afghanistan/afghanistan-ngo-safety-office-anso-quarterly-datreport-q-1-2012

Calha. (2014). Special Rapporteur Afghanistan—Post-ISAF. Accessed December 19, 2016, http://www.nato-pa.int/default.asp?SHORTCUT=3792file:///C:/Users/Ahmad%20Elyas/Downloads/054_dsc_15_e-special_miranda_calha_afghanistan.pdf

Equality for Peace and Democracy. 2014. Looking BACK to move FORWARD. Accessed December 19, 2016, http://www.epd-afg.org/wp-content/uploads/2014/03/WPS-paper.pdf

Goodhand, J., and Hakimi, A. 2014. "Counterinsurgency, Local Militias, and Statebuilding in Afghanistan." United States Institute for Peace: Peaceworks. Accessed December 19, 2016, http://www.usip.org/publications/counterinsurgency-local-militias-and-statebuilding-in-afghanistan

Human Rights Watch (HRW). 2011. *Just Don't Call It a Militia: Impunity, Militias, and the Afghan Local Police.* Accessed December 19, 2016, https://www.hrw.org/sites/default/files/reports/afghanistan0911webwcover.pdf

Husarska, Anna. 2009. The Militarization of Afghan Aid. Accessed December 19, 2016, http://foreignpolicy.com/2009/07/31/the-militarization-of-afghan-aid/

Oxfam. 2010. *Quick Impact Quick Collapse: The Dangers of Militarized Aid in Afghanistan.* Accessed December 19, 2016, https://www.oxfam.org/sites/www.oxfam.org/files/file_attachments/quick-impact-quick-collapse-jan-2010_9.pdf

Pessin, A. 2010, July 13. Pentagon Defends Afghan Local Police Plan. VOA News. Accessed December 19, 2016, http://www.voanews.com/content/pentagon-defends-afghan-local-police-plan-98459414/166022.html

United Nations Security Council. *Conflict-related Sexual Violence Report of the Secretary-General,* (S/2015/203). Accessed December 19, 2016, http://www.securitycouncilreport.org/atf/cf/%7B65BFCF9B-6D27-4E9C-8CD3-CF6E4FF96FF9%7D/s_2015_203.pdf

Young. 2010. Development at Gunpoint? Accessed December 19, 2016, https://www.foreignaffairs.com/articles/2010-12-19/development-gunpoint

Women Regional Network. 2014. *Surviving War and Transition: Perspectives from Afghan Women.* Accessed December 19, 2016, www.womensregionalnetwork.org/images/uploads/CC_Afghanistan.pdf

10

What Happened to Nepal's Women Maoists?

Bishnu Raj Upreti and Gitta Shrestha

Ten years of armed conflict waged by the Communist Party of Nepal (Maoist) ended with the Comprehensive Peace Agreement (CPA) in November 2006. However, the integration and rehabilitation of the Maoist ex-combatant remained a major issue for another six years. The insurgency was grounded in Nepal's deep social and economic problems. What started as a small rebellion, over the years, developed into a brutal armed conflict with gross human rights violations on both sides leading to 17,846 killed, 1,530 disappeared, 3,142 kidnapped, 8,935 injured, 9,000 widowed, 620 orphaned, 17,484 properties captured, and 75,571 people displaced (Rawal 2015). The conflict had a major impact on the prevalent structure of the geographical, social, and gender inequities in Nepal. For the first time in Nepalese history, women in unexpected numbers joined the war as guerrillas, activists, and supporters.

The image of "women with guns" during the decade-long conflict reflected an extraordinary transformation in Nepal's patriarchal society, fighting against multiple discriminations—caste, class, and gender. A woman holding a gun became the metaphor for empowerment. Literature on women combatants is severely limited, with most writings focused on analyzing the factors which motivated women to join the Maoist movement. There is little research on the experiences of women combatants during the conflict and the post-conflict reintegration process, especially the challenges faced by the former women combatants on their return to community.

The possibility of the Maoist led "Peoples War" providing an opportunity for empowering women is contested among scholars who point out that the majority of women combatants were from indigenous groups who traditionally enjoyed greater gender equality than caste oppressed Indo-Aryan women. Moreover, leadership positions in the movement were largely held by high caste Hindu women. Also, anecdotal information reveals that whatever the social "gains" made in the war period, they proved unsustainable as evident in the difficulties the former combatants confronted in the process of post-conflict social reintegration. Indeed, they were compelled to revert back to traditional gender roles.

Women Guerrillas in the "Peoples War"

In Nepal, the number of women fighter remains contested. The Maoist claim of 40 percent female combatants is challenged by the United Nations Mission in Nepal (UNMIN) verification process. The Maoist leadership had specified that the People's Liberation Army (PLA) comprised 32,250 male and female cadres; however, the UNMIN verification process whittled this down to 19,602 combatants, sifting out 4008 identified as minors. Eventually, out of the 19,602 considered eligible, only 3846 were women, that is, approximately 20 percent of the combatants. Arguably the exaggeration was intended to legitimize the movement's egalitarian and empowering claims (Advocacy Forum and ICTJ 2010: 25). Nonetheless, even if scaled down from 40 percent, the UNMIN verified figure of 20 percent is significant in the context of Nepal's gender stereotyped society. A report of the Nepal Women's Commission (2003) estimated that women comprised a third of the Maoist peoples' militia in some districts, and as high as 50 percent in the more mobilized Maoist districts.

In estimating numbers, it needs to be kept in mind that women combatants often slip through the cracks of formal international demobilization registration processes. In some cases, female combatants are kept out of the demobilization process by the commanders, to hide away abducted women/girls, for fear of legal and social consequences. Researcher Shrestha-Schipper draws attention to the many former women combatants who, like their male colleagues, also deserted and crossed the border into India for work, but whose stories never made headlines like that of the Maoist male cadres. Ariño (2008: 6) and Colekessian's (2009: 14) studies corroborate that the fear of social stigmatization led many to self-exclude themselves from the benefits available to those participating in the post-conflict reintegration and security sector reform process.

Women's motives for joining as guerrilla fighters are political, structural, ideological, and personal (Advocacy Forum and ICTJ 2010; Manchanda 2004). Young girls were first recruited as part of the cultural team or as couriers at the beginning of the conflict, and gradually they were "educated" and ideologically motivated and engaged in combat. Female recruits were largely in their teens and belonged to marginalized Dalit, ethnic, and indigenous communities. Girls, in particular, were also attracted to the Maoist cultural propaganda units which specialized in song and dance. A large number of illiterate or semi-literate youth were mobilized by their teachers who were Maoists supporters. Others were encouraged by close relatives and friends who were sympathizers, political activists, militia members, or PLA combatants. Some joined the movement for reasons of revenge against the brutality caused during the course of search operations of the security forces (Onesto 2005). Most girls/women came from lower socioeconomic backgrounds marginalized by the state and feudal social structures (Advocacy Forum and ICTJ 2010: 24; Pettigrew and Shneiderman 2004).

According to top ranking Maoist woman leader Comrade Parvati (2003) alias Hisila Yami, women were drawn to the movement in opposition to the existing system of gender oppression, women's double burden of work, early marriage, and the legal practice of polygamy. Indo-Aryan women from caste-structured societies joined the Peoples Liberation Army (PLA) in protest at early marriage; Tibeto-Burman women were basically against the vicious circle of a rigorous and monotonous life of toil and reproduction; and Dalits were in opposition to their traditional exploitation as bonded labor. A majority of women ex-combatants credited the Maoists insurgency with curbing domestic and sexual violence, alcoholism, ensuring equal rights and opportunity, and providing a quick justice system in the form of the "dry law and parallel justice system" (Bharadwaj et al. 2007; Shah 2007; Sharma and Prasain 2004: 152). Many Maoist women emerged as role models and many young girls were attracted to the image of politically and physically liberated women. Also, quite a few joined because they fell in love with men combatants; others were driven by revenge and justice.

It should be added that alongside women flocking to the movement, there was significant involuntary recruitment of young girls into the militia involving abduction and coercion. Schipper argues: "Ideological campaign alone would not have produced the expected result on the recruitment of youths in the Maoist ranks." She cites case studies from Jumla, where the Maoist recruitment method of "one house, one Maoist," forced daughters to join the insurgency in order to save the "sons" of the house (Shrestha-Schipper 2008–09: 107).

Challenging Gendered Stereotypes

Women in the movement were combatants, organizers, mobilizers, trainers, transporters, scouts, spies, porters, cooks, nurses, messengers, care givers, and cultural activists (Sharma and Prasain 2004: 153; Upreti 2009). In the PLA, women showed equal mettle in battle, marking a major milestone in the gender resocialization process. Apart from the gendered exigencies of the reproductive cycle (pregnancies and birth), sexual division of labor was minimal in the PLA. Women cut off their long hair and wore combat dress like their male comrades. They served as role models for other women members, socializing them into the PLA. Women were vice-commanders at the battalion level, commanders and vice-commanders at company level and political commissars at the battalion level. At militia level, they constituted the vanguard protecting regional and district level revolutionary people's councils (Yami 2007).

In the initial stages when there were few women, male commanders regarded them as of little more than propaganda value and relegated them to the side lines. Women fought hard to prove their competence, going through the same physical training as men, suppressing their "femininity" and projecting a "masculine" demeanor, struggling to get equal opportunities in battle. At first, when there were only two women to a squad, it was hard for women to confide in their male comrades about their constraints during menstruation in undertaking the arduous physical routine. However, as the number of women commanders increased, it became common practice to swap duties during menstruation.

As the insurgency intensified, the need for more women in the battlefield led to programs for developing the leadership ability of female fighters by constituting all "women platoons." Eventually, women became commanders leading both male and female combatants. However, female leadership remained undervalued as Onsari Gharti, a former combatant admitted that "the party was reluctant to give important responsibilities to women" (IDEA 2012: 547). Brigadier Commissar was the highest post to which women were appointed in the PLA, and achieved by only two or three women cadres (IDEA 2011: 338). Maoist Chairman Prachanda, in an interview to Onesto acknowledged the patriarchal prejudice that stood in the way of accepting women in leadership positions in the PLA (Onesto 2005). Also, women's reproductive functions acted as a disruption. According to Yami, one could hardly find women above 25 years old in the combat ranks. Many of them had to switch from the combat front to the party organization after having children. Many had to leave their children with others to continue work in combat bodies. Gender relations remained unequal, as evident in the attitude of the party to the institution of marriage, as a means of controlling women's sexuality. Moreover, while the encouragement to intercaste marriages was socially bold and progressive, its instrumental aspect was no less significant, to prevent combatants from leaving the Maoist movement and returning to society.

Some cases have been documented of female combatants forced to marry against their wishes. Since unmarried cadres were viewed with suspicion, females were obliged to marry their fellow combatants (Onesto 2005: 180). A few analysts suggest that women in the PLA were sexually exploited by their male colleagues (Shakya 2003: 39). UNFPA studies corroborate that some Maoist women were coerced into satisfying the sexual urges of Maoist men (Ward and Marsh 2006: 6). However, it is significant that there are hardly any allegations of the PLA being implicated in sexual violence during the conflict, especially in contrast to the then Royal Nepal Army.

Post-War—Life in Cantonments

As per the CPA 2006, combatants (men and women) were confined in 7 main and 21 satellite cantonment sites, and remained there for more than six years. Although political and military training continued inside the camps for four years, a majority complained of boredom and a sense of isolation, while they waited for a decision on their uncertain future (Ogura 2009, 2010; Saferworld 2010: 8). Poor living conditions in the camps drove many families to leave the cantonments and the country in search of jobs. Cantonment life was difficult, especially for pregnant women and lactating mothers due to inadequate housing, bedding, clean drinking water, and health services. A significant number of mothers left the cantonments, due to regulations disallowing women combatants with children younger than three years to live in the camps. In 5th division alone, nearly 250 women were forced to leave. Nursing mothers took maternity leave and lived in rented rooms outside the camps. Many returned to participate in the regrouping process (Shah 2012).

Integration of the Maoist forces in Nepal's security forces or security sector reform was a crucial milestone in Nepal's roadmap to peace. Prolonged for nearly six years, finally in 2011, the regrouping of combatants began with the involvement of the UN Mission in Nepal (UNMIN). Three options were provided to ex-combatants— integration into the army, rehabilitation, and voluntary retirement. A maximum of 6500 personnel were eligible for integration as per the standard norms of the Nepal Army, with some concessions made on age (three years), education level (one level), and marital status. A total of 4008 Verified Minors and Late Recruits (VMLRs), one-third of whom were young girls, were found ineligible for integration into the Army and were offered special rehabilitation packages.

A total of 15,624 ex-combatants (12,170 males and 3,454 females) opted for voluntary retirement cash package and 6 males opted for rehabilitation. A major deterrent was demotion to a lower post in Nepal Army due to the education criteria (Ingdal and Holter 2010: 14). On July 4, 2013, a total of 1,422 officially joined Nepal Army. Only 104 female ex-combatants joined the Nepal Army. Only 4 women out of 70 former Maoist combatants joined the Nepal Army as officer-cadets, after finishing nine months of basic training (NIPS 2013). Initially, more than 3,000 female combatants had wanted to join the national army, but opted for voluntary retirement because of marriage and children. In the cantonments, combatants had been encouraged to marry. Consequently, by the time of integration, a majority were pregnant, nursing or with young children, and therefore ineligible for integration despite being qualified (Shah 2012; International Crisis Group 2011: 5).

Both combatants and women's rights activists had demanded a gender-friendly approach in terms of assignment of rank (including high rank), promotion and training in Nepal Army while integrating female ex-combatants in the security forces (Saferworld 2012). The major political parties had agreed to concessions on educational qualification, marital status, and age while integrating the former rebel soldiers in the security forces. Few female combatants had higher education.

Social Rehabilitation

The ex-combatants were offered gender stereotypical vocational trainings in tailoring, beauty care, shop keeping, health care, and education packages with the support of United Nations Interagency Rehabilitation Program (UNIRP). The prospect of support for dependents (child care services and family allowances) in the microcredit package encouraged many women to opt for the microenterprise package (296 out of 476) over vocational training (22), education (137), and health training (21) (DFID 2013). The emphasis was on economic reintegration rather than social integration (Subedi 2011). This was despite evidence of the social risks faced by the female ex-combatants on their return back to the entrenched patriarchal communities (Saferworld 2010). As the women/girls combatants had challenged the social and gender order, a significant number of them opted to relocate to different communities or urban centers rather than face rejection in their original caste communities or those they had married into, especially in the case of intercaste marriages, encouraged by the Maoists (Colekessian 2009: 12).

The armed conflict had directly and indirectly exerted pressure for changes in gender relations. Following the lead of the Maoists, the Nepal Army in 2004 adopted a policy of recruiting women in the general armed services and the officer ranks. However, women are less than 2 percent of the armed forces. Feminist discourses have questioned the desirability of the mobilization of women into armies (state and nonstate) as it contributes to the militarization of the entire society. Moreover, feminists fundamentally challenge the empowering potential of women in the militaries.

We contend that the militarization of women as soldiers in PLA, offered girls mobility and exposure to the outside world, and the possibility of a more equal environment. Sustaining those social gains of conflict has proved a very formidable task. As regards the Maoist women, a minority who were able to consolidate their new agency in post-conflict structures are yet to devise new ways to support their fellow female combatants. Initiatives such as *Purwa PLA Mahila Sangathan* (ex-PLA Women's Association) are important in strengthening the autonomy of the Maoist women.

Bibliography

Advocacy Forum and International Centre for Transitional Justice. 2010. *Across the Lines: The Impact of Nepal's Conflict on Women*. Kathmandu: Advocacy Forum and International Centre for Transitional Justice.

Ariño, M.V. 2008. "Nepal: A Gender View of the Armed Conflict and the Peace Process." *Escola de Cultura de Pau*. Accessed November 8, 2016, http://escolapau. uab.cat/img/qcp/nepal_conflict_peace.pdf

Bharadwaj, N. Dhungana, S.K., and Upreti, B.R. 2004. "Electoral Bottlenecks and Problems of Governance in Nepal." *Kasarinlan: Philippine Journal of Third World Studies*, 19(2): 54–74.

Colekessian, Ani. 2009. *Reintegrating Gender: A Gendered Analysis of the Nepali Rehabilitation Process*. The United Nations International Research and Training Institute for the Advancement of Women (UN-INSTRAW), Santo Domingo.

Comrade Parvati (Hsila Yami). 2003 "Women's Leadership and the Revolution in Nepal." *Monthly Review*. Accessed November 8, 2016, http://monthlyreview.org/commentary/womens-leadership-and-the-revolution-in-nepal.

DFID. 2013. DFID Nepal Operational Plan. Kathmandu: DFID.

IDEA (International Institute for Democracy and Electoral Assistance). 2011. *Women Members of the Constituent Assembly*. Kathmandu: Women Caucus.

Khadka, Sarada. 2012. "Female Combatants and Ex-combatants in Maoist Revolution." MA thesis, University of Tromsø, Norway.

Manchanda, R. 2004. "Maoist Insurgency in Nepal: Radicalizing Gendered Narratives." *Cultural Dynamics* 16: 237.

Nepal Women's Commission. 2003. *Violence against Women*. Kathmandu: NWC.

Ogura, Kiyoko. 2009. *A Chapamaar's Peace*. A Report at Himal South Asia (July 2009). Accessed December 19, 2016, http://old.himalmag.com/component/content/article/565-a-chapamaars-peace.html

———. 2010. *View from the Cantonment*. A Report at Himal South Asia (March 2010). Accessed December 19, 2016, http://old.himalmag.com/component/content/article/86-view-from-the-cantonment.html

———. 2012. "How Women Chapamaars Changed in the Maoist Insurgency." Thesis, Central Department of Sociology/Anthropology Tribhuvan University, Kathmandu, Nepal.

Onesto Li. 2005. *Dispatches from the People's War in Nepal*. London: Pluto Press.

Pettigrew, J., and Sara Shneiderman. 2004. "Women and the Maobaadi: Ideology and Agency in Nepal's Maoist Movement." *Himal Magazine*, 17 January, 19–29.

Rawal, Ram Bahadur. 2015. "Completion of the Transition: New Beginning from the Promulgation of New Constitution." *Nepal Weekly Magazine*, 27 September–4 October, pp. 24–29. Nepal: Kantipur News Group.

Saferworld. 2010. *Common Ground? Gendered Assessment of the Needs and Concerns of Maoist Army Combatants for Rehabilitation and Reintegration*. London: Saferworld.

———. 2012. *Women and Security in Nepal Report*. Kathmandu: Saferworld.

Subedi D. B. 2011. "Rehabilitation and Reintegration of the Maoist Ex-combatants in Nepal: Issues, Challenges and Potential Lessons," *Contributions to Nepalese Studies*, 38(2), pp. 143–70.

Shah, Shaubhagya. 2007. "Paradise Regained and Lost? April's Sizzle and February's Chill," in *The Inclusive State: Reflections on Reinventing Nepal* edited by Anand Aditya, pp. 230–35. Kathmandu: SAP-Nepal.

Sharma, Mandira, and Dinesh Prasain. 2004. "Gendered Dimensions of the People's War: Some Reflections on the Experiences of Rural Women," in *Himalayan People's War: Nepal's Maoist Rebellion* edited by Michael Hutt, pp. 151–54. London: Hurst & Co.

Shakya, S. 2003. "The Maoist Movement in Nepal: An Analysis from the Women's Perspective," in *The People's War in Nepal: Left Perspective* edited by Karki, A. and Seddon, D. New Delhi: Adroit Publishers.

Shrestha-Schipper, Satya. 2008–09. "Women's Participation in the People's War in Jumla." *European Bulletin of Himalayan Research* (33–34): 105–22. Accessed December 2, 2016, http://himalaya.socanth.cam.ac.uk/collections/journals/ebhr/pdf/EBHR_33&34_05.pdf

Upreti, Bishnu Raj. 2006. *Armed Conflict and Peace Process in Nepal: The Maoist Insurgency, Past Negotiation and Opportunities for Conflict Transformation*. New Delhi: Adroit Publishers.

———. 2009. *NEPAL: From War to Peace, Legacies of the Past and Hopes for the Future*. New Delhi: Adroit Publishers.

Yami, H. 2007. *People's War and Women's Liberation in Nepal*. Kathmandu: Janadhwani Publication.

11

FATA "A Permanent War Zone": Breaking the Silence

Noreen Naseer

Tribal Agencies—Discriminated Deprived

In the global terrorism discourse, the Pakhtun tribal areas of northwest Pakistan straddling the Afghanistan border are projected as the "natural" epicenter of militancy and extremism. Pakistan's semi-autonomous border region, the Federally Administered Tribal Areas (FATA) is considered to be a highly volatile border region with geostrategic significance, as Al-Qaida and the Taliban are actively present in the area. But curiously, the perspective of the people of FATA and especially women are absent from any academic debate at the national or international levels. This is compounded by institutional regulations and cultural codes that silence the people. Tribal people are not allowed to speak or participate politically because of the Frontier Crimes Regulation (FCR) and *Pakhtunwali,* the cultural code of the Pakhtun tribes. This paper is an attempt to bring into the conflict discourse, the perspective of the conflict-affected peoples, especially the impact of conflict on women and children. It also draws upon interviews conducted with internally displaced persons from Kurram, Khyber, North and South Waziristan, and Bajaur and Orakzai agencies housed in camps in Peshawar, Khyber Pakhtunkhwa.

FATA is a mountainous region largely made up of seven "agencies." According to the FATA Development Authority, the region's population is officially estimated to be 3.17 million (unofficial estimates 7 million). FATA is the poorest, least developed part of Pakistan with nearly 66 percent of the population below the poverty line. Literacy is barely 17 percent (national average 40 percent) with only 3 percent of the women, literate (national average 32 percent). FATA's forbidding terrain serves to isolate the tribes from markets, health and education services, and external influences (Shinwari 2008).

The British accorded a unique administrative and political status to contain the tribal peoples through a strategic mix of political agents, Frontier Crimes Regulations (FCR) and tribal elders, and left alone their traditional practices and internal independence. That relationship essentially continued after the transfer of colonial power in 1947 to the new state of Pakistan.

The draconian FCR was retained and became a tool of oppression and militarization of tribal people. The law states that three basic rights are not applicable to the residents of FATA—appeal, *wakeel*, and *daleel* (the right to appeal a court conviction, the right to legal representation, and the right to present reasoned evidence). The jurisdiction of Pakistan's courts does not extend to FATA, and by inference, fundamental rights are denied to the people living in FATA. FCR gives collective punishment to family or tribe members, for crimes of individuals. Articles 246 and 247 of the 1973 Constitution accord a special status to FATA, which keeps tribal areas away from the legislative process. As a result, members from the FATA agencies elected to the national assembly and senate can legislate for the rest of Pakistan but not for their own constituencies in FATA. FCR is a set of regulations dating back to the colonial period and it accords a special status to FATA under which the president of Pakistan has all powers to legislate and execute laws.

In 2011, Pakistan President Zardari introduced some amendments moderating some draconian aspects of the FCR, including the setting up of a FATA judicial tribunal (an appellate body) and exemption of women, children, and elderly from collective punishments. These amendments were overshadowed by the simultaneous promulgation of the policy of—"Action in Aid of Civil Power" in 2011. It once again gave the military absolute power. The policy was stark evidence of the military's opposition to reforms which threatened their authority.

Harsh terrain, poor education, and poor infrastructure have widened the social and economic gaps between Pakistan's tribal belt and the rest of the nation. Moreover, FATA's economic, political, and social sectors have been neglected by Pakistan's governing structure. Closer social and economic interaction exists across the large porous border with Afghanistan. Pakhtun people living in the tribal areas divided by the Durand line have earned much of their income from cross-border trade.

Tribal customs and traditions provide the governing structure and the *Maliks* (tribal elders) play a major role. FATA's strategic location tempted the state establishment and successive governments to give generous allowances to the Maliks to keep control of the area. In addition, Mullahs too were funded but discreetly, receiving funds from Middle-East states to fight jihad in Afghanistan against Soviets and other forces. The result of this blindsided policy has converted FATA into a permanent war zone.

History and Constructed Narrative

Militarization and radicalization of the Pakhtun border areas, that is, FATA has a long history dating back to the beginning of the 18th century, when Syed Ahmed Shaheed mobilized armed tribals with religious zeal to fight Sikh rule in the Punjab. The British further militarized the tribal areas by setting up cantonments in the border region and raising levis and militias to contain Afghan and Russian Czars (Barfield 2007). During the first Kashmir War in 1948, Pakistan state agencies sent armed tribal raiders to Kashmir fired by the slogan— Islam is in danger. In the popular imagination in Pakistan, the tribal *Razakars'* involvement to free Kashmir reinforced the notion and myth of the archetypal tribal man—a warrior and defender of the fortress of the Islamic state of Pakistan.

In the proxy war against the Soviet takeover of Afghanistan, with Pakistan positioned by the US as the frontline state, FATA became the launching pad to fight war in Afghanistan and also to assist Kashmir mujahideen. Hundreds of religious seminaries (madrasas) were set up in the FATA and the border areas to wage a holy war. In the process, the culture and values of the Pakhtun peoples were radicalized and militarized casting Pakhtuns as a warring nation. Backed by oil rich Arabs and the capitalist West, more than 15,000 Arabs, Uzbek and Chechens, mujahideens, were settled in FATA to fight the 10 year holy war against the Soviets (Rana 2010:13). With the Soviet withdrawal in 1989, the international community abandoned an Afghanistan (and the border areas) full of armed men. The Afghan crisis also left in its wake a FATA saturated with weapons. Civil war and anarchy created the conditions for the formation of the Taliban government in 1995–96 with support of Pakistan and Saudi Arabia (Johnson and Mason 2006: 72–74).

Talibanization of FATA: Impact on Women and Children

Thirty years of war in Afghanistan resulted in a major social and economic upheaval in the tribal agencies, but the fallout of 9/11 terrorist attack again transformed FATA into a war zone. The Afghan Taliban retreated to FATA to continue fighting. Since 2001, the Pakistan military has undertaken multiple operations against the Taliban as well as negotiations for ceasefire and peace. Caught in between has been the civilian population. In some areas of FATA, the Taliban formed a de-facto government and issued *fatwas* (diktats derived from Islamic *Sharia*). It is important to remind that US and Pakistan support for the jihadi elements produced the Talibanization of Pakhtun tribal society with dramatic implications for education, health, women's security, and their participation in the economy.

Education

The Taliban are opposed to scientific and critical education. Consequently, they have created an environment of fear to deter the tribal people from sending their children to school. The Taliban have attacked schools and massacred boy students; fired mortar shells at school vans taking girls to schools; set fire to schools and attacked girls going to school. Hardly surprising, that school attendance dropped to barely 1 percent. Out of 458 educational institutions, 317 schools have been destroyed by militants. The contagion is affecting the settled adjacent areas of Khyber Pakhtunkhwa, especially after the Taliban threw acid on Kohat University female students in Lower Kurram.

Health

The Taliban also targeted the health sector in FATA, which was already weak and grossly inadequate. Only 41 hospitals serve a population of nearly 7 million assisted by poor paramedic staff. According to Save the Children, under-five mortality in FATA is 135 per 1,000 live births and infant mortality is 86.8 percent per 1,000 live births (Rana 2010). Taliban targeted health workers and staff, making access to health facilities even more difficult for tribal people (International Crisis Group 2015).

The Taliban made an example of health worker Suryia Bibi from Parachinar. She was ambushed on her way back from Peshawar in an ambulance, raped and killed, and a CD of the incident was sent to her family and circulated through mobile phones as a warning. After the Suryia Bibi incident many women health workers resigned or went on indefinite leave. Few came back.

Continuing attacks against polio workers and the ban on polio immunization drops in FATA have created a health emergency. Already oppressed by a highly patriarchal tribal culture, tribal women are further restricted by the Taliban's interpretation of an "Arabized" Islamic culture. Many women and children die of minor infections due to nonavailability of drugs and inaccessibility to hospitals in the cities. Food shortages and malnutrition have a detrimental effect on the fragile health conditions of children and women. It is important to note that in FATA, a chronic poverty-affected area, the prices of staple food items are vulnerable to manipulation due to the non-application of national tax laws. But tribal people are indirectly taxed under Rahadari (passage permit) system, which results in corruption and inflated prices. In FATA there is a permit for everything that is brought in, except the coffin of someone who has died.

Women's Participation in FATA Economy

In spite of the patriarchal structure of tribal society, traditionally 60 percent of the work force in the agriculture sector were women and children. However, after the Taliban took control, women were stopped from working in the fields. Even those in the non-Taliban areas quit working, fearing attacks by other armed groups. As a result, poor families have been pushed into absolute poverty. Many women working as teachers, health workers, and running vocational training centers for embroidery and tailoring in FATA were also stopped and threatened. In FATA, women do not have right to inherit property. On the death of male members, lands and properties are grabbed by relatives with help of Taliban, leaving dispossessed women in destitution and despair.

Women and Children Abducted and Trafficked

In just a single incident of violence, more than 6,000 women and children fled across the Pak–Afghan border during the Kurram Agency sectarian violence spearheaded by Taliban. According to local journalists, women from different villages were taken to Khost, Paktia, and Makeen (South Waziristan) by Taliban and were sold or taken as war bounty (*Mal-e-Ghanimet*). Families declared them missing or dead. Similarly in other agencies during the action of local peace forces (Aman Lashkers) many women and children were lost, forcibly displaced and taken by force.

Internally Displaced[2] Women

Conflict leaves many women widowed, raped, crippled, mutilated, and forcibly displaced. Rarely is there any assistance available in flight, emergency relief, and return/resettlement. Women in camps, rented accommodation, and informal settlements in different villages suffer from dire physical and economic distress in crowded unhygienic conditions of displacement. Surveys of IDPs settled outside the camps have recorded a sharp drop in mothers' breast feeding, for lack of privacy (IRIN 2012).

Moreover, the impact of conflict, flight, and displacement has left many highly traumatized. Conservative cultural norms and traditions inhibit them from seeking help or counseling. Many women have started taking opium for pains and mental trauma.

More than 700 families in Durrani, Shasho, and Eidgah camps in Kurram Agency were headed by women with no men to look after them (World Food Programme Report 2011). Moreover, World Food Program had to discontinue supplying food rations to various camps due to the deteriorating law and order situation, affecting women and children most. Born and raised in protective environment, women and young girls did not feel safe around other strange men (WRN 2016).

Games of War Peace Played on the People of FATA

Endless military operations in the FATA have devastated the lives of the tribal people. There are 21 jihadi and 39 sectarian groups operating in Pakistan, and they support some 50 Taliban groups stationed in FATA, under the umbrella of Tehrik-e-Taliban Pakistan. According to media reports, since 2002, the Pakistan military, as a part of the global "war on terror" strategy, has launched twelve major operations. These military operations have completely militarized the social and economic life of FATA.

Intermittently, cycles of conflict are broken by efforts to engage the Taliban in peace negotiations, the most recent being Prime Minister Nawaz Sharif's overtures to the Taliban in 2014 which collapsed after the Taliban's bloody massacre of children in a military public school in Peshawar. It propelled the launch of the Zarb-e-Azb[3] military assault on FATA. The population was given 45 hours to flee, while the military operation took weeks to plan.

Earlier, between 2007 and 2009, thirteen peace agreements were signed by the government and the Taliban. The local population was not involved and there was no representation of women in all these peace agreements signed with the militant Taliban. Only the power elite of Islamabad were involved, and they had no understanding of the local dynamics vis-à-vis the Taliban. The traditional leaders of the tribal society, the Maliks, had been sidelined or eliminated. More than fifteen hundred tribal elders (Maliks) had been targeted and killed and around five hundred injured both by Taliban and the military under different pretexts (Nawaz 2009).

Military operations in the tribal belt led to the displacement of more than 3 million people in all. The largest displacement is from North Waziristan Agency where it has been completely over-run by the military. Nearly 1 million people have been displaced in the latest military operation, cutting off tribes from their lands, customs, and culture and creating an identity crisis among the young generation growing up in the camps. In South Waziristan as well, schools and colleges have been converted into military camps. Numerous military check posts have been established, completely controlling the movement of tribal people inside and outside tribal areas. In South Waziristan, the military with the help of the administration refuses entry into the agency without a permit. There are growing complaints about the military looting property of people who have had to flee.

For over a decade, FATA has been in the grip of perpetual war and operations, destroying its forests, mountains, and water resources. Tribal areas, once considered the most beautiful parts of Pakistan are now polluted with fumes of gun and powder. These areas are experiencing extreme weather conditions, floods, and droughts. Agriculture activities have been badly hit not only by ongoing militancy but by unpredictable weather conditions and have reduced the people to near-famine conditions.

In the tribal areas, the military has established an economic monopoly setting up bakeries and grocery stores and squeezed out local business. In Kurram Agency, the military has displaced local transporters by using their military vehicles to safely transport the Turi tribesmen of Kurram, but at ten times the cost. Rumors abound of the military taking advantage of conditions of curfew and difficult market access to sell essential foodstuffs at inflated prices. Tribes people interviewed in displacement camps in Peshawar claimed that some military personal were involved in illegal trade across the border areas of Khyber and Orakzai, and in league with local smugglers and drug dealers, and Taliban.

Following the Pakistan President's promulgation of an ordinance on June 2011 titled "Action in Aid of Civil Power in the Federally

Administered Tribal Areas," FATA has been completely taken over by military. The law provided a legal framework for the armed forces to conduct operations in tribal areas against miscreants waging war against Pakistan, attacking infrastructure, raising unlawful private armies and trying to assert unlawful control over the territories of Pakistan. Frontier Crime Regulations draconian judicial/administrative regulations, devoid of human rights are in practice, which in itself is militarized arrangement for the tribal areas. Some of its clauses are reformed but is not abolished, unfortunately, federal government also introduced 'Regulation to Provide for Actions in Aid of Civil Power' in FATA, giving sweeping powers to military to counter terrorism such as detention of any suspect for 120 days, military right to occupy tribals property and court can award punishment on the testimony of any military officer. Thus, neutralising the reforms introduced in the FCRs. Military "occupation" has particular consequences for tribal women in the FATA, already bound within customary Pashtunwali traditions, and now rendered further oppressive after the encounter with extremist Taliban's misogynist ideologies.

Participation of Tribal Women in Peacebuilding and Demilitarization

There is a striking absence of women's representation in the jirga or any government scheme for the tribal areas. It is pertinent to mention that women in FATA are not organized in any kind of pressure group. Neither is there any forum through which they can address their concerns or increase their security. Women social activists who run service-based NGOs face huge security risks. In 2012, Farida Afridi of Savera from Khyber Agency, on her way to a meeting was assassinated in Hayatabad, Peshawar. She was running an NGO called Savera in Khyber Agency that provided computer training plus other vocational trainings to young tribal girls and boys. She had been threatened by the Taliban like other tribal women working in NGOs or businesses and forced to quit. In contrast, tribal women in the settled areas and cities of Karachi work without risk in the service sector and other professions. In the tribal areas, tribal women are forced to take up jobs that do not involve them going outside their homes.

Unless the tribal areas are integrated into Pakistan, and settled and developed like the rest of the country, piecemeal social reform will be futile. The deliberate vacuum created in the FATA as regards judicial, political, and economic development has led to the present situation. As a beginning, the special status of FATA and the FCR that underpins it should be abolished. Any peace agreement signed with the Taliban must involve the local people, and women should be included so that their grievances are addressed. Tribal women affected by conflict should be taken in confidence in all aspects of repatriation and resettlement arrangements. Judicial, political, and economic reforms are needed to counter militarization as well as Talibanization in FATA.

Notes

1. Editor's Note: Following the revelation of the false hepatitis vaccination program in July 2011, an infuriated Taliban vowed to avenge the deception and imposed a ban on legitimate vaccination programs including polio. In June 2012, the Taliban-blocked polio vaccination in North Waziristan, issued fatwa against polio vaccination and carried out attacks. See Declan Walsh, "Taliban Block Vaccinations in Pakistan," *New York Times*, June 18, 2012.
2. Editor's Note: In 2014, Pakistan IDP population is estimated at 1.9 million and it has the dubious distinction of having the third largest population of IDPs. For many tribes in FATA Afghanistan was a more proximate destination for flight. An estimated 6,452 people from North Waziristan had crossed the border into the proximate eastern parts of Afghanistan, while the overwhelming majority of the nearly one million displaced from FATA and Khyber agency became IDPs in Pakistan (IDMC 2015).
3. Operation Zarb-e-Azb was a joint military offensive conducted by the Pakistan Armed Forces against various militant groups, including the Tehrik-i-Taliban Pakistan (TTP), the Islamic Movement of Uzbekistan, the East Turkestan Islamic Movement, Lashkar-e-Jhangvi, al-Qaeda, Jundallah and the Haqqani network. The operation was launched on June 15, 2014 in North Waziristan along the Pakistan–Afghanistan border as a renewed effort against militancy in the wake of the 8 June attack on Jinnah International Airport in Karachi and the gory incident of Army Public School for which the TTP and the IMU claimed responsibility. 30,000 Pakistani soldiers were involved in Zarb-e-Azb, described as a "comprehensive operation" to flush out all foreign and local militants hiding in North Waziristan.

Bibliography

Barfield, J. T. 2007. *Weapons of the Not So Weak in Afghanistan: Pashtuns Agrarian Structure and Tribal Organization for Times of War & Peace*. New Haven, Connecticut: Yale University.

FATA. April 2012. "FCR Amendments: A Way Forward or Hurdle for Peace and Development in FATA." Seminar Series, March Seminar Report, Islamabad, 1–32. Accessed December 19, 2016 http://fatada.gov.pk

FATA Civil Secretariat. 2006. *Sustainable Development Plan 2007–2015*, 12–24. Peshawar: FATA. Accessed December 19, 2016, https://www.fata.gov.pk/

FATA Research Centre. 2013, September 17. "Social and Psychological Consequences of Violence in FATA." Seminar Report, Islamabad. Accessed November 9, 2016, https://www.academia.edu/9173163/Seminar_Report_FATA_Research_Centre_committed_to_Peace_and_Development_for_FATA_Region_in_Pakistan_Social_and_Psychological_Consequences_of_Violence_in_FATA_Acknowledgment?auto=download

International Crisis Group. 2015, October 25. "Winning the War on Polio in Pakistan." *Asia Report No. 273*. Accessed November 9, 2016, http://www.crisisgroup.org/~/media/Files/asia/south-asia/pakistan/273-winning-the-war-on-polio-in-pakistan.pdf

IRIN. 2013, May 3. "Tough Times for IDPs Living Outside Camps." Accessed November 9, 2016, http://www.irinnews.org/report/95401/pakistan-tough-times-for-idps-living-outside-camps

Johnson, H. T., and C. M. Mason. 2006. *Understanding the Taliban and Insurgency*. Foreign Policy Institute. Washington DC: Elsevier Ltd.

Khan, Z. A. 1988. *Pakistan's Security: The Challenge and the Response*. Lahore: Progressive Publishers, 78–89.

Nawaz, S. 2009. *FATA A Most Dangerous Place, Meeting the Challenge of Militancy and Terror in Federally Administered Tribal Areas*. Washington DC: Center for Strategic International Studies, 16–37.

Naz, Rukhshanda. 2016. *Women IDPs from N/S Waziristan*. Peshawar: WRN. Accessed November 30, 2016, www.womensregionalnetwork.org

Rana, A. M. 2010. *Dynamics of Taliban Insurgency in FATA*. Islamabad: Pak Institute for Peace Studies, 190.

Shinwari. N. 2008. "Understanding FATA: 'Attitudes towards Governance, Religion Society in Pakistan's Federally Administered Tribal Areas'," *CAMP*, II: 1–4.

PART III

JUSTICE, IMPUNITY, AND ACCOUNTABILITY

12

Challenges for Transitional Justice in South Asia

Warisha Farasat

Addressing Post-conflict Justice

When in January 2007, Louise Arbor, the Secretary General of the Office of the High Commissioner for Human Rights (OHCHR) addressed the Exhuming Accountability conference at Kathmandu, I remember in great detail the electrifying energy and enthusiasm in the room (International Center for Transitional Justice and Himal Southasia 2007). A historic Peace Agreement with a serious promise for rule of law had just been signed between the Seven Party Alliance (SPA) and the Communist Party (Maoist) in Nepal. Even years later whenever I recall that evening, I have no doubt that if there was ever a hope for accountability for the crimes committed during the 10-year old conflict in Nepal, it was then and there.

It was one of those moments where the promise of rule of law and justice had seemed immediate. But as the peace process unraveled in Nepal, the promise of that day grew more distant. Although the 2006 Peace Accord had specifically mentioned that a Truth and Reconciliation Commission and a Disappearances Commission should be formed, the draft laws of both these Commissions fell gravely short of international standards. Eventually nearly eight years after the Accord, the Commission for Truth and Reconciliation Commission (TRC) and the Commission of Investigation on Enforced Disappeared Persons (CIEDP) were formed in February 2015.

The term transitional justice also found its way into the vocabulary of the Nepali peace process as it has in other peace processes such as in Sri Lanka, Afghanistan, Kashmir, Northeast India, and the Chittagong Hill Tracts. Unlike the concept of human rights and justice, the term transitional justice was new and unfamiliar. In Nepal, many activists felt that the translation of "transitional justice" into Nepali as *sankramankaleen nyaya* was not only confusing but also misleading. There were many legitimate questions asked. Why was justice only transitional (and not permanent)? Did we not need justice in peace times? What did this term really mean? Did it mean a Truth and Reconciliation Commission?

The concept of a Truth Commission to address past human rights abuses was integrated into the Peace Agreement, which also carried other elements of transitional justice processes, including vetting, a term that seemed like an imposition to the Nepalis. The concept of transitional justice was eventually demystified through the gradual process of advocacy by local human rights groups in collaboration with their international counterparts, including the United Nations Mission in Nepal (UNMIN) and OHCHR.

One of the major contributions of the field of transitional justice globally, has been its emphasis on victim groups, with a singular focus to provide primacy to their voices and expectations to address human rights violations. There is no clear consensus on when transitional justice became a term that gained currency in the international human rights language, but it is quite clear that the experiences of dealing with past repressive regimes and their legacy of human rights violations in Latin America and South Africa contributed largely to the initial understanding of transitional justice. Transitional justice thus came to be understood as spanning a multiplicity of approaches to address past human rights abuses in societies transitioning from authoritarian rule to democracy as well as in a range of post-conflict scenarios.

Essentially, it meant that during these times of transition in any country, past human rights abuses cannot simply be wished away while moving ahead toward a resolution. Instead, the only way to ensure that these conflicts do not recur in the future is to deal with the perpetrators of the human rights abuses with unflinching firmness. While it is essential, because the victims of human rights violations deserve justice as a right, the serious prospect of a firm action against the perpetrators actually acts as a huge deterrent as well.

The elements of uncovering the truth about these violations; prosecution of perpetrators; reparations for victims and their families; institutional reform measures such as vetting and finally reconciliation, have formed the cornerstone of what came to be understood as transitional justice.[1] Moreover, one of the additional benefits that accrued from confronting past abuses was the ability to inform future generations about the truth of the occurrences during the conflict. There was consensus that people outside these regions were often uninformed about the existing human rights violations in these conflict zones, and creating a historical record of these abuses may also help prevent them from occurring in the future.

But gradually, the Truth and Reconciliation Commission (TRC) became synonymous with the term transitional justice, and in many cases a TRC was privileged over other transitional justice mechanisms such as prosecutions or even reparations. In a sense, the entire focus was then given to the formation of a TRC that was increasingly seen as a panacea for everything in deeply fractured and polarized societies.

In South Asia, there has been a tradition of forming Commissions of Inquiry to investigate incidents of human rights violations or communal massacres. Most South Asian countries including India, Nepal, Sri Lanka, Pakistan, and Bangladesh have their own Commission of Inquiry Act which bestow investigatory, subpoena, and recommendatory power to these bodies. Essentially, a Commission of Inquiry if formed of independent commissioners would have similar investigatory powers such as that of Truth Commissions that were formed in Latin America or South Africa. Like a Truth and Reconciliation Commission, a Commission of Inquiry can only recommend prosecutions and not punish perpetrators.

But one significant difference between the TRC and the traditional Commissions of Inquiry has been the focus. Almost all the TRC's are victim-centric and provide the victims with a viable platform to share their experiences, recording their pain, anger, and expectations. While typical Commission of Inquiries have also recorded testimonies from victims and their families, they have been more narrowly focused on investigating the crimes rather than holding public hearings or providing victims and their families a platform to share their experiences.

Gendering Post-conflict Justice

Transitional Justice advocacy has also opened up new opportunities for engaging with the question of women in post-conflict transitions. The International Criminal Tribunal of Rwanda and that of Yugoslavia greatly expanded the concept of rape and sexual violence, and defined the context under which these crimes would constitute crimes against humanity and genocide. Sexual violence and rape was also put firmly within the framework of Torture, thus ensuring that serious civil and political rights violations include rape and sexual violence.

Furthermore, the UN Security Council adopted the landmark UN SC Resolution 1325 on October 31, 2000 on women, peace, and security that for the first time dealt with specific issues of peace, security, and justice for women in conflict and post-conflict situations.[2] The fundamental principles enshrined in UN SC Resolution 1325 were further reaffirmed by UN SC Resolution 1820, most notably that rape and other forms of sexual violence can constitute a war crime, a crime against humanity, or a constitutive act with respect to genocide.[3] A string of UN Security Council Resolutions—1888 (2009), 1889 (2009), 1960 (2010), 2106 (2013), 2122 (2013), and 2242 (2015)—have further reiterated and expanded on the urgency to ensure peace, security, and justice for women in situations of armed conflict.

The greatest challenge in making effective these principles as with other international human rights laws and treaties, is that of implementation. Although there has been a significant norm setting with regard to women and conflict at the international level, the commitment to women's rights is still substantially weak during peace processes and afterwards. There is also a question as to how effective transitional justice mechanisms have been in addressing questions of security and impunity for rape and sexual violence. Again, experiences globally and across the South Asian countries have differed.

Development of the Field of Transitional Justice

With transitional justice becoming a popular way to address post-conflict justice issues, confusion around it grew even further. Adding to this dilemma of privileging a Truth Commission over other mechanisms was the vastly different understanding of transitional justice mechanisms by human rights groups and the UN bodies on the one hand and the political actors on the other. While the proponents of transitional justice including the human rights groups saw it as a mechanism to address past human rights violations more effectively with a view to further the goal of justice, those that had to implement these mechanisms increasingly tried to scuttle them with the intention to impede justice. A clear reason for these different approaches to transitional justice stemmed from the fact that political actors who came to power after peace negotiations were themselves, often, responsible for serious violations, and did not want to account for the past except to say that "reconciliation" must happen between communities.

And finally, the Western countries have not only tried to appropriate the discourse of transitional justice but also misused it. The trial of Saddam Hussein was clearly an example of victors' justice over transitional justice (Nesiah 2013). In Iraq, the West substituted the real principles of due process and fair trial as propounded by transitional justice for political expediency. Thus, the trial of Saddam Hussein was not an example of transitional justice as claimed by the US and its allies but that of victors' justice. This gradual taking over of the agenda of transitional justice by the West has meant that something that evolved in the developing countries, has increasingly been appropriated by the West to advance its larger political agenda under the pretext of human rights and democracy.

Moreover, while the value of transitional justice was its "south" to "south" exchange of knowledge and approaches to human rights and justice, increasingly these mechanisms came to be incorporated in a top down way in peace agreements without a proper understanding of what they entailed. Since transitional justice mechanisms had emerged from the experience-based learning of developing countries, most notably in Latin America and Africa, it seemed that they would be useful in other contexts in the global south, where nations were coming out of repressive regimes or conflicts. But as seen in Iraq and elsewhere, transitional justice has been misused as a tool in the hands of the West, which has eroded its legitimacy to a certain extent.

The overemphasis on the South African model and a limited understanding of the role and functioning of the TRC in South Africa, meanwhile, has hampered a holistic understanding of transitional justice mechanisms. Even in Nepal, initially there was great enthusiasm amongst the political class to incorporate a Truth and Reconciliation Commission in the peace agreement, but this may have stemmed in part due to the fact that the South African TRC was one of the only models that was presented to the Nepalis, and for them the South African TRC was a good example of writing amnesty into the law. Successive draft bills of Nepal's Truth and Reconciliation Commission and the Disappearances Commission have had amnesty writ large in the texts.

It needs to be emphasized that while the ultimate decision to formulate a truth commission lies with the government, its legitimacy is closely associated with the process of its formation. Each transition is unique and a truth commission should respond to the local demands of the context and history of the conflict. However, at all stages a truth commission should be informed by best practices and international standards. The credibility of a truth commission is largely dependent on the degree of consultations with relevant stakeholders, both prior to enacting the legislation and during the life of the truth commission. This includes broad consultations during the conceptualization process with members of local and international human rights groups and victims' groups.

In this connection, Liberia is a good example to show how Truth Commissions should be created after broad national consultations. A Comprehensive Peace Accord that concluded in 2003 in Liberia, provided for the establishment of a Truth and Reconciliation Commission. The Liberian Truth and Reconciliation Act was enacted subsequent to extensive national consultations in five counties. These nationwide consultations were aimed at ascertaining priorities and expectations of the various stakeholders from the truth commission process.

The following sections examine the challenges in implementing transitional justice mechanisms in a number of South Asian contexts, bringing out the experiences of individual countries and the region as a whole.

Nepal Truth and Disappearance Commissions—Alibis for Injustice

In Nepal, there was immense pressure on the Ministry of Peace and Reconstruction from the local and international human rights community to conduct widespread consultations, before the formation of the Truth and Reconciliation Commission (TRC) as well as the Disappearances Commission. Organizations such as OHCHR, International Center for Transitional Justice (ICTJ), Human Rights Watch (HRW), Amnesty International and some of the embassies worked with the government and civil society to conduct nationwide consultations with stakeholders including victim groups. But when it came to incorporating these suggestions into the draft Bills for the Commission on Truth and Reconciliation and the Commission to Investigate Enforced Disappearances, the government failed to do so.

Under international law, legitimate consultations require the government to maintain and share the information regarding what inputs they received, what they accepted/incorporated or denied and the reasons for doing so. Serious attempts should be made by the government to engage with the recommendations and opinions collected during the process. Of course, it is not possible to include all recommendations that come out of these consultations, but the Nepali government ignored even the most significant recommendations. Most importantly, there was overwhelming demand from both international human rights community and local civil society groups to remove the amnesty clause from the draft TRC Bill, but the government managed to retain the clause in some form or the other.

The legality of the provisions for amnesty alongside a few other clauses in the Truth and Reconciliation Bill were challenged before the Nepali Supreme Court. While the matter was still subjudice before the Supreme Court, the Nepali Government in February 2015, hurriedly formed the Truth and Reconciliation Commission and the Commission to Investigate Enforced Disappearances, disregarding the stiff opposition from human rights and victims' groups. Subsequently, the Supreme Court of Nepal held that amnesties were illegal and could not be granted by a TRC in Nepal.

In spite of the Nepali Supreme Court's ruling, the controversial amnesty provisions continue to exist in the guise of mediation in the current TRC Act. The five persons appointed to each of these two Commissions were largely assessed by local human rights groups and the media as political appointees rather than being independent and impartial. Most victim and human rights groups have distanced themselves from the functioning of the newly formed commissions, thus leaving the fate and legitimacy of these bodies uncertain. Commissions which flout fundamental guarantees inscribed in the Nepali constitution as well as international law norms, cannot be expected to dispense truth or justice or challenge entrenched impunity. Many victims feel that there is little movement toward truth or justice (Human Rights Watch 2005; National Human Rights Commission 2006, 2008; UNHCHR n.d.).[4]

The inclusion of women's issues in the transitional justice agenda in Nepal has been an uphill task. It was only because of the concerted effort of the international community and local human rights and women's groups that the peace and security concerns of women found some space. A UN SC 1325 group was formed under the aegis of the UNIFEM (now UN Women) comprising of international and national groups. This group met regularly to recommend ways in which the ongoing transitional justice process could be made gender sensitive. While a few of the recommendations of this group found their way into the legislations being drafted, most of the suggestions were ignored by the Nepali transitional government. The delay in the formation of the two Commissions further meant that most of the issues of women's security and human rights violations during the conflict remain unaddressed.

During this protracted hiatus period, Nepali courts including the Supreme Court, have refused to prosecute persons responsible for human rights violations saying that these cases specifically fall within the jurisdiction of the TRC or the CIED, and must await their constitution. Although these Commissions have now been instituted, they cannot be a substitute for the courts. The Commissions have powers to investigate but do not have the power to prosecute. They are not judicial bodies; their powers are limited to establishing the truth of what happened and recommending prosecutions. They are envisaged as complementary to the judicial mechanism. However, confusion about their mandate and role has meant that in conflict-related cases, which should be getting prosecuted in the regular courts are not moving forward and impunity for serious crimes committed during the Nepali civil war remains entrenched. The Supreme Court has clarified that conflict era crimes can be investigated and prosecuted by the regular criminal courts, but in reality that has not happened.

Even though a handful of emblematic cases in which robust evidence has been gathered with a view to bring these cases to courts, these processes of accountability have moved very slowly within Nepal.

The Maina Sunuwar case illustrates how the expected formation of the TRC and the DC has been used as an alibi for not delivering justice. There has been meticulous collection of evidence and lobbying around the Maina Sunuwar case in Nepal. Fifteen-year old Maina Sunuwar was tortured and killed by members of the Nepali army on February 17, 2004. After sustained campaigning by Maina's mother Devi Sunuwar, local and international human rights groups, one of the alleged perpetrators—Major Niranjan Basnet, was repatriated from the United Nations (UN) Peacekeeping Mission in Chad in December 2009.

In the preface to a December 2009 report on the torture and subsequent killing of Maina Sunuwar, her mother Devi Sunuwar had said:

> A lot of human rights activists and national and international journalists visit me and tell me that the story of injustice meted out to my daughter is known around the world. Furthermore, the human rights defenders tell me that the case of my daughter is "emblematic". But I am at a loss what this "emblematic" is. Perhaps, a case becomes emblematic if the injustice involved crosses all reasonable bounds? Or when the state promotes the criminals to high-ranking posts and awards them with other prizes despite persistent pressure from national and international circles to bring the perpetrators to book?

Devi's cynicism is a stark reminder of the arduous struggle to bring perpetrators to justice, even in those cases that receive immense international support and attention. However, it also points to the fact that thorough documentation and the sustained campaign of victim families in conjunction with local and international human rights groups can go a long way in challenging impunity. Maina's case not only brought attention to the egregious abuse of a 15 year old girl by the Nepali army, but also the larger issue of enforced disappearances that plagued Nepal during the conflict. Unfortunately, there have been no prosecutions for large-scale enforced disappearances. The government sidesteps the question of accountability by stating that the TRC and CIED would take care of these crimes, knowing fully well that these two Commissions do not have the power to prosecute perpetrators.

Women such as Devi Sunuwar have been at the forefront of the struggle against impunity for human rights violations in Nepal. Many of the families that were affected by the conflict lost their male members to enforced disappearances and extrajudicial killing. In addition to suffering rape and sexual violence, women were massively affected by human rights violations against the male members of their families. The violence committed against women during the conflict or their family members, however, have not been recognized by the political parties after the signing of the Peace Accord. The Ministry of Peace and Reconstruction that was responsible for drafting the TRC and Disappearances Commission Bill, initially lacked an understanding of incorporating elements of UN SC 1325 in these drafts, and it was only with consistent prodding from the local human rights and women's groups and the international community that it even begun to recognize the importance of gendering these Bills.

Although, the TRC Act partially recognizes the crimes of rape and sexual violence, the system in effect provides for amnesty for serious crimes including sexual violence, as it imposes a 35 day statute of limitation. There are also some problematic provisions that could force survivors of sexual violence to reconcile with alleged perpetrators (Advocacy Forum & International Center for Transitional Justice 2010). A comprehensive framework to deal with issues of reparation and rehabilitation is sorely lacking. Till today, no steps for investigation and prosecution of sexual violence during the conflict have been taken.

In fact, women's issues were not even taken seriously during the signing of the Peace Accord in Nepal. There were no women negotiators nominated by any of the parties during the peace process. Interestingly, when the Nepali Congress members were asked why they did not nominate a woman legislator, they quipped that if they had done so, the Maoists would not have taken them seriously. Similarly, the CPN (Maoists) stated that had they included women in their team, the Nepali Congress would have dismissed her interventions (Warisha and Hayner 2009).

Sri Lanka Blocking Accountability, Entrenching Impunity

After her maiden trip to Sri Lanka in 2013, the UN High Commissioner for Human Rights Navi Pillay, was extremely critical of the dismal record of the Sri Lankan government in addressing serious human rights violations. Instead of engaging with the recommendations made by the High Commissioner, the Sri Lankan government launched vicious personal attacks against Pillay by questioning her credibility, as she is a South African of Tamil descent.

In Sri Lanka, the issue of ensuring accountability for the crimes that were committed during the conflict, remains. The Sri Lankan government's complete unwillingness to account for the crimes that were committed in the past has meant that there have been no genuine attempts, officially, to address the past (Nesiah 2009). After the end of the civil war in 2009 and in face of stiff international and local pressure, the government decided to form the Lessons Learned and Reconciliation Commission (LLRC) in Sri Lanka. In 2010, President Mahinda Rajapaksa formed the LLRC. It has been widely reported and documented by many groups that, the Sri Lankan Army committed serious war crimes and human rights violations against the Tamil civilian population in the offensive that it had launched to annihilate the LTTE. These atrocities committed against Tamil civilian population during the last months of the war in Sri Lanka have been well-documented, not only by various Sri Lankan groups but also by credible international organizations.

Although the LLRC was formed, the Sri Lankan government's purpose behind this move was not honest. Their aim was primarily to relieve the immediate international pressure. From its inception, the mandate and credibility of the LLRC was seriously questionable. The Commission was formed without any consultation with the stakeholders and its mandate was thoroughly compromised. The government had also appointed a weak set of Commissioners.

As expected, LLRC did exactly what the Sri Lankan government wanted it to do. Despite irrefutable evidence of war crimes and crimes against humanity having been committed by the Sri Lankan forces, the LLRC gave a clean chit to the army and the Sri Lankan government. While evaluating the conduct of the Sri Lankan army and the government during the final stages of the war in 2009, the Commission erroneously concluded:

> In evaluating the Sri Lanka experience in the context of allegations of violations of International Humanitarian Law (IHL), the Commission is satisfied that the military strategy that was adopted to secure the LTTE held areas was one that was carefully conceived, in which the protection

of the civilian population was given the highest priority. The Commission also notes in this regard that the movement of the Security Forces in conducting their operations was deliberately slow during the final stages of the conflict, thereby evidencing a carefully worked out strategy of avoiding civilian casualties or minimizing them. (Report of the Commission of Inquiry 2011: 328)

The tone and tenor of the entire LLRC report was hinged on reiterating the Sri Lankan government narrative that the conduct of the forces was exemplary during the final assault against the LTTE, and all care was taken to ensure minimal civilian casualties. Any violations that may have happened were only aberrations and not systematic or deliberate on part of the government forces.

Unlike the LLRC, the Report of the UN Secretary General's Panel of Experts on Accountability on Sri Lanka that was mandated to advise on the issue of accountability, and conducted its own fact finding came up with conclusions and recommendations that differed substantively from the Sri Lankan government appointed LLRC (Report of the Secretary General's Panel 2011).

Thus, in conclusion, the Panel found credible allegations that comprise five core categories of potential serious violations committed by the Government of Sri Lanka: (i) killing of civilians through widespread shelling; (ii) shelling of hospitals and humanitarian objects; (iii) denial of humanitarian assistance; (iv) human rights violations suffered by victims and survivors of the conflict, including both IDPs and suspected LTTE cadre; and (v) human rights violations outside the conflict zone, including against the media and other critics of the Government.

The Panel's determination of credible allegations against the LTTE associated with the final stages of the war reveal six core categories of potential serious violations:

(i) using civilians as a human buffer; (ii) killing civilians attempting to flee LTTE control; (iii) using military equipment in the proximity of civilians; (iv) forced recruitment of children; (v) forced labor; and (vi) killing of civilians through suicide attacks. (ibid.)

As the findings of a credible UN Panel of Experts completely contradicted the LLRC's report, it was clear that the Sri Lankan government had manipulated the LLRC to give an absolute clean chit to its forces.

What is even more disturbing is how the Sri Lankan government created a completely compromised body, called it a "Commission of Inquiry (COI)," with a deceitful purpose to pass it off as a credible investigative Commission. This is indeed problematic because Commissions of Inquiry have been usually formed in South Asia to investigate human rights violations in the aftermath of mass or communal violence or massacres. These COIs are primarily used as mechanisms to tide over the immediate crisis and their recommendations are not followed. Nonetheless, these COI's have served an important purpose in investigating serious crimes, documenting the patterns of violations, fixing responsibility on perpetrators and providing a set of recommendations for ensuring truth, justice, and reparations in varying measure. Usually, governments across the region have failed to implement the recommendations of these Commissions.

In Sri Lanka, the Presidential Commission of Inquiry that was formed to investigate the disappearances could not achieve much as the government failed to implement its recommendations, but nonetheless provided an important historical and factual account of the serious crimes of disappearances that it set up to investigate. However, the LLRC is such a compromised Commission from the start that it even failed to independently investigate the crimes committed by the parties to the conflict, including the Sri Lankan government forces and at least affix responsibility on the perpetrators.

This is indeed dangerous as now the Commission of Inquiry is not only completely biased and farcical, but also failed to fulfill the basic role of an independent investigating body. The setting up of a sham Commission as the LLRC has taken the debate on impunity to a new low.

In a polarized context like Sri Lanka where there is such little faith in government institutions, it would augur well for the new government, if it was serious, to invite either a UN-backed body such as the Panel of Experts or a team comprising of international Commissioners to investigate the allegations of war crimes and crimes against humanity in the country. With the Rajapaksa government voted out of power, and a new government in Colombo, fresh possibilities have opened up for addressing the crimes of the past decades, but it is still unclear if there is the requisite political will to do so.

Indeed, it is also important to acknowledge that the question of accountability for serious human rights violations in Sri Lanka is not only to ensure justice for those who suffered during the last stages of the war in 2008–09 but also for the crimes of enforced disappearances, extra judicial killing, sexual violence, and torture during the two preceding decades.

Bangladesh: Compromising International Standards

During the 1971 Bangladesh War of Independence, civilians witnessed egregious abuses both at the hands of the Pakistani army as well as *razakars* or local Bangladeshis who were supporting the Pakistani army. Moreover, there were also massacres of Bihari Muslims at the hands of some Bangladeshi nationalists supporting the independence struggle. Most of these crimes have not been accounted for even today, as an amnesty for serious crimes committed during the Bangladeshi War of Independence has been in place. Finally, in 2009, the Awami League government set up the International Crimes Tribunal (ICT) to investigate and prosecute the perpetrators of the genocide committed during the Bangladesh Liberation War. Prior to that, there had almost been no trials for these crimes, and only a Liberation War Museum that commemorated the 1971 War was opened in Dhaka. These memorialization efforts were important in keeping the memory of the horrible crimes that had occurred during the 1971 Liberation War.

The formation of the ICT was initially welcomed both by Bangladeshis as well as the international community as finally there was going to be some accountability for the crimes committed during the Liberation War. Nonetheless, while the Tribunal was called International Crimes Tribunal, the statute itself fell short of international standards and best practices. There were due process concerns raised by a host of international human rights organizations. The most contentious clause was the inclusion of a death penalty for serious crimes. Most international Tribunals including ICTY and ICTR did not provide for death penalty even for serious war crimes, crimes against humanity or genocide as it was seen to be antithetical to human rights principles. The argument of many Bangladeshis including human rights activists who supported the ICT was that till the time death penalty was on the criminal statute books of Bangladesh, it could be one of the options for the ICT. However, the objections of the international human rights groups was that if the ICT purported to be an International Crimes Tribunal and not merely domestic, then it should be informed by international law.

The issue of death penalty for war crimes committed during the 1971 War remained extremely contentious and divisive. It came to a head when Jamat-i-Islami leader Abdul Qader Mollah was convicted on five counts of crimes against humanity and given a life sentence. He came out of the court brandishing a victory sign, which infuriated many Bangladeshis who thought that he had been let off too lightly for very serious crimes. What followed thereafter were spontaneous and massive protests—now known as Shahbagh protests of 2013—demanding the death penalty for Mollah as well as the banning of the Jamat-i-Islami party of Bangladesh, a religious party that was seen by Bangladeshis as being complicit in the crimes committed in 1971 Liberation War.

Subsequently, the International Crimes (Tribunal) Act, 1973 was amended by the Bangladeshi government and Mollah's original life sentence was enhanced to a death sentence in February 2013. The Bangladeshi government finally hung Mollah in December 2013 just before the national elections. Several international human rights organizations raised concerns upon this retroactive application of the death sentence claiming that it sidestepped due process and fair trial standards that are inextricably linked to the legitimacy of any judicial process (International Center for Transitional Justice 2013).

The reopening of cases from the 1971 Bangladesh war was a significant move, particularly because serious crimes were committed during the period; however, if fair process standards are not followed, then can the ICT really claim to be a legitimate Tribunal? While the concept of the ICT neatly fits within prosecutions discourse of transitional justice, the objections raised about due process yet again illustrates the limitations of international law in relation to domestic tribunals. The government in Bangladesh selected only aspects of international criminal jurisprudence or transitional justice and applied it to the ICT, but disregarded the fundamental tenets of these theories. So what will happen when the past abuses are addressed but due process concerns are not followed? The Tribunal is still underway, but for the ICT to bolster its legitimacy, it will have to move toward ensuring internationally recognized procedural safeguards and due process for individuals facing criminal charges.

'Kashmir' Avoidance and Subversion of Justice

Kashmir is another region in South Asia that has witnessed protracted conflict that remains unresolved even after two decades. It cannot be said that Kashmir is post-conflict or that transitional justice would have the same meaning there as in the other South Asian contexts. However, given the grievous abuses that have been committed during the conflict, transitional justice mechanism would necessarily have some relevance for Kashmir. The then Jammu and Kashmir Chief Minister Omar Abdullah had proposed the formation of a Truth and Reconciliation Commission to "heal the wounds of Kashmiris" who had hugely suffered during the conflict.

While the conflict is still ongoing in Kashmir with no signs of any political resolution to the issue, local human rights groups rightly apprehend that if the government forms such a Commission, it would be only used to further entrench impunity. The prevailing situation in Kashmir is such that there have been almost no prosecution of perpetrators of serious violations, the fate of the forcibly disappeared persons remains unknown, and extrajudicial killings and sexual violence continues. If the government is sincere about implementing transitional justice mechanisms, then it should begin by granting sanction for prosecution of security force personnel involved in human rights violations, repeal laws such as the AFSPA, Public Safety Act and ensure that the guilty are punished.

The insistence of the state government under the then Chief Minister Omar Abdullah, to form a Truth and Reconciliation Commission over other transitional justice mechanism, has meant that there is a political motive to impede justice processes through the normal courts by forming a TRC. Why doesn't the government instead invite the UN Working Group on Disappearances to ascertain the fate of the thousands who have disappeared, or ensure that there are swift prosecutions in cases of human rights violations?[5]

Besides, the formation of a Truth Commission cannot be a replacement to the political resolution of the conflict. Neither can it replace the demand for punishment of the perpetrators of serious crimes including disappearances. Also, how could a TRC be feasible if human rights abuses continue to happen in Kashmir? Perhaps the

Omar Abdullah government had envisaged the TRC as a never-ending process, which will shift the focus from the demands of justice. Cynicism as regards the sincerity of the TRC proposal is further reinforced by the context within which the Omar Abdullah government mooted the idea. It is a context in which the government has repeatedly failed to investigate and prosecute perpetrators of human rights violations. Moreover, at the time that Omar Abdullah spoke of a TRC, public attention was centered on the mass graves unearthed by the State Human Rights Commission which is the government's own body. Indeed, there was a general sense in Kashmir that the concept of the TRC was put forward by the Omar Abdullah government to hoodwink public opinion.

Most importantly, why was the government not investigating and prosecuting the mass rapes of Konan Poshopra, a village in North Kashmir, carried out by the armed forces? Even when the District Judge reopened the investigation in 2013, 22 years after the incident, the concerned government agencies refused to investigate and submit a final report despite a court order to do so within three months. Moreover, when the successor PDP–BJP government led by Mufti Mohammad Sayeed took over in early 2015, the state government challenged the JK High Court granting compensation to the Konan Poshpora rape victims in Supreme Court. In the Shopian rape and murder case of 2009 also, there have been no authoritative investigations that have led to prosecution (International People's Tribunal on Human Rights and Justice in Kashmir 2009; Independent Women's Initiative for Justice 2009; Warisha 2013).

The variables of truth, justice, and reconciliation are not mutually exclusive and it is difficult to ascertain the order in which they form a part of any peace process. Like reconciliation, justice is a key component of lasting peace. There is no agreement on what reconciliation exactly means. Broadly, it entails an end to, and acknowledgement of the past historical injustice supplemented with measures to repair the wrong. A common experience of human rights abuse does not necessarily translate into a common way to deal with the past. Thus, reconciliation needs to address not only the conflicting historical narratives of different communities but also the way they want to deal with the past. But reconciliation should not become an excuse to subvert justice. Political transitions occur in many different ways and there is no one magical formula for these widely divergent contexts.

When you talk to various human rights groups in Kashmir, they would not say that they are against a Commission of Inquiry but that they would like to see a credible set of Commissioners, which would mean that there is a UN-led or international community led effort that investigates the human rights violations that have occurred over the past two decades. International actors, civil society or those groups with no local vested interests in the political issue were perceived as most legitimate to start or support a process of truth and justice, as well as be actively involved in commission of inquiry if set up. Impartial agencies drawn from international organizations or a body in which all sides have faith were thought best to start a process of justice over establishment of a Truth Commission that would sabotage justice.

Epilogue

There appears to be a pattern in the application of transitional justice mechanisms in South Asia. The victims of gross human rights violations and the human rights groups perceive transitional justice mechanisms as something that delivers truth, justice, and reparations to them. The political class, however, does not necessarily see the implementation of transitional justice mechanisms as their desirable goal. For them, in contexts such as Nepal, Sri Lanka or even Kashmir, reconciliation forms the most attractive part of the transitional justice framework. But as can be seen from the example of Bangladesh, the desire for legal justice or punishment of perpetrators does not go away even after four decades of the commission of these crimes. The demand for death penalty in large part represented the anger and frustration of a complete denial of past human rights violations for so many years.

This entire dichotomy between promoting the agenda of Reconciliation over Truth, Justice or Reparations is also evidenced in the politics of funding over transitional justice in South Asia. While the USAID was promoting the Local Peace Committees and the entire model of reconciliation as part of transitional justice in Nepal, it was surprising that the pressing question of impunity did not cross the minds of either the US or India. How could the issue of uncovering the truth in cases of enforced disappearances or punishment for perpetrators of serious crimes not be seen as integral to any transitional justice process? Reconciliation is not an abstract concept, but heavily dependent on peace and justice between communities. To expect that reconciliation is possible without some measure of justice or reparations is unrealistic. In Nepal, Sri Lanka and Kashmir, the governments have tried to artificially import the idea of transitional justice through the mechanism of forming Truth and Reconciliation Commissions with the sole purpose of subverting truth and justice.

In Nepal, the "Nepal Transition to Peace Initiative" (NTTP) funded by USAID was an ardent supporter of the Reconciliation model. The argument is not that the focus on reconciliation is problematic *per se*, but if it becomes the only form of transitional justice then it impedes justice.[6] In furtherance of their goals, the NTTP had vehemently argued that including amnesties as part of the Truth and Reconciliation Commission was permissible under international law, and lobbied alongside the Nepali Ministry of Peace and Reconstruction when the UNMIN, OHCHR, international and local human rights groups as well as victim groups were completely against the amnesty clause of the draft TRC Bill. It prepared and presented an entire memo arguing that amnesties were permissible under international law for serious crimes including torture.

Reparations are another mechanism of transitional justice that is not understood properly by political actors who are trying to implement them in their countries or regions. In most cases, reparations are simply understood to be ex-gratia relief or monetary compensation and nothing more. In fact, the concept of reparations under international law is premised on the concept of acknowledgment of the wrongdoing. But in all these countries including India, Nepal, Sri Lanka, Pakistan or Kashmir whenever money has been paid for human rights violations, it has never been accompanied with the requisite acknowledgment that the state failed to protect the rights of the citizens or that the state was complicit in carrying out these violations in the first place.

The discourse on transitional justice also does not acknowledge enough the efforts of civil society and victim groups in the documentation of egregious crimes, or even in holding unofficial People's Tribunals or other fact-finding bodies. This is a major lacunae in the current discourse on transitional justice, especially in the context of South Asia that has a rich tradition of unofficial or People's Tribunals that collect victim testimonies and other relevant information to expose grave human rights violations. Meticulous human rights documentation contributes in setting the ground for examining the past, and is integral to all human rights work. Since governments would most likely deny, delay or destroy any evidence related to human rights violations, it is important to preserve and collect evidence as far as possible. In this context, it is therefore important to strengthen and provide impetus to the existing documentation.

Moreover, developing documentation of human rights abuses in conjunction with the local groups, where the information or data collected is jointly owned has contributed to official commissions. There is no doubt that official commissions of inquiries have greater powers to investigate and since the government appoints them, it is harder for them to deny their findings. Nonetheless, the role of these unofficial bodies is also significant and has not found their rightful place in the transitional justice narrative.

Notes

1. It is broadly premised on the following principles. The first is that conflicts are based on retribution and the role of retribution is vengeance. In effect a model of prosecution solely based on retribution will be unable to break the cycle of violence. In order to break this cycle of violence, there is a need to "transfer the responsibilities from apportioning blame and punishment from victims to public bodies acting according to the rule of law." Second, prosecutions are limited and selective in nature and in instances of mass violence are unable to punish the multiple perpetrators. Thirdly, transitional societies need to confront ordinary crimes as they seek to address the past. With limited resources, prosecutions for all perpetrators may be difficult, but that does not mean that there should be no accountability for them.
2. See http://www.un.org/en/ga/search/view_doc.asp?symbol=S/RES/1325(2000) (accessed November 30, 2016).
3. See http://daccess-dds-ny.un.org/doc/UNDOC/GEN/N08/391/44/PDF/N0839144.pdf?OpenElement
4. 671 people were allegedly disappeared by the state security forces, and 299 abducted by the Maoists.
5. For the entrenched impunity for human rights violations in Kashmir, see Human Rights Watch (2006); *Indian Express* (2011); and Lowenstein (2009).
6. For further information of the NTTP on the Nepali Peace Process, see Farasat and Hayner (2009).

Bibliography

Advocacy Forum and International Center for Transitional Justice. 2010, December. "Across the Lines: The Impact of Nepal's Conflict on Women." Accessed November 30, 2016, http://ictj.org/sites/default/files/ICTJ-Nepal-Across-Lines-2010-English.pdf

Aukerman, Miriam J. 2002. "Extraordinary Evil, Ordinary Crime: A Framework for Understanding Transitional Justice." HHRJ 15: 60.

Human Rights Watch. March 1, 2005. "Clear Culpability: 'Disappearances' by Security Forces in Nepal." Accessed Novermber 30, 2016, https://www.hrw.org/reports/2005/nepal0205/

———. 2006. "Impunity Fuels Conflict in Jammu and Kashmir." Accessed November 26, 2016, http://hrw.org/reports/2006/india0906/

Indian Express. 2011, August 21. "2156 Unidentified Bodies in 38 Graves in Kashmir: State Human Rights Panel Inquiry. Accessed November 30, 2016, http://archive.indianexpress.com/news/2156-unidentified-bodies-in-38-graves-in-kashmir-state-human-rights-panel-inquiry/834890/

Independent Women's Initiative for Justice (IWIJ). 2009. "Shopian: Manfacturing a Suitable Story—A Case Watch." Accessed November 30, 2016, http://www.countercurrents.org/iwj.pdf

International Center for Transitional Justice. 2013, September 19. "ICTJ Concerned by Retroactive Sentencing in Bangladesh Genocide Trial." Accessed November 30, 2016, http://www.ictj.org/news/ictj-concerned-retroactive-sentencing-bangladesh-genocide-trial

International Center for Transitional Justice and Himal Southasia. 2007, January 23–25. "Exhuming Accountability" Conference Kathmandu.

International People's Tribunal on Human Rights and Justice in Kashmir (IPTK). 2009. *Buried Evidence: Unknown, Unmarked and Mass Graves in Indian Administered Kashmir—A Preliminary Report.* Srinagar: IPTK.

Lowenstein, Allard K. 2009. "The Myth of Normalcy: Impunity and the Judiciary in Kashmir." International Human Rights Clinic, Yale Law School. Accessed November 30, 2016, https://www.law.yale.edu/system/files/documents/pdf/Intellectual_Life/Kashmir_MythofNormalcy.pdf

March 31, 2011. "Report of the Secretary General's Panel of Experts on Accountability in Sri Lanka. Accessed November 30, 2016, http://www.un.org/News/dh/infocus/Sri_Lanka/POE_Report_Full.pdf

Minow, Martha. 1998. *Between Vengeance and Forgiveness: Facing History After Genocide and Mass Violence.* 11–12.

National Human Rights Commission. January 9, 2006. *Report by the Special Rapporteur on Torture and other Cruel, Inhuman or Degrading Treatment or Punishment, Manfred Nowak, Mission to Nepal* (E/CN.4/2006/6/Add.5). New Delhi: National Human Rights Commission.

National Human Rights Commission. 2008, August 30. *Report on the Situation of Forcefully Disappeared People during the Period of Armed Conflict in Nepal.* New Delhi: National Human Rights Commission.

Nesiah, Vasuki. 2009, August 16. "Unpacking the Truth." *Sunday Island.* Accessed November 30, 2016, http://www.island.lk/2009/08/16/features5.html

Nesiah, Vasuki. 2013. "'The Law, This Violent Thing'": Dissident Memory & Democratic Futures." Neelan Tiruchelvam Memorial Lecture. Accessed November 30, 2016, https://www.colombotelegraph.com/index.php/the-law-this-violent-thing-dissident-memory-and-democratic-futures/

Nino, Carlos S. 1991. "The Duty to Punish Past Abuses of Human Rights Put Into Context: The Case of Argentina." *Yale Law Journal* 100: 2635.

November 2011. "Report of the Commission of Inquiry on Lesson Learnt & Reconciliation." Accessed November 30, 2016, http://groundviews.org/wp-content/uploads/2011/12/FINAL-LLRC-REPORT.pdf

UNHCHR. *Report of the Working Group on Enforced or Involuntary Disappearances on its Visit to Nepal* (E/CN.4/2005/65/Add.1). Geneva: UNHCHR.

Warisha, Farasat. 2013, May 11. "Understanding Impunity in Jammu & Kashmir." *Economic & Political Weekly,* XLVIII: 19. Accessed December 19, 2016, http://www.epw.in/journal/2013/19/commentary/understanding-impunity-jammu-and-kashmir.html#sthash.wYEMvnO6.dpuf

Warisha, Farasat, and Priscilla Hayner. 2009, July. "Negotiating Peace in Nepal: Implications for Justice." Accessed December 19, 2016, http://www.initiativeforpeacebuilding.eu/pdf/Negotiating_Peace_in_Nepal.pdf

Participant Analysis
and
Field Notes

13

Against Forgetting: Gendered Justice in "Post-conflict" Bangladesh

Dina M. Siddiqi

Mapping the Terrain of Gender Justice

In this essay, I map the terrain of gendered justice for women at the margins of the nation today, taking the abduction and as yet unresolved disappearance, over 20 years ago, of the outspoken indigenous rights activist, Kalpana Chakma,[1] as a signpost. The trajectory of her case points to the asymmetric political, historical, and cultural landscapes traversed by Pahari/Jumma women, imagined as "*outside* the Bengali nation," (emphasis added) in relation to their Bengali counterparts. Without wishing to overstate its significance, I also explore the multiple and continuing reverberations of this missing female body on mainstream feminist politics.

In a broader context, I assess the possibilities for justice in the post-Chittagong Hill Tracts Peace Accord period, that is, since 1997. I conclude that the situation has not altered dramatically in the interim. The "post-conflict" situation in the CHT is anything but conflict-free. Rather, the existence of the Accord renders invisible the ongoing militarization of everyday life in the area. In the circumstances, the prospect of justice for indigenous peoples, regardless of gender, appears minimal. Notably, the Accord did not broach the subject of gendered crimes by state or nonstate actors. For its part, the Bangladeshi state has sought systematically to erase the forcible disappearance of CHT women activist Kalpana Chakma, and even that of her military abductor from political memory.

Outsiders in the Bengali Nation

From the outset, the fate of the CHT has been captive to the (i) logic of colonial politics and post-colonial state making processes. Upon annexing the area in 1860, British authorities appointed three circle chiefs, or rajas, whose main responsibilities were tax collection on behalf of the state, help with land administration, including jhum lands, and dispensing "traditional" justice through local forms of dispute resolution. As part of a broader strategy to minimize "hills–plains" conflict and to protect a stable source of revenue, the colonial state also placed legal restrictions on in-migration and declared much of the CHT as reserved or protected forests. This protected status was to generate much resentment among Bengalis in independent Bangladesh.

Culturally, religiously and linguistically distinct from Bengalis, the Paharis/Jumma were marginal to political and cultural life in East Pakistan. Increasingly militant Bengali demands for greater recognition and a more equitable distribution of resources and employment in the 1950s and 1960s resonated little with Pahari chiefs and traditional leaders. Conversely, Pahari populations experienced forms of displacement and dispossession by the Pakistani state's developmental policies not captured by the demands of the Bengali autonomy movement.

The onset of war in 1971 ruptured a carefully cultivated "neutrality" on the part of Pahari Chiefs. Local political contingencies persuaded the Mong circle chief to ally himself with pro-liberation forces, while the Chakma circle chief, Raja Tridib Roy, decided the interests of his people would be best served by open allegiance to Pakistan. In the eyes of Bengalis fighting a murderous war unleashed by the Pakistani army, Tridib Roy's decision could only be interpreted as a treasonous act. Since Roy was de-facto spokesperson for all Paharis, the stain of "collaborator" stayed with the Chakmas and others long after independence. Despite enormous differences among the eleven officially recognized groups in the CHT, Paharis tend to be conceived as a monolithic entity in the dominant imagination. This homogenization makes it easier to cast all Jumma peoples as anti-liberation/pro-Pakistani, although many Jumma peoples and other adivasis took up arms against the Pakistanis.

Suspicions of disloyalty to the nation are folded into older, racial stereotypes of inferiority and civilizational backwardness. Jumma women, in particular, are viewed by most Bengalis as immodest (especially in dress), morally lax, and therefore sexually available.

As with all such projects, the ethnolinguistic terms of Bengali nationalism were by definition exclusionary. The state's political project hinged upon the production of a culturally homogenous population of ethnic Bengalis (Mohsin 1997 cited in Roy 2004). During his first visit to the CHT, Sheikh Mujib called on Paharis/Jummas to forgo their language and culture and *become* Bengalis and so, by implication, full citizens of the country. The 1972 constitution did not recognize the existence of indigenous peoples inside Bangladesh; ethnicity and citizenship were folded into each other. After 1975, successive military regimes systematically "Islamized" the state and its representational practices, thereby reifying the Bangladesh citizen as Muslim, and rendering all non-Muslims including indigenous peoples, invisible (Karim 1998).

Pre- and Post-conflict Geographies of Occupation

Anthropologist Kamala Visweswaran reminds us that occupation rarely names itself as such (Visweswaran 2013: 3). So it is that the material violence and symbolic domination of everyday life in the CHT are recast as matters of territorial and cultural integrity, economic development, and national security. Narratives of militarism and counter-insurgency, interwoven with discourses of development and ecological sustainability, reproduce the CHT as a troubled space that must be tamed; they also serve to erase relations of power between Bengalis and others. As we shall see, Pahari/Jumma women's bodies are fundamentally implicated in the everyday practices required to secure occupation, and to produce the cultural/racial "Other" of the Bengali nation.

Typical of conflicts between indigenous populations and centralizing states, contestations over land rights shape the CHT struggle in fundamental ways. State resettlement of around 400,000 indigent Bengalis between 1979 and 1985 was partially justified by the widely held misconception that unlike the rest of Bangladesh, the hills were sparsely populated; existing "surplus" land could and should be redistributed to landless people from the plains. In practice, mass population transfer was part of a broader counter-insurgency strategy that worked through the often violent eviction of indigenous families from ancestral lands or the reallocation of "reserved forests" for other purposes.

In turn, sexual violence or its threat constituted a fundamental feature of forced relocation and eviction from early on in the conflict. CHT activists often cite the rape of indigenous women by Bengali security forces in the 1970s, as a significant factor in the PJCSS's decision to take up arms. Threats of rape, abduction and sexual harassment served a double function: the ostensible emasculation of Pahari men who appear unable to protect the "honor" embedded in "their" women's bodies and the heightening of insecurity and fear in everyday life.

Although security personnel initially accounted for the majority of rapes, the conditions of occupation, and especially impunity, encouraged and enabled Bengali settlers to, "violently take over lands belonging to the Jummas, evicting hundreds from their homes, using sexual violence against indigenous women, and committing massacres [...] (Chakma and Hill 2013: 139)." The Peace Accord makes no provisions for survivors of sexual violence to seek redress or "rehabilitation" (Mohsin 2002). Post-conflict, women's bodies continue to be sites of violence for settlers as well for security forces. A disturbing new trend observed by the Kapaeeng Foundation is that a large number of victims/survivors are very young girls or adolescents. Increasingly, the majority of perpetrators are Bengali settlers with powerful political ties (Kapaeeng Foundation 2015).

A hostile legal justice system, coupled with the indigent circumstances of most indigenous people, make legal redress a distant or unreachable goal. It is not unusual for those seeking justice to be forced into settling out of court or threatened with retribution (ibid.). Moreover, as elsewhere in Bangladesh, powerful patrons invariably patronize and shelter criminals. In the prevailing system, those without political ties have little chance of securing justice.

Sections of the military and paramilitary have always expropriated indigenous land to expand their activities and to "secure" their bases. The acquisition of indigenous land proceeds through other "legal" means as well—such as the enactment of laws that ostensibly protect the environment or further economic development (Chakma and Hill 2013: 138). The Forest Department can seize land belonging to indigenous peoples in the name of creating additional "reserve forests," much of which ends up denuded by corrupt officials. The civil administration can lease out land (primarily from "unclassified forests," used traditionally for jhum cultivation, herding, and other commons based activities) for the establishment of industrial plants and commercial plantations. Leases generally go to powerful Bengalis, including military officials, political leaders, professionals, business entrepreneurs, and their relatives.

The overall effect of such policies has been to shift the demographic composition and cultural cartography of the CHT. The 1991 census reveals that almost 50 percent of the CHT population is now non-indigenous Bengali, a stunning increase of 150 percent since 1974.

The fundamental power equation has not changed since the signing of the CHT Peace Accord in December 1997. The Accord had promised demilitarization, the settlement of land disputes, and the devolution of authority to indigenous institutions and representatives, but these commitments remain partially implemented, if at all. No longer officially a war zone the signs of occupation are everywhere in the CHT. Most visibly, military camps are ubiquitous. The military maintains six cantonments in the three districts that comprise the CHT, while the remaining 61 districts of the country share 14 cantonments among themselves. That is, a full third of the nation's army is stationed in an area that is a tenth of the total land mass and contains one percent of the total population of Bangladesh (International Workgroup for Indigenous Affairs 2012). This context enables the numerous mass attacks—the burning down of homes, massacre of people, and sexual violence—on indigenous villages.

Less tangibly, the military continues to be heavily involved in administrative matters. The latter has been made easier by retention of the counter-insurgency executive order, known as Operation *Uttoron* (Uplift), that authorizes army intervention in civil matters beyond its official jurisdiction. As a consequence, the army presence directly or indirectly mediates all relationships between Bengali settlers and Paharis (D'Costa and Chakma 2012). In effect, the Accord has invisibilized the ongoing militarization of everyday life in the area. Post-conflict, it could be argued, is another name for constant surveillance, an environment of fear, intimidation and self-censorship, and little prospect of justice.

Memory and Other Sites of Resistance

On the occasion of the first national indigenous women's conference held in Dhaka in April 2012, the Kapaeeng Foundation observed that, "[D]ue to non-implementation of CHT Accord of 1997, no basic and noteworthy progress has been made for indigenous women's participation in development processes, education, and health care in CHT. The biggest concern in rape (cases) and other violence against indigenous women both in CHT and plain land is the lack of access to justice and absolute impunity that perpetrators enjoy" (Kapaeeng. org 2012). A month later, a memo submitted on 27 May 2013 to the visiting UN Special Rapporteur on Violence Against Women, Rashida Manjoo, by eight indigenous people's organizations noted increasing violence against women and the absolute impunity of perpetrators—both Bengali settlers and members of law enforcement agencies—as major concerns in the CHT (kapaeeng.org/indigenous-women-leaders-submit-a-joint-statement... 2012). The memo touched on the equally troubling phenomenon of forced intermarriage, following abduction and forcible conversion to Islam. Articulated in policy or not, forced marriages serve as instruments of assimilation into Muslim Bengali society, yet another strategy for shifting the demographic profile of the region.

The instrumentalization of sexuality as a counter-insurgency measure may have a longer institutional history; reportedly in 1983, army officers received a secret circular encouraging them to marry indigenous women (CHT Commission 1991: 88). Nationbuilding, in this imaginary, requires the literal occupation of indigenous women's bodies. Chakma and Hill suggest that this memo functioned not only to encourage voluntary intermarriage but resulted in a violent turn with marriages between army officers and indigenous women taking place through intimidation and abductions (Chakma and Hill 2013: 142). It is more than likely that the (talk of the) existence of the memo encouraged acquiescence to or the condoning of the coercive aspects of such marriages.

The framing of the memo recalls a racialized Bengali imagination shot through with an "incorrigible romanticism" and "lecherous exoticism" regarding indigenous peoples in the hills (Rahman 2010: 192). Sexualized stereotypes of Paharis—imagined as closer to nature, pristine like the landscape that surrounds them, virgin territory—abound in popular culture and offer endless prospects for "corruption" or conquest by the Bengali male. Thus, the "incentive for those arriving in the CHT, in addition to all the financial benefits of land grabbing, is the fantasy of the uninhibited consumption of 'sexy Chakma girls' (ibid.: 193, emphasis added)." The scaffolding for this fantasy is a common sense understanding of CHT cultures/religions as backward, uncivilized, and in need of salvation/reform. Thus, the discursive construction of Pahari women as the essential, cultural "Other" allows for the colonization of their bodies and the "civilizing" of their minds. Ostensibly, this brings all Paharis into the orbit of the civilized Bengali nation, erasing the violence carried out in the name of national integration and peacemaking.

Kalpana's Story

Jumma women have consistently resisted the practices of occupation, formally and informally, through poetry as well as politics. At one point in time, the Hill Women's Federation, of which Kalpana Chakma was the organizing secretary, epitomized such resistance in the political arena. Kalpana Chakma's brief life and the afterlife of her disappearance are emblematic of the high cost of speaking out in a context of power asymmetries and the culture of impunity. Kalpana fearlessly spoke out against the occupation of the CHT, demanded the right to self-determination but also "represented a new generation of indigenous women who would not shy away from raising uncomfortable questions in their own communities (Naher and Tripura, 2010: 196)."

By no means a separatist Kalpana wanted to belong to the nation, but on terms of equality rather than of domination or assimilation. Kalpana Chakma was allegedly abducted by Lt. Ferdous of Rangamati Kojoichori army camp in June 1996, a day before the much anticipated national elections. Her abduction may have been linked to her support of a pro-Pahari political candidate. However, human rights organizations also report that she had already had an altercation with Lt. Ferdous after several houses in her village were burned. In either case, the timing may reflect the kind of nation imagined into being by those responsible for her disappearance: not only a refusal to make space for voices of dissent, but also a felt need to excise such "dangers" from the body politic. Kalpana Chakma's disappearance could also be read as a failed attempt at "colonization through marriage." An explanatory note on a Facebook page set up in her memory states that, "it is feared that she might have been killed if [sic] she did not agree to marry Lieutenant Ferdous, the army officer who led the abduction."

Kalpana's brothers witnessed the abduction and recognized at least one of the abductors. Twenty years after her abduction, neither Lt. Ferdous nor the military establishment has been held accountable. At the time, it was difficult for her family to even lodge a case with the police. Since then, her brothers have been legally harassed, threatened with violence and otherwise intimidated in a bid to persuade them to withdraw the case.

Despite a number of investigations, the state has failed to name any suspects. The principal accused, Lt. Ferdous, has never been questioned by the police. Curiously, the military now claims to have no record of him. It appears he too has been "disappeared," erased from official memory. Nevertheless, indigenous activists, in collaboration with organizations such as the Chittagong Hill Tracts Commission, have persisted in keeping up pressure on the state.

In January 2013, the court rejected the latest "Final Report" into the investigation of Kalpana's disappearance, and gave instructions for a further investigation, stating that every effort should be given to "rescuing the victim Kalpana Chakma." The deadline for the new report has long passed and the Police Superintendent of Rangamati Hill District has since stated that it is difficult for her to investigate the case "uninterruptedly."

Keeping the story of Kalpana Chakma alive works as a powerful form of resistance to Bengali domination. The Bangladeshi state and the armed forces would like to erase the entire Kalpana Chakma episode. Indigenous activists, and many of their Bengali counterparts, have resisted the willed forgetting of the state and its institutions. For instance, Shahidul Alam and Saydia Gulrukh's powerful exhibition, Searching for Kalpana Chakma: A Photo Forensic Study 2013, seeks to produce tangible visuals of a scene that has been made invisible through the passage of time, and to break a silence that successive Bangladeshi governments have carefully nurtured (Guhathakurta and Van Schendel 2013; Mohaiemen 2010).

In an important and insightful analysis, Lamia Karim notes that it was easy for many middle-class Bangladeshis to dismiss the problem of a missing Chakma woman by appealing to a narrative of romance or a discourse of terrorist separatism. Those whose identities were invested in and produced through the Bengali nation-state, were deeply uncomfortable taking up the cause of someone whose political demands appeared to threaten territorial integrity. Drawing on a language of equality and rights, these activists argued that since the constitution guarantees freedom of movement, they could not endorse protected areas status for the CHT. Karim observes that this line of argument assumes that all subjects enter the nation-state as full citizens and with the same rights. She writes that, "[a]lthough the body of the missing Chakma woman served to bond the human rights activists and organizes them against the gendered violence of the state; it simultaneously immobilizes their action because the Chakma's woman stake in self-determination, at least potentially, undermines the Bangladeshi nation-state." (Karim 1998)

The provenance of feminist and human rights activism has expanded considerably since the time Karim wrote at the turn of the millennium. Today, "the CHT problem" is firmly located within the orbit of the national question. It is instructive that the 17th anniversary of Kalpana Chakma's abduction was commemorated in 2013 at the auditorium of the *Mukti Juddho Jadughor* (The Liberation War Museum), a bastion of secular Bengali nationalism.

Yet inclusion is tenuous and conditional upon demonstrating loyalty to the Bengali nation. The anxiety this generates may explain the urgent quest on the part of some indigenous activists to locate Pahari freedom fighters in the 1971 war. Witness also the unfolding of the Shahbagh movement, in which indigenous activists tried to carve out a space for themselves but remained on the margins. Difference, "sisterhood" and nationalism do not sit together well.

Notably, dominant Pahari representations of Kalpana tend to foreground her as someone who sacrificed her life for the Jumma cause. Somewhat constrictive and highly nationalized, the meanings attached to her absent body are produced under deeply fraught conditions of occupation. Indigenous feminists are conscious of the dangers inherent in the difficulties of resisting this mode of representation.

It could be argued that an exclusive or selective focus on Kalpana Chakma courts serious pitfalls. In the highly mediatized social spaces of activism, the figure of Kalpana can be rendered celebrity status, albeit a disappeared one. Non-Pahari activists might feel good rallying around this individual case, without any need to reflect on the everyday, systemic abuses in which their own privilege is implicated. Other pressing issues may not receive this kind of attention.

In the final analysis, the intractable question of difference—in feminist theory and politics—remains. A major difficulty stems from the meanings brought to bear on the disappeared body of the missing activist. Calls for justice framed within a narrow prism of "violence against women," including violence perpetrated by the state, are inherently problematic. The obscuring or displacement of structural violence is built into analyses that privilege gender as the primary (if not exclusive) axis of inequality. Context and specificity—histories of colonialism, nationalist politics, class, or ethnicity—can be ignored or erased in this kind of liberal feminist framing. Kalpana's body, then, can stand for all female bodies everywhere; her injuries can be understood, and resisted, as an outcome of the universal condition of being a woman. The liberal feminist fighting for gender-equality can speak out on behalf of the oppressed "Other," leaving intact the highly unequal structuring of gender, nation, and difference (in this case ethnicity).

Building on Karim's analysis, I would argue that the language of women's rights and equality has severe limitations when it operates on uneven terrain, as it invariably does. Without recognition of the military occupation and its consequences, calls to ensure the bodily integrity and rights of Chakma women effectively mask differential inclusions/exclusions into the nation in the name of gender-equality. This decontextualized emphasis on violence enacted on the individual body obscures structural difference and obfuscates the systemic violence against those perceived to belong to a particular collectivity (Paharis, indigenous peoples and so on). Structural violence can then be relegated to the margins, if engaged at all, or even naturalized. The Bengali woman's place of privilege in the nation need not be called into question even as she extends solidarity to her Pahari sisters.

Nation, Gender, and Difference: Struggles for Accountability

The Kalpana case revealed deep fissures in the feminist and human rights movement of the time. It brought to the fore the troubled relationship of nation, gender, and difference. Most Bangladeshis continue to embrace the narrative of the occupying nation, perpetrating a kind of epistemological violence in the process.

In March 2015, the Home Ministry issued an order prohibiting Paharis from speaking to foreigners—or to Bangladeshi citizens outside the CHT—except under the direct supervision of military or government personnel. Notably, the prohibition did not extend to Bengali inhabitants of the CHT. The Ministry also imposed strict restrictions on the entry of foreigners to the area; potential visitors would be required to submit applications at least a month ahead of time. Permission was contingent on clearance by intelligence agency. The order represented a blatant attempt to silence Jumma voices of resistance and to institutionalize racial/spatial hierarchies. In a related absurd twist, Paharis married to either foreign nationals or nonlocal Bengalis were effectively barred from bringing their partners to their hometowns. In the face of massive local and international outrage, the government was forced to withdraw the order. It is precisely the production of this kind of exclusionary citizenship in the name of national security of which activists must remain vigilant.

An occupation by any other name is still an occupation (cf. Visweswaran). Post-Accord CHT has the same basic structures of domination as in the past. It is in within the existing "geography of occupation" and "history of forgetting" that we must locate the gendered aftermath of conflict, the multiplying incidents of sexualized violence against Pahari/Jumma women since 1997, and Pahari/Jumma struggles for state accountability.

Bengalis need to rethink a more "just" nationalism: one in which Bengali privilege does not depend on the exploitation of the cultural Others and that does not call for assimilation as the condition for citizenship and equality. Only then can we begin to address meaningfully the question of gender(ed) justice for Jumma women.

Note

1. I would like to thank Prashanta Tripura for pushing me to reflect more fully on the consequences of the sustained focus on Kalpana Chakma's disappearance.

Bibliography

CHT Commission (Chittagong Hill Tracts Commission). 1991. "Life is Not Ours: Land and Human Rights in the Chittagong Hill Tracts," Bangladesh. Accessed November 10, 2016, http://www.iwgia.org/iwgia_files_publications_files/0129_Life_is_not_ours_1–108.pdf

Chakma, Kabita, and Glen Hill. 2013. "Indigenous Women and Culture in the Colonized Chittagong Hill Tracts of Bangladesh." In *Everyday Occupations: Experiencing Militarism in South Asia and the Middle East*, edited by Kamala Visweswaran. Philadelphia: University of Pennsylvania.

Chakma, Suhas. 2001. "Behind the Bamboo Curtain: Racism in Asia." In *Racism against Indigenous Peoples*, edited by Suhas Chakma and Marianne Jensen. Copenhagen: International Workgroup for Indigenous Affairs.

D'Costa, Bina. 2011 *Nation-Building, Gender and War Crimes in South Asia*. London: Routledge.

D'Costa, Bina, and Kabita Chakma. 2012. "Chittagong Hill Tracts: Diminishing Conflict or Violent Peace?" in *Diminished Conflicts in the Asia-Pacific: Why Some Subside and others Don't* edited by Edward Aspinall, Robin Jeffrey and Anthony Regan. London: Routledge, pp. 101–14.

Guhathakurta, Meghna, and Willem Van Schendel (eds.). 2013. *History, Culture, Politics*. Durham: Duke University Press, pp. 291–366.

International Workgroup for Indigenous Affairs. 2012. *Bangladesh: Militarization in the Chittagong Hill Tracts—The Slow Demise of the Region's Indigenous People*. IWGIA Report 14, p. 12. Shimin Gaiko Centre.

Kapaeeng Foundation. 2015, August 12. "CHT: Indigenous Women Targets of Sexual Violence." *Kapaeeng Foundation Statement*. Accessed November 10, 2016, http://unpo.org/article/18471

Karim, Lamia. 1998. "Pushed to the Margins of the State: Adivasi Peoples in Bangladesh and the Case of Kalpana Chakma." *Contemporary South Asia* 7 (3): 301–16.

Mohsin, Amena. 2002. *The Politics of Nationalism: The Case of the Chittagong Hill Tracts Bangladesh*. Dhaka: The University Press Limited.

Naher, Ainoon, and Prashanta Tripura. 2010. "Understanding Violence against Indigenous Women in Bangladesh." *Journal of Social Studies* 123.

Panday, Pranab Kumar, and Ishtiaq Jamil. 2009. "Conflict in the Chittagong Hill Tracts of Bangladesh: An Unimplemented Accord and Continued Violence." *Asian Survey* 49 (6): 1063.

Rahman, Biplob. 2010. "Pristine 'Fairies' and 'Sexy Pahari Girls'," in *Between Ashes and Hope: Chittagong Hill Tracts in the Blind Spot of Bangladesh Nationalism*, edited by Naeem Mohaiemen. Dhaka: Drishtipat Writers' Collective.

Roy, Chandra K. 2004. *Indigenous Women: A Gendered Perspective*. Norway: Resource Centre for the Rights of Indigenous Peoples.

Visweswaran, Kamala. 2013. "Geographies of Everyday Occupations." In *Everyday Occupations: Experiencing Militarism in South Asia and the Middle East*, edited by Kamala Visweswaran. Philadelphia: University of Pennsylvania.

14

Beyond Transitional Justice: Accountability Initiatives in Nepal

Mandira Sharma

In the decade-long internal conflict in Nepal from 1996–2006, both the warring parties—the state forces and the Maoist rebels were implicated in serious human rights abuses. It is estimated that the conflict claimed 17,265 lives, left 1,302 individuals disappeared, 4,305 disabled, 78,675 dispossessed and displaced, thousands of civilians tortured, and hundreds of women and girls raped and sexually abused (Media Foundation 2011: 72–75). A recent report by the United Nations Office of the High Commissioner of Human Rights (OHCHR) stated that, "there exists a credible allegation amounting to a reasonable basis for suspicion that a violation of international law has occurred" in Nepal and that, "these cases merit the prompt, impartial, independent and effective investigation by competent judicial authorities" (OHCHR 2012: 28).

The commitment to establishing transitional justice mechanisms, to address the legacy of violations during the conflict was formally inscribed in the Comprehensive Peace Accord (CPA), signed between the Seven Party Alliance (SPA) and the then Communist Party of Nepal-Maoists (CPN-Maoist) in September 2006, and later reiterated in the Interim Constitution of Nepal 2007. However, the proposed mechanisms including a Truth and Reconciliation Commission (TRC) and a Commission of Inquiry on Disappearances (CID) took nearly a decade to materialize, owing to an open confrontation between successor governments and the civil society backed victims, national and international human rights organizations, and sections of the diplomatic community. At issue, were questions over the formation and power of the commissions and amnesty provisions, which continue to undermine the accountability process.

This paper, in discussing Nepal's stuttering transitional justice process, foregrounds the parallel justice initiatives taken by Nepali civil society to address impunity for human rights abuses committed during the conflict.

I

Leveraging Human Rights in Peace Process

Advocacy on human rights by Nepali groups during the conflict had succeeded in putting Nepal under the international oversight of the UN's human rights body, OHCHR, and galvanized international support in favor of human rights and democracy in Nepal. Many analysts maintain that the increased monitoring presence of the UN, the support of international aid agencies to human rights monitoring by national bodies such as the National Human Rights Commission and Nepali NGOs played a substantial role in decreasing the incidence of serious human rights violations (Frieden 2012: 100). It also played an important role in creating an environment conducive to the negotiation of a ceasefire, and the space for national actors to push a human rights and prodemocracy agenda, culminating in the April 2006 People's Movement, and the signing of the Comprehensive Peace Agreement (CPA) in November 2006 (Rawski and Sharma 2012: 175).

Consequently, the CPA makes 18 references to human rights, provides for specific rights, refers to international human rights instruments and explicit commitments to the setting up transitional justice mechanisms—TRC and CID—to root out impunity and establishing accountability. Even during the conflict, the Maoist rebels had repeatedly reiterated their commitments to abide by the

Geneva Conventions and other relevant international human rights law (Human Rights Watch 2004: 22–23). As for the government, it was obliged under the state's national laws and international treaty obligations to prosecute serious human rights offenses. Ethically and circumstantially, the signatories to the CPA were not in a position to condone human rights atrocities committed during the conflict.

In the aftermath of the CPA, national and international human rights organizations led by OHCHR and NHRC focused attention on accountability for conflict-related violations. Victims were vociferous in their demands for justice and reparation. The Supreme Court kept up the pressure, directing the government to establish transitional justice mechanisms, criminalize serious violations and provide reparations to victims (ICJ and NBA 2012). Also, international treaty monitoring bodies directed the government to provide effective remedies and take appropriate legislative measures to prevent the future commissions of crimes (UN Human Rights Committee 2011: para 9). Nepal's successive governments were not in a position to ignore these pressures.

Dilemma of Peace Versus Justice

Establishing accountability mechanisms to deal with human rights violations committed in the past is a tough task, made all the more challenging in the context of a negotiated political transition like that of Nepal. The "undefeated" armed parties to the conflict were being called upon to hold themselves accountable for human rights abuses, that is, the Maoists, who had emerged as the major political party after democratic elections and the Nepal Army which remained a powerful institution resistant to security sector reforms.

Moreover, as the peace process unfolded, other agendas claimed priority of attention, elections, and power sharing among parties, the management of arms and Maoist Combatants. The proposed Commissions were delayed and surrounded by controversies as Nepal's various governments withdrew cases against political activists, attempted to grant amnesty to those involved in serious human rights crimes and continued to defy court orders.

The "peace vs justice" (Teitel 2002: 28) dilemma that so problematically hangs over peace processes haunted the Nepali transition. On the one hand, there were a lot of victims who had suffered at the hands of the Maoists and granting blanket amnesty to the rebel leaders and cadres meant legitimizing the reprehensible crimes committed by them during the conflict. On the other hand, targeting the state security apparatus was argued as unjustifiable and the coalition of "old" political forces, the SPA, opposed the idea. The "Myth of Equivalency" as Mallinder termed it, was in operation in Nepal and the governments sought stratagems to push the issue of accountability off the track (Mallinder 2008).

The TRC process in Nepal started with the unveiling of the draft TRC bill by the Ministry of Peace and Reconstruction in June 2007. Exploiting the rhetoric of national reconciliation, the government tried to introduce blanket amnesty via a controversial clause in the draft bill for the establishment of the TRC: Sec 25. However, joint advocacy by national and international human rights organizations in Nepal pushed for the withdrawal of the bill. Fresh consultations with victims and relevant stakeholders were initiated, and a revised TRC bill was issued. The amnesty clause was dropped for certain serious violations such as murder, rape, and torture. It also retained the discretionary authority of the Attorney General, a political appointee, to determine whether to prosecute cases recommended by TRC.

In these public consultations, no separate consultations with women victims and women's groups were held. Also, there was no attention to crimes such as enforced pregnancy, enforced prostitution, and other crimes of gender-based sexual violence, which victims and human rights groups had demanded be placed in the non-amnesty category of crimes. Also, despite numerous reports of rape and other forms of sexual violence, and documented evidence of the widespread and systematic practice of torture and conflict-related trauma—these categories of victims were not included in the "interim relief" schemes.

Negotiating Accountability

Parallel to the TRC process, both the Maoists and the political parties (SPA) had agreed to publicize the whereabouts of the disappeared within sixty days of the signing of the CPA. Even after a decade this promise still remains unfulfilled. The Interim Constitution 2007

(Article 33q) had reiterated that it was the duty of the state "[t]o provide relief to the families of the victims, on the basis of the report of the Investigation Commission constituted to investigate the cases of disappearances made during the course of the conflict."

Meanwhile, the Supreme Court in response to 83 habeas corpus petitions filed by "disappeared" victim support groups, directed the government to criminalize disappearances as an offense outside amnesty provisions. The order of the Supreme Court also called upon the government to deliver on the commitment to establish a "credible, competent, impartial and fully independent commission to address the issue of the disappeared during the conflict." (SC Dahal vs GoN writ no. 3575, July 2007) Under pressure, the government introduced a draft bill on Enforced Disappearances (Charge and Punishment) 2008 but was forced to withdraw it in the face of criticism by international agencies such as International Commission of Jurists (ICJ) and Nepali Members of Parliament (Advocacy Forum 2009).

Victim families assisted by human rights organization, like Advocacy Forum, began registering First Information Report (FIR), demanding criminal investigation, while the courts started issuing directives to involved authorities. However, the police, the army, government agencies and the former rebels routinely defied court orders. Instead, the government acted as a protective shield by defending war crimes and gross violations as politically motivated crimes, withdrawing criminal cases and awarding alleged violators with high-ranking posts and ministerial berths, promoting public officials implicated in serious violations and sending them to lucrative UN Peacekeeping Missions.

Police authorities, on their part, refused to register FIRs deferring the cases to the jurisdiction of the proposed transitional justice mechanisms (Human Rights Watch and Advocacy Forum 2008). The Nepali judiciary, which had upheld the right to speedy delivery of justice and overruled suspending justice in anticipation of a future transitional justice mechanism, began to defer to the executive's prerogative of amnesty decrees by withdrawing cases (Advocacy Forum 2010). The withdrawals were based on the Faustian clause in the CPA that committed the signatories "to withdraw accusations, claims, complaints and cases under consideration leveled against various individuals due to political reasons" (CPA: clause 5.2.7).

The government made a number of attempts to establish TRC and CID via an executive decision as done earlier in setting up

Commissions of Inquiry. But activists lobbied for a law to be enacted by Parliament with an explicit independent mandate and structure. The demand was for a victim-centric framework. In particular, human rights groups warned against victims being forced to mediate with their perpetrators in the name of reconciliation.

After the legislature parliament was dissolved in 2012, the caretaker government sought to bring in through the backdoor an ordinance on the formation of a composite Disappearance, Truth and Reconciliation Commission. Finally in 2014, the government, despite the contrary directive orders of the Supreme Court, the views of international treaty bodies and the protests of victim groups introduced a new bill and passed it as law, The Commission on Investigation of Disappeared Persons, Truth and Reconciliation Act. The process itself was alarming, as no debate in parliament was allowed, and certainly no amendments possible.

More than 230 victims of the conflict from across the country filed the writ of Mandamus in the Supreme Court of Nepal, challenging sections of the Act. They also declared a boycott of the activities of the Commissions pending the Supreme Court's verdict. Nepali human rights activists supported their call. In February 2015, the Supreme Court ruled that several sections of the Act were in breach of Nepal's constitution and its international obligations.

A year of these commissions has lapsed but the Act has not been amended. OHCHR in February 2016 announced its inability to support these mechanisms for their mandate to grant amnesty even to those involved in serious human rights violations. International law clearly sets the permissible limits on amnesty. Amnesty for genocide, war crimes, crimes against humanity, or gross violations of human rights, such as extrajudicial, summary, or arbitrary executions; torture and similar cruel, inhuman, or degrading treatment; slavery, and enforced disappearance, including gender-specific instances of these offenses is prohibited under international law (OHCHR 2009).

Alienation from the Commissions has been compounded by the government's politicized procedure of appointing the Commissioners with scant attention to their expertise, experience, or human rights credentials. As a result, the legitimacy of the work of these commissions is at stake.

II

Parallel Justice Initiatives

As the prospects of providing justice to the victims and addressing impunity through transitional justice mechanisms was not that promising, Nepal's human rights community has been helping conflict-victims seek justice nationally and internationally by adopting different advocacy tactics and strategies, keeping alive the victims' hopes of justice and not letting the space shrink further. Followings are some of the initiatives that human rights organizations, especially Advocacy Forum—Nepal, have undertaken to challenge impunity in a context where not a single perpetrator of human rights violations has been prosecuted in civilian courts.

Filing Cases before the UN Human Rights Committee

Nepal is a party to the First Optional Protocol of International Covenant on Civil and Political Rights (ICCPR), which allows individuals, whose countries are party to the ICCPR and the Protocol, to submit written communications to the UN Human Rights Committee (HRC) in case of a breach of rights guaranteed by ICCPR, after they have exhausted domestic legal remedies in the pursuit of justice. Human rights organizations have assisted victims taking cases from Nepal to the Human Rights Committee. Cases before the HRC include torture, disappearances, extrajudicial execution, and rape. Such initiatives have brought international attention to the problems of victims of human rights violations in Nepal and the denial of justice. They also have jurisprudential implications for Nepal's national legal framework.

Vetting Measures

Nepali civil society has focused on UN Peacekeeping as a means of leveraging greater attention to human rights in the performance of

Nepal's security personnel on the ground. Also, it has been a staunch advocate for a policy at the UN to screen troops serving in the UN Peacekeeping Operations. The Nepali civil society organizations requested the UN Department of Peacekeeping Operations to repatriate individual peace keepers after it became known that there was *prima facie* evidence of their involvement in serious human rights violations in Nepal, but regardless of that they had been sent on peacekeeping missions. Captain Niranjan Basnet, co-accused in the Maina Sunuwar murder case pending before the Kavre district court, was recalled from a peacekeeping mission to Chad in 2009. Deputy Superintendent of Police Basanta Kunwar, against whom a case under the Torture Compensation Act was pending in the Kathmandu District Court was recalled from Liberia in August 2011. In doing this, Nepali human rights organization joined hand with three other major troop contributing countries—India, Bangladesh, and Nigeria to successfully demand screening policies for UN peace keepers (Human Rights Screening of UN Personnel, Decision No 2012/18).

Likewise, the human rights community has been successful in its advocacy of foreign embassies to deny visas to alleged human rights violators. Australian and the US authorities have refused senior Maoist politician Agni Sapkota a visa, on the basis of "serious and specific human rights allegations associated with his conduct during the insurgency" (Advocacy Forum and Human Rights Watch 2010: 10).

Although human rights groups were unable to prevent the appointments of Sapkota and Dong (another senior indicted Maoist politician) to key government positions. Human rights groups were influential in the case of promotion of one of the co-accused in Dhanusha case as chief of police. The Supreme Court directed government to devise a vetting policy to screen those involved in serious human rights violations. The Government is yet to devise a policy on vetting.

Breaking the Silence on Victims of Sexual Violence: Initiating Emblematic Cases

Nepali women and girls bore the brunt of the impact of armed conflict in Nepal. However, social, legal, cultural, and economic constraints have obliged Nepali women who experienced violence, including sexual violence to suffer in silence. Women whose men folk were disappeared, widows who were left to manage on their own—are still waiting for truth, justice and reparation. Women's access to justice is extremely limited, especially for survivors of sexual violence who are left to struggle with emotional trauma, pain of victimization and the social stigma of the aftermath. Despite the repeated promises of ending sexual violence and the adoption of National Plan of Action under UN Security Council Resolution 1325, 1820, no cases of conflict-related sexual violence has been brought to justice. On top of social stigma, the victims of sexual violence continue to face numerous hurdles, especially the statutory limitation of 35 days in filing complaints, and the rules of evidences.

There are others, the wives of the disappeared, like Purnimaya Lama whose husband Arjun was picked up by a Maoist unit allegedly led by aforementioned Agni Sapkota and disappeared. In her quest for justice, the mother of four children had to face destitution, intimidation, and frustration (AFAD 2011). However, in the case of Purnima (alias), with national remedies exhausted (the police refused to register an FIR; Supreme Court refused to order the police to investigate the case), the case was brought before the UN Human Rights Committee and is under consideration.

The problem of impunity for conflict-era crimes of sexual violations carries over post-conflict as evidenced in the case of Sita Rai which triggered the year-long public protest called "Occupy Baluwatar" in 2013. It symbolized the difficulties that victims of sexual violence face, and persisting impunity.[1]

Universal Jurisdiction

Nepali civil society's struggle to establish the victims' right to effective remedy achieved a significant success when a serving Nepali army officer, Colonel Kumar Lama, was arrested by the British police under universal jurisdiction powers provided under the CAT and Section 134 (1) of the UK Criminal Justice Act, on charges of torture alleged to have taken place in Gorusinghe Army Barracks in Kapilvastu district, Nepal during the armed conflict. This case changed the discourse on how accountability has to be dealt in relation to the conflict-related crimes of human rights violations in Nepal. Col Lama is currently awaiting trial in the UK.

Conclusion

Nepal's transitional justice process has been embroiled in controversy from the beginning, because of different expectations that different actors have from this process and lack of principled guidance on the issue. As there is no record of the positions different parties had taken while negotiating the provision of Truth and Reconciliation Commission in the text of CPA, it is not clear what was promised while agreeing to the TRC in the CPA. Perhaps the transitional justice terminology might have entered the Nepali lexicon without a nuanced understanding of what in fact it meant and whether it would address the needs of Nepal. As transitional justice is a holistic concept entailing truth seeking, prosecution, reparation, institutional reforms and guarantee of nonoccurrence, the selective use of any of these components cannot help to achieve what it is meant to achieve.

Nonetheless, even in the midst of these controversies and the contradictory positions of different actors, Nepali human rights activists are finding ways to keep the justice agenda alive, by initiating different parallel initiatives such as invoking international criminal justice system, vetting policies, special procedures under UNHRC invoking international criminal justice such as Universal Jurisdictions. These initiatives have helped not only to remove the many obstacles that victims of human rights violations face but also to develop knowledge-based jurisprudence on these issues which have far reaching implications on how Nepal should deal with its difficult past of human rights violations.

Note

1. See https://en.wikipedia.org/wiki/Occupy_Baluwatar (accessed November 10, 2016).

Bibliography

Advocacy Forum. 2009. *Bepatta Ko Kanoon ma Ke Hudaichha*. Kathmandu: Advocacy Forum.
———. 2010. *Evading Accountability by Hook and by Crook*. Kathmandu: Advocacy Forum.

Advocacy Forum and Human Rights Watch. 2010, December. "Indifference to Duty: Impunity for Crimes Committed in Nepal." Accessed December 14, 2016, http://advocacyforum.org/_downloads/indifference-to-duty-english-version.pdf

Asian Federation Against Involuntary Disappearances. 2011. "Purnimaya's Quest for Justice." Accessed November 10, 2016, https://afadsecretariat.wordpress.com/2011/06/16/364/

Frieden, Jorg. 2012. "A Donor's Perspective on Aid and Conflict." In *Nepal in Transition: From People's War to Fragile Peace*, edited by Sebstian Von Einsiedel, David M. Malone, and Suman Pradhan, 100–113. Cambridge, MA: Cambridge University Press.

Human Rights Watch. 2004, October. "Between a Hard Rock and a Hard Place: Civilians Struggle to Survive in Nepal's Civil War." Accessed December 14, 2016, https://www.hrw.org/reports/2004/nepal1004/4.htm

Human Rights Watch and Advocacy Forum. 2008. *Waiting for Justice: Unpunished Crimes from Nepal's Armed Conflict*. Accessed December 14, 2016, https://www.hrw.org/sites/default/files/reports/nepal0908web_0.pdf>

ICJ and NBA. 2012. *Transitional Justice and Right to Remedy*. Kathmandu: ICJ and NBA.

Mallinder, Louise. 2008. *"Amnesty, Human Rights and Political Transitions: Bridging the Peace and Justice Divide."* Hart Publishing.

Media Foundation. 2011. *Healing the Wounds: Stories from Nepal's Transitional Justice Process*. Kathmandu: Media Foundation.

OHCHR (Office of the High Commissioner for Human Rights). 2009. *Rule of Law, Tools for Post-Conflict State, Amnesties*. Geneva: OHCHR.

———. 2012. *Nepal Conflict Report: An Analysis of Conflict-related Violations of International Human Rights Law and International Humanitarian Law between February 1996 and 21 November 2006*. Geneva: United Nations Office of the High Commissioner for Human Rights.

Rawski, Frederick, and Mandira Sharma. 2012. "A Comprehensive Peace? Lessons from Human Rights Monitoring in Nepal." In *Nepal in Transition: From People's War to Fragile Peace*, edited by Sebastian Von Einsiedel, David M. Malone, and Suman Pradhan, 175. Cambridge, MA: Cambridge University Press.

Teitel, Rudi G. 2002. *Transitional Justice*. Oxford University Press.

UN Human Rights Committee. 2008. *Yasoda Sharma vs Nepal*, Communication No. 1469/2006, CCPR/C/94/D/1469/2006.

———. 2011. *Ywraj Giri vs Nepal*. Communication No. 1761/2008, CCPR/C/101/D/1761/2008.

15

No Peace without Justice in Afghanistan

Najla Ayubi

In the last 35 years of war and conflict, all of Afghanistan has been affected by violence both directly and indirectly. In the context of war, Afghan citizens, women, men, and children suffered the violence of torture, harassment, rape and sexualized assaults, massacres, looting, and impoverishment. War destroyed Afghanistan's infrastructure and its governing institutions, including the parliament and the judiciary. The experience of violence was accentuated by ethnic and gendered identities.

Afghanistan is a multiethnic and traditional society with a long history of governance along tribal lines by a weak central state. The conflict reinforced social, political, economic, religious, and ethnic fault lines, dividing the society and creating a lack of trust among Afghans. In addition, the long years of war and violence and the resulting unstable political and economic situation had a particularly cruel impact on women. Traditionally, Afghan women have been discriminated, systematically marginalized, and accorded a subordinate status. The ideological framework of the Taliban further entrenched historically rooted gender-discrimination to create "gender apartheid," and heightened violence against women and the violation of their being human.

Challenges to Accountability

After the fall of Taliban through the intervention of the international forces and the signing of the Bonn Agreement in 2001, it was expected that the peace process would provide for accountability mechanisms to address war-related human rights violations, and lay the foundation for restoration of the rule of law, and reconciliation with justice. But unfortunately that opportunity was missed. No attention was given to addressing past war crimes. Feminist legal activists observed that, "The Bonn Agreement, the roadmap for the first five year of the state building process, did not include a framework for transitional justice" (Ayub, Kouvo, and Sooka 2009). Instead, it provided for an Independent Human Rights Commission to be established. With Transitional Justice not incorporated in the design of the Bonn Process, decision makers—national and international—with their eyes set on working out power sharing arrangements (including with ex-warlords), found it politically expedient to bypass accountability and reconciliation.

This was despite documented evidence by the Afghanistan Independent Human Rights Commission (AIHRC) demonstrating that the majority of the Afghan people wanted accountability. Nationwide consultations distilled in the AIHRC publication "A Call for Justice" revealed that an overwhelming majority of the population wanted justice. The AIHRC Consultation had covered more than 4,000 respondents and held 200 focus group discussions. It was the first time the Afghans had been asked about their experience of the conflict and their opinions of how Afghanistan should move forward. The voice of the people of Afghanistan showed that 86.8 percent wanted the enforcement of justice, 20.2 percent wanted justice through reconciliation, 49.1 percent wanted justice through the prosecution of the criminals and 84.8 percent of the people wanted enforcement of justice carried out through restitution of the victims (AIHRC 2005a).

The AIHRC Report revealed that 70 percent of Afghans or their family members have been victims of war crimes and human rights violations. AIHRC assessment was that "the number of victims have been huge, more than a million. In Kabul alone, more than 100,000 people were killed during the years of the civil war during 1992–96." *The Survey showed Afghans singling out reconciliation as one of the most important and fundamental components of the peace process.* It corroborated the AIHRC's advocacy that without justice and accountability, human rights will become nothing more than rhetoric (AIHRC 2005b).

But these victims were powerless to pursue justice against the warlords who were in power not only within the government system but also in their local communities. Instead of a comprehensive peace and justice program, the government of President Karzai undertook some small initiatives. President Hamid Karzai responded to the AIHRC report by announcing in December 2006, the Action for Peace, Justice and Reconciliation to take forward some of the recommendations of "A Call for Justice" report. The Action Plan identified five major activities to be completed within the ambitious time frame of three years: (a) acknowledgment of the suffering of the Afghan people, (b) ensuring credible and accountable state institutions, (c) truth-seeking and documentation, (d) promotion of reconciliation and national unity, and (e) establishment of effective and reasonable accountability mechanisms.

In particular, the Action Plan emphasized the participation of women in the consultations for establishing truth-seeking mechanisms. In these consultative processes with civil society, academia, community leaders, and religious leaders, special consideration was to be shown to enable women to participate especially on "how to deal with gender-based violence and other crimes against women." Unfortunately this gendered aspect of the action plan was not implemented by the government.

Political will apart, lack of integrity in the judicial system and the poor capacity of the justice sector presented a huge challenge to investigate and prosecute war crimes. The Action Plan failed to incorporate in its implementation structure, the vital need to reform the judiciary. Further undermining the possibility of ensuring justice for past crimes, the Afghan House of Representatives approved the "Peace and Reconciliation Bill" (the amnesty law). It stipulated that all those who were accused of the crimes of the past decades including Mullah Omar and Gulbuddin Hekmatyar should not be prosecuted, the dignity of the Mujahideen should be respected and their contribution appreciated.

The UNAMA and the international community were against the passing of such an amnesty law, but in the larger interest of maintaining their relationship with the Afghan government they did not persist in their opposition and accepted the policy and power games of the Afghan government. In the end there was not enough political pressure to support the voice of voiceless, the victims of grave human rights violations.

It was the AIHRC—a nongovernmental organization—and other local and traditional civil society organizations which, along with the national and international media, kept the voices of the victims alive. This was despite the threats that these organizations, directly and indirectly, received from the accused. For instance, AIHRC came under intense hostile pressure over its report "Conflict Mapping in Afghanistan Since 1978," (2012) which detailed the locations and details of 180 mass graves of civilians or prisoners, many of the sites secret and none of them yet excavated properly. The figures accused in the report of playing a role in mass killings included some of the most powerful figures in Afghanistan's government and ethnic factions, including the Northern Alliance, that fought the Taliban in 2001. The Commissioner associated with the Report, Nader Nadery, was removed from the AIHRC and the publication suppressed. While the UN supported the publication of the mass graves report, a US Embassy official was quoted by the media as saying "it would open up old wounds" (Nordland 2012).

Gendered Consequences

In the three decades of war and political crisis, women and children were the majority of victims affected by the war crimes in Afghanistan. The failure to establish accountability mechanisms for securing even minimal justice has had serious implications for the security and life chances of women. As indicated above, one of the main reasons preventing access to justice was the capture of public institutions by powerful people and groups who were accused of war crimes. They were able to stop the effective functioning of the rule of law in these cases. Also, gender-based crimes are particularly sensitive from a cultural, religious, and social point of view. Consequently, they often go unreported. Women and their families preferred not to report crimes like mass rape, sexual violence, sexual abuse, forced marriage, forced pregnancy or situations in which women were forced to offer sex to survive, that is, in exchange for food, shelter, and protection.

The social impact of the conflict for women's security and rights has been particularly damaging. There has been a dramatic deterioration in the social and ethical values in Afghan society, especially in regard to women. The impunity with which women have been killed, kidnapped, and publicly harassed by armed groups, and the failure of the official justice institutions to investigate these cases has made women much more vulnerable to violence. According to "Afghanistan Rights Monitor," the Afghan Government has done almost nothing inside Afghanistan to effectively prosecute the murderers of Afghan women and girls. The president has compromised justice and accountability to keep his warlord allies satisfied. "In some cases the so-called 'unknown armed men', the second largest category identified as responsible for killing of women leaders and activists, are hidden behind some of the most powerful warlords who are well represented in the government" (Nemat and Samadi 2012).

The High Peace Council includes powerful warlords closely affiliated to the armed groups. The Afghan peace process roadmap lacks any vetting process and talks only about reintegration, not about reconciliation. For instance, the Provincial Peace Committees set up by the HPC over the last few years have focused on integrating not insurgents but largely criminals. According to a survey undertaken by the Peace Training and Research Organization (PTRO) tiled "Unheard Voices," many respondents questioned the credibility of the reintegration program. More than 50 percent of all respondents saw the reintegration process as mostly benefiting criminals (PTRO 2012). Questioned on whether people supported the peace process or not, the survey showed that there is widespread support for the national peace process with an overwhelming 90 percent hopeful that it would be successful. But the PTRO survey also showed that "40 percent feared it could result in a loss of rights instead." This fear is particularly acute for women in such insecure provinces as Helmand. In Marjah district, 90 percent of women respondents voiced fears of a likely loss of rights. Values seen as under threat included women's equality, freedom of expression, and democracy.

In the last few years, women's security has been at greater risk. The government, by incorporating into its security network additional layers of poorly trained and irresponsible armed groups, has made women even more vulnerable. In particular, the setting up of the

Afghan Local Police and Afghan Community Police, and distribution of weapons to these forces has increased insecurity. The ALP is not as institutionalized as the ANP, in terms of recruitment policy, training, hierarchy, reporting, and accountability mechanisms (Keizer 2013). Increasingly, media reports have drawn attention to increasing incidents of women becoming victims of rape, kidnapping, murder, and facing sexual violence and harassment. Perpetrators were either powerful local commanders, local police, or affiliated with some illegal armed groups or members of the Afghan parliament. Moreover, even cases with a high level of media attention were not investigated properly. Unfortunately, the judicial system does not have a monitoring mechanism to ensure women's access to justice.

Accessing Justice for VAW

The implementation and enforcement of the Elimination of Violence Against Women (EVAW) law has been an important achievement in the struggle for rights and justice for Afghan women. In the past six years since the EVAW law was passed by a legislative decree of the president in 2009 (though not legally ratified by parliament), the law criminalized 23 acts of violence against women, including child marriage, forced marriage, rape, and physical abuse, while also identifying punishment for the perpetrators. However, misguided efforts to get Parliament to ratify the bill in 2013 produced a huge setback, with conservative parliamentarians arguing that some of the provisions of the law were not Islamic. The international community's disengagement from Afghanistan can only strengthen these conservative forces. Although weakened, the EVAW still remains a potentially empowering tool for women. In March 2014, the government published its first report on the Elimination of Violence Against Women in Afghanistan, registering 4505 incidents (March 2012–13) of which 3,396 constituted acts liable to prosecution under the EVAW law (UNAMA–OHCHR 2015).

The 2014 civil society monitoring report on UNSCR 1325 finds that there is a visible increase in the number of reported cases to AIHRC, and the slight improvement of the implementation of the EVAW law could be a result of civil society efforts to improve women's access to justice (UNSCR 1325 in Afghanistan 2014). It underscored the importance of enactment of the EVAW law and the independent workings of the AIHRC.

Also, AIHRC remains an important institution for protecting women against the violation of their human rights, especially to bodily integrity. In 2013, AIHRC stated that reported cases of domestic abuse have increased over the past years. In addition to household violence, there has been an unprecedented number of high-profile attacks on female government officials and police officers. For instance, a female member of the Afghan National Police (ANP) in Helmand province died from wounds suffered in a targeted attack by unidentified gunmen. The officer had replaced a previous high-ranking female officer who was killed under similar circumstances back in August 2013.

Amidst much that is making for greater insecurity, there also is a renewed hope of new president and chief executive who promises to be more sensitive to the challenges faced by Afghan women. Upon President Ghani's initiative, a regulation was drafted on the prohibition of harassment of women in the public sphere. In conjunction with the Government's ongoing review of the Criminal Code, there have been proposals to integrate criminal provisions of the EVAW law into the revised Criminal Code.

One of the basic issues affecting the meaningful implementation of laws for ensuring women's rights and security, is the plural existence of three different legal systems in Afghanistan's justice sector: the constitutional law, *Sharia* and customary laws. When women face violence, there is no specified place to report their case. Sometimes they turn to the informal justice systems. Here, they rarely secure redress as most of the decisions are based on extremely patriarchal and even misogynist customary laws, or based on a misinterpretation of the Sharia.

Even the constitutional laws applicable in the government's juridical system are often applied in an ineffectual manner and with little uniformity. There are no specific plans to bring in legislative and judicial reforms, and apply a uniform system of accountability. In particular, there is no integrity (fair process, transparency, and consistency) in the selection process of the female judges or in the Supreme Court staff recruitment process. Also, the high-advisory council lacks representation of women. It is argued that women cannot be appointed to such high-level positions in the Supreme Court, because the Sharia does not allow it. However, in July 2015, in a landmark decision President Ashraf Ghani appointed Anisa Rassouli to be Afghanistan's first female Supreme Court judge. Later she fell short of nine votes during the parliamentary vote of confidence and failed to be appointed. Clerics and conservatives criticized the choice of Rassouli and claimed that only men were fit to sit in the highest court in the country, and a woman was not fit to try criminal cases. With Rassouli's appointment one could have hoped for some overhaul in a sexist legal system. The battle is on for the president to nominate another female as a Supreme Court judge.

Overall, women's participation in the justice system has improved in the past years, especially in comparison with other, more sluggish sectors such as the security sector (UNSCR 1325 in Afghanistan 2014: 17). However, many women in the judicial system feel that women are uncomfortable about reporting violence, and confronting a law and order system that is corrupt financially and politically. They are only too aware that it is men who are able to manipulate the system and there is very little space for women judges and professionals to practice their knowledge or expertise (Table 15.1).

Also, in a context in which there is little political will on the government's side to back the AIHRC to support implementation of the laws and regulations related to women, progress is bound to be slow, if not even regressed. Developments such as the nomination

Table 15.1 Index of Women's Participating in the Justice Sector in 2013 and 2014

	Number of Women	*Number of Men*	*Percentage of Women*
2013			
Judges	139	1,654	8
Lawyers	386	1,575	20
2014			
Judges	182	1,620	10
Lawyers	484	1,735	22

Source: The Supreme Court and the Afghanistan Independent Bar Association (AIBA) (December 2013 and September 2014).

of ex-mujahideen or former members of the Taliban movement (Mawlawi Abdul Rahman Hotak) as Human Rights Commissioners reveals the government's lack of commitment to human rights. These people cannot be expected to believe in human rights issues and particularly in women's rights. According to the UN Human Rights Commissioner Navi Pillay, such persons fail to meet eligibility standards of independence, popular trust, political impartiality and human rights commitment (Abrahimkhil 2013).

Mounting pressures from a weak government, resurgent warlords, and illegal armed groups are weakening the capacity of the AIHRC and the governing structure of accountability for human rights violations. This has grave consequences for Afghan women's access to justice, especially in a context of deteriorating security and greater vulnerability.

Bibliography

Abrahimkhil, Shakeela. 2013. "UN Human Rights Chief Worried About Afghan Regress." Accessed November 10, 2016, http://tolonews.com/en/afghanistan/11963-un-human-rights-chief-worried-about-afghan-regress

AIHRC. Accessed November 10, 2016, http://www.aihrc.org.af/en/annual-reports/527/aihrc-annual-report-1-january-2005-31-december-2005.html

———. "Action Plan of the Government of the Islamic Republic of Afghanistan." Accessed November 10, 2016, http://www.aihrc.org.af/media/files/Reports/Thematic%20reports/rep29_1_05call4justice.pdf

———. 2005a. "Call for Justice: A National Consultation on Past Human Rights Violations in Afghanistan." Accessed November 10, 2016, http://www.aihrc.org.af/media/files/Reports/Thematic%20reports/rep29_1_05call4justice.pdf

———. 2005b. "Annual Report." Accessed November 10, 2016, http://www.aihrc.org.af/en/annual-reports/527/aihrc-annual-report-1-january-2005-31-december-2005.html

Ayub, Fatima, Sari Kouvo, and Yasmin Sooka. February 2009. "Addressing Gender-specific Violations in Afghanistan." *International Center for Transitional Justice*. Accessed December 01, 2016, http://ictj.org/sites/default/files/ICTJ-Afghanistan-Gender-Violations-2009-English.pdf

Keizer, Cornlieke. 2013. "In Focus: The Rights of Afghan Women during the Transition Period." Accessed November 10, 2016, http://ihrfg.wordpress.com/2013/06/07/in-focus-the-rights-of-afghan-women-during-the-transition-period-cordaids-preliminary-research-findings/

Ministry of Women's Affairs, Government of Afghanistan. 2014. Kabul: EVAW. Accessed November 10, 2016, http://mowa.gov.af/Content/files/EVAW%20Law%20Report_Final_English_17%20%20March%202014.pdf

Nemat, Ozala Ashraf, and Ajmal Samadi. 2012, December. "Forgotten Heroes: Afghan Women Leaders Killed in Impunity Ignored in Justice." *Afghanistan Rights Monitor.* Accessed November 10, 2016, http://www.arm.org.af/site_files/13551528791.pdf

Nordland, Rod. 2012, July 22. "Top Afghans Tied to '90s Carnage, Researchers Say." *New York Times.* Accessed November 10, 2016, http://www.nytimes.com/2012/07/23/world/asia/key-afghans-tied-to-mass-killings-in-90s-civil-war.html?_r=0

PTRO. 2012. "Unheard Voices—Afghan Views on the Challenges of the Peace Process—A Report from the Peace Training & Research Organization." Accessed November 10, 2016, http://afghanistan101.blogspot.co.uk/2012/03/unheard-voices-afghan-views-on-peace.html

UNSC Resolution 1325 in Afghanistan. 2014. "Civil Society Monitoring Report 2014." Kabul: *Afghan Women's Network.* Accessed November 10, 2016, UN%20Security%20Council%20Resolution%201325%20in%20%20%20Afghanistan%20-%20November%2018.pdf

UNAMA–OHCHR. 2015. "Justice through the Eyes of Afghan Women." Accessed November 10, 2016, https://unama.unmissions.org/Portals/UNAMA/UNAMA-OHCHR/UNAMA_OHCHR_Justice_through_eyes_of_Afghan_women_-_15_April_2015.pdf

16

State Intervention to Transitional Justice in Sri Lanka

*Bhavani Fonseka**

Sri Lanka faces many questions in the aftermath of a near three-decade war. Is reconciliation possible? Will the truth ever be known? What of accountability? In defining a post-war identity and exploring ways of moving forward, questions of truth, justice, accountability, and reconciliation are crucial. More than six years after the war ended, opinions vary as to what is best for Sri Lanka to bridge the gaps resulting from the brutal war.

The joint statement by the secretary general of the United Nations and the president of Sri Lanka at the end of the war in May 2009 remains an important marker, in that it was the first recognition of the need to address past violations: "The Secretary-General underlined the importance of an accountability process for addressing violations of international humanitarian and human rights law. The Government will take measures to address those grievances" (un.org, sg 2159). This was subsequently followed by resolutions at the United Nations Human Rights Council (UNHRC) and a human rights investigation

---

*This chapter was written in 2013, with some updates made in 2016 to reflect recent developments in transitional justice in Sri Lanka.

by the Office of High Commissioner for Human Rights (OHCHR) into Sri Lanka's past abuses.

International Pressure as a Catalyst for Transitional Justice

The former President Mahinda Rajapaksa's government used the term "home grown" to present their ideal model of transitional justice, indicative of the preference toward a national process over an international one. The term "home grown" emerged in the midst of intense pressure for an international investigation into violations perpetrated by both the Sri Lanka government and the Liberation Tigers of Tamil Eelam (LTTE) during the war. The result was the establishment of the Lessons Learnt and Reconciliation Commission (LLRC) in 2010, another addition to Sri Lanka's long list of Commissions of Inquiry, none of which have resulted in genuine truth and justice for the victims.

The failure of the LLRC led to continuing pressure for more effective accountability mechanisms, and is internationally reflected in the UNHRC's four resolutions 2012–15, on the need for a credible judicial process. In 2014 in particular, the UNHRC in a contentiously debated resolution exhorted the need for a "comprehensive approach to transitional justice incorporating the full range of judicial and non-judicial measures," including individual prosecutions, reparations, truth-seeking, institutional reform, and vetting of public employees and officials (A/HRC/RES/25/1, preamble). It resulted in the initiation of a human rights investigation on Sri Lanka during the same period covered as the LLRC. The Report of the OHCHR Investigation on Sri Lanka (OISL) indicted the widespread and systemic nature of violations which point to the possible perpetration of international crimes by both sides (A/HRC/30/CRP.2).

The election of President Maithripala Sirisena in January 2015 and the promise of greater openness toward instituting truth and justice measures saw the UNHRC adopt a consensus resolution titled "Promoting reconciliation, accountability and human rights in Sri Lanka" in October 2015 (2015 Resolution). The 2015 Resolution provided a framework on transitional justice including the establishment of a credible judicial process, with international participation. Although the Government of Sri Lanka backed the resolution, there is criticism of it being too internationally interventionist by the Sinhala fundamentalists and not sufficiently international by some sections of the Tamil polity.

This chapter focuses on past state interventions at truth and justice, with questions raised whether transitional justice is possible in Sri Lanka. The chapter briefly comments on the role of women in different processes and makes the case that women are often sidelined or ignored in such initiatives of the state. Despite this, women play an active role engaging with state and nonstate initiatives in the search for and pursuit of truth and justice. The chapter also briefly examines what is needed if transitional justice is to be viable in the "polarized" context of Sri Lanka (Uyangoda 2012). It argues for much needed reform and attention to gender in exploring viable modalities to address the past and options for the future.

Commissions of Inquiry and Other State Initiatives

Prior to examining recent initiatives, it is important to briefly note some key developments during the war in terms of truth, justice, and accountability. Sri Lanka has a history of Commissions of Inquiry and Committees established by successive governments to deal with political violence. For instance, Commissions of Inquiry into the Involuntary Removal or Disappearance of Persons was appointed in December 1994, followed by an "All Island" Commission in 1998 (Human Rights Watch 2008). The Commissions of Inquiry emphasized the excessive use of state power and identified several suspected perpetrators. Another commission titled "The Presidential Commission on Ethnic Violence" was appointed in August 2001 to investigate ethnic violence during the period 1981–84, a period not covered by the previous four commissions (UN Human Rights Committee Oct 18, 2002).

Former President Rajapaksa's government also appointed several commissions and committees to investigate and inquire into human rights violations (CPA 2012a). In 2006, a commission was established to investigate and inquire into 16 cases of past violations. A novel component of the investigation was the appointment of an International Independent Group of Eminent Persons (IIGEP) to monitor and observe commission proceedings. Several questions regarding the flawed process were raised by civil society, international organizations, and the IIGEP, including the independence and impartiality of the process, state interference, and the lack of witness and victim protection. The IIGEP concluded its work within a year of appointment, critiquing the process for a "lack of political will" by the government to investigate human rights. Two cases investigated by this Commission of Inquiry—the killing of five youth in Trincomalee in January 2006 and the killing of 17 aid workers in Muttur in August 2006—continue to receive widespread national and international attention. A decade after, accountability for these and many other crimes elude Sri Lanka.

Cases where justice was possible for serious human rights crimes stand out as the rare exception such as in the abduction, rape, and murder of 18 year old Tamil student, Krishanthi Kumaraswamy and the subsequent murder of her mother, brother, and a neighbor in Jaffna in 1996. The Krishanthi Kumaraswamy case and the Embilipitiya cases are two cases in which perpetrators were held accountable (Pinto-Jayawardhena 2010). The Embilipitiya case involved the enforced disappearance of 32 school children in 1989–90, as a part of the counter terror strategy against the JVP insurgency (Hoole 2014). Most recently, the conviction in 2015 of four soldiers in the rape case in Vishvamadu area demonstrates justice is possible, but at a cost with many challenges with investigations and prosecutions including protection issues (Women's Action Network 2015).

Most state initiatives in the past were seen as tokenism, affecting no real change on the ground toward realizing truth, justice, and accountability. Moreover, independent institutions became increasingly politicized and investigations were delayed. Promises of legislative and policy reform such as the introduction of witness and victim protection mechanism were delayed for years, with the enactment of legislation only happening in 2015. Despite an Authority being established to address protection issues, concerns still remain. Questions are also raised about the necessary expertise, capacity, and political will for establishing an effective transitional justice process. All this has contributed to a culture of impunity, further exacerbated by delays in introducing the promised reforms.

Women in the Search for Truth and Justice

In examining the role of women in state initiatives, it is important to consider women's participation in previous investigations and inquiries as well as their engagement with the overall justice process. The "All Island" Commission established to look into involuntary removal or disappearance of persons was headed by Manouri Muttetuwagama, a prominent female civil society activist. Since then women have been appointed to most commissions, though questions must be posed as to whether women are appointed more as a tokenistic effort to demonstrate gender presence or with the actual intention of incorporating a gender perspective.

Furthermore, past commissions and committees witnessed a significant number of women engaging with such processes, largely due to mobilization by women's groups and civil society. However, the challenges have been numerous as in the case of LLRC process. Security issues including fear of reprisals and practical difficulties inhibit women's inability to participate. Several women who came before the LLRC reported subsequent harassment by the military and intelligence agencies for reporting disappearances. Similar concerns were raised with the subsequent commission on missing persons known as the Paranagama Commission.

In addition to security issues, affected communities including women had to travel long distances and face hardships so as to attend the public sessions of the LLRC, with no guarantee of being heard. Many who made it to the LLRC public sessions in their areas complained of limited time and lack of a process to sufficiently take note of their grievances. The LLRC has been critiqued for its flawed process and analysis, however on a more positive note, there is the LLRC's acknowledgment of the challenges faced by women, including women-headed households.

In discussing women's participation in transitional justice mechanisms, it is important to examine it within the larger context of Sri Lankan women's activism in search of their "disappeared" loved ones, and their demand for accountability during the war years. The Mother's Front in Sri Lanka emerged in response to the disappearances, abductions, and killings during the 1980s. Many other initiatives came into being during the war and post-war period. The post-war period has seen that activism continue, with women in search of loved ones engaging with state initiatives such as the LLRC and going to court. For example, in 2013, thirteen women filed habeas corpus cases in Vavuniya petitioning the courts on the disappearances of their family members, a brave move by women who continue to undergo immense difficulties in their search for truth and justice. This case is one of the many initiatives taken by women to continue to keep the issue of past abuses alive, and to engage with state initiatives in the pursuit of truth and justice.

Post-war State Interventions

Since the 2009 joint statement of the UN and the government acknowledging the need for accountability in post-war Sri Lanka, calls for independent investigations have persisted by national and international groups. Ultimately, it resulted in the United Nations Secretary General appointing a Panel of Experts (POE) to advise him on whether war crimes and crimes against humanity had occurred during the war. The Sri Lankan government insisted on a home grown solution and established the LLRC.

Although the LLRC was constituted in response to calls for investigation, its mandate had no real investigative powers. Established under the Commissions of Inquiry Act, its mandate included inquiring into root causes of war (*Gazette Extraordinary* 2010). LLRC set up in June 2010 held public and private hearings across Sri Lanka. However, one of its major weaknesses was the question of independence of its commissioners. For example, the chair of the LLRC was a former Attorney General and a member of the then government's delegations defending government policies abroad (Amnesty International 2011). Also, of the LLRC's eight commissioners, only one was a woman.

The shortcomings of the LLRC resulted in several key actors refusing to make formal submissions in person (CPA 2012b). Many others, including people directly affected by the war and living outside of Colombo, made written and personal submissions. In the North and East, the LLRC only had a few days of public sittings in certain locations. Regardless of the difficulties, large numbers made representations. Notwithstanding the flaws in the process, the need to know the truth, seek justice, and reparations resulted in a significant number of people coming forward. In the absence of any other process at that time in Sri Lanka, the LLRC was seen by many as the only option to find loved ones and obtain justice.

Frustration is high with the lack of progress made since the LLRC report was handed to the then government. A statement by a woman who went before the LLRC captures the sentiment shared by many:

> We went to the LLRC hoping that they will give us an answer, all we got was a report, what do I do with a report? Show it to my child and say here is you[r] father? [Women's Action Network March 2013]

Confronted with mounting dissatisfaction, the then government fell back on its practiced strategy of producing documents to fend off criticism. A National Action Plan to implement the LLRC was subsequently introduced. The National Action Plan contained timelines and identified government actors tasked with the implementation of specific recommendations (Fonseka, Ganeshathasan, and Raheem 2012). One recommendation that did not require significant effort was to sing the National Anthem in both Sinhala and Tamil languages. Another was to share detainee lists with family members. Nearly six years after the war ended and three years since the LLRC report was made public, this was one of the many recommendations not implemented. The National Anthem was sung in both Sinhala and Tamil languages at an official event at the Independence Day celebration on February 4, 2016, sending a symbolic message of reconciliation.

In 2013, the then President Rajapaksa proposed a three-member commission on disappearances, another initiative seen by many as an attempt to allay criticism for inaction on the ground (*Reuters* 2013). The three-member Presidential Commission of Inquiry into Complaints of Abductions and Disappearances (Paranagama Commission), has two women commissioners. At the time of writing, the Paranagama Commission had received around 24,000 complaints and was reported to be finalizing their work. This chapter has already briefly discussed some of the previous commissions appointed by previous governments to deal with disappearances. More recent initiatives of the government have all been Colombo-centric with limited presence in the affected areas. This contributes to the affected communities not having ownership of the process.

State interventions have not been limited to Commissions of Inquiry. Several committees and advisers have been appointed to focus on different issues of transitional justice and reconciliation by successive governments. Despite these efforts, there has been limited progress as regarding the four pillars of transitional justice.

Since the present government came into office, the 2015 Resolution provides a framework on transitional justice. At the time of writing, the draft legislation to establish the Office of Missing Persons was approved by the cabinet of ministers and it is to be seen when and how the OMP will operate. Similarly, the government is committed to establish a Truth and Reconciliation Commission, a hybrid court with special counsel and an Office for Reparations. The present government also appointed in 2015 the Office of National Unity and Reconciliation (ONUR) headed by former President Chandrika Kumaratunge. The ONUR is meant to focus on different issues relevant to reconciliation, including women's issues and livelihoods. It is to be seen how these institutional interventions will work with existing line ministries and other entities in furthering transitional justice. 2015 also witnessed the present government establishing a National Centre for Female Headed Households, but information available on its mandate is too limited to make any assessment. The existing and proposed mechanisms and other commitments at reform are ambitious, but it is to be seen whether they will break with the past and deliver on transitional justice, and if gender perspectives will be considered.

Transitional Justice: Is it Viable in Sri Lanka?

The 2015 Resolution provides a framework that addresses the four pillars of transitional justice. The primary responsibility is with the Government of Sri Lanka to take action in a meaningful way. The OISL Report asserted that "the design of any mechanisms, such as a truth-seeking mechanism or future institution to deal with disappearances, must be through a process of genuine, informed and participatory consultation, especially with victims and their families" (OHCHR 2015: para 1274). More contentiously, it urged the need to go beyond a domestic accountability mechanism and examine the possibility of hybrid special courts integrating international judges, prosecutors, lawyers, and investigators (ibid.: para 1278). The 2015 Resolution on Sri Lanka similarly calls for the international participation in a domestic accountability mechanism.

There is now a considerable opening of space to discuss issues relevant to transitional justice and reconciliation. Compared to the time when there was limited public discourse and the "home grown" model was promoted by the then government, there is presently vibrant debate on transitional justice including divisions with the composition of an accountability mechanism. In a survey conducted in 2016, 47.3 percent of Sri Lankans stated mechanisms should be an exclusively domestic one, 37.3 percent indicated that the mechanism should be hybrid and 9.2 percent stated it should be an exclusively international one (CPA 2016). The Government must engage with a cross section of society, including victims, in the design and implementation of policy, legislation, and mechanisms. This should be done in partnership with nonstate actors including victim groups, ensuring the process is inclusive and transparent.

The lack of a genuine effort at addressing transitional justice by successive governments can be attributed to "a lack of political will" to address past violations. There is now the promise of greater political commitment on the need for accountability and it is to be seen how the present government adheres to and implements its own commitments. However, a major inhibiting factor remains the weakness in the legal and policy framework which requires urgent reform, including amending legislation to incorporate international crimes. The government needs to ensure that the domestic legal framework is in line with international standards. In addition, attention must be on building the capacity of officials and others who are likely to be involved in transitional justice, ensuring the required expertise is brought in to deal with investigations and related issues.

More than seven years after the war ended, much needs to be done toward reconciliation. The government of President Maithripala Sirisena has committed to an ambitious roadmap. The coming months and years will be indicative as to whether the present government is willing and able to keep to its promises and whether there will be gender sensitivity in the design and implementation of processes and mechanisms. In moving forward, one must remember that the victim's right to truth, justice, and reparations cannot be ignored. Failing to heed to their calls will result in the promise of peace and reconciliation being mere token words.

Bibliography

2011. *Report of the Lessons Learnt and Reconciliation Commission.* Accessed November 30, 2016, http://www.defence.lk/warcrimes/lessons_learnt_and_reconciliation_commission_final_report.html

2011. *Report of the Secretary–General's Panel of Experts on Accountability in Sri Lanka.* Accessed November 30, 2016, http://www.un.org/News/dh/infocus/Sri_Lanka/POE_Report_Full.pdf

Amnesty International. 2011. "When Will They Get Justice? Failures of Sri Lanka's Lessons Learnt and Reconciliation Commission." Accessed November 30, 2016, https://www.amnesty.org/en/documents/ASA37/008/2011/si/

———. 2013, August 5. "Sri Lanka: Investigators of Alleged Army Killings of Protesters Should be Truly Independent." Accessed November 10, 2016, http://www.amnesty.org/en/news/sri-lanka-investigators-alleged-army-killings-protesters-should-be-truly-independent-2013-08-05

CPA (Centre for Policy Alternatives). 2012a. *A List of Commissions of Inquiry and Committees Appointed by the Government of Sri Lanka (2006–2012).* Colombo: CPA.

———. 2012b. *Statement on the Release of the LLRC Report.* Otawa, Ontaria: CPA.

———. 2016. *Survey on Democracy in Post-war Sri Lanka, Social Indicator—Centre for Policy Alternatives.* Otawa, Colombo: CPA.

Fernando, Ruki. "Disappearances in Sri Lanka and the Visit of the UN Working Group on Disappearances." Accessed November 10, 2016, https://rukiiiii.wordpress.com/2015/11/12/disappearances-in-sri-lanka-and-the-visit-of-the-un-working-group-on-disappearances/

Fonseka, Bhavani, Luwie Ganeshathasan, and Mirak Raheem. 2012, August. *Commentary on the National Plan of Action to Implement the Recommendations of the LLRC.* Colombo: CPA.

Human Rights Watch. 2008. "Recurring Nightmare: State Responsibility for 'Disappearances' and Abductions in Sri Lanka." Accessed November 30, 2016, https://www.hrw.org/report/2008/03/05/recurring-nightmare/state-responsibility-disappearances-and-abductions-sri-lanka

Hoole, Rajan. 2014, May 9. "Embilipitiya Schoolboys' Affair—The Thin End of the Wedge." *Colombo Telegraph.* Accessed November 10, 2016, https://www.colombotelegraph.com/index.php/embilipitiya-schoolboys-affair-the-thin-end-of-the-wedge/

OHCHR. February 2013. *Report of the Office of the United Nations High Commissioner for Human Rights on Advice and Technical Assistance for the Government of Sri Lanka on Promoting Reconciliation and Accountability in Sri Lanka, 22nd Session—Human Rights Council.* Geneva: OHCHR.

―――. 2015. *OHCHR Investigation on Sri Lanka* (OSIL). Geneva: OHCHR.

Pinto-Jayawardhena, Kishali. 2010. *Post War Justice in Sri Lanka: Rule of Law, the Criminal Justice System and Commissions of Inquiry.* International Commission of Jurists.

Reuters. 2013, July 26. "Sri Lanka's President Orders Probe into War-time Disappearances." Accessed November 10, 2016, http://www.reuters.com/article/2013/07/26/us-srilanka-rights-idUSBRE96P0LC20130726

UN. 2009. "Joint Statement by UN Secretary-General, Government of Sri Lanka." Accessed November 10, 2016, http://www.un.org/News/Press/docs/2009/sg2151.doc.htm

UNHRC Resolutions on Sri Lanka 2012, 2013, 2014 and 2015.

Uyangoda, J. 2012. "Healing after War: Thinking beyond the Solitudes." In *Healing the Wounds: Rebuilding Sri Lanka after the War*, edited by D. Herath and K. T. Silva. Kandy: International Center of Ethnic Studies, pp. 18–32.

Women's Action Network. March 2013. "Militarized North-East Sri Lanka: Muslim and Tamil Women Systematically Crushed by Lawlessness and Expropriation," Statement by the Women's Action Network. Assessed November 30, 2016, http://srilankabrief.org/2013/03/militarized-north-east-sri-lanka-muslim-and-tamil-women-systematically-crushed-by-lawlessness-and-expropriation/

―――. 2015, October. "Statement on the Vishvamadu Rape Case." Accessed November 30, 2016, http://www.tamilguardian.com/files/File/Womens%20Action%20Network/WAN%20statement%20on%20Vishvamadhu%20rape%20case%2007Oct2015.pdf

About the Editor and Contributors

Editor

Rita Manchanda is an established writer, scholar-researcher, and human rights activist specializing in conflicts and peace-building in South Asia with particular attention to vulnerable and marginalized groups, that is, women, minorities, indigenous peoples, and forcibly displaced persons.

Professor Manchanda has over 15 years of experience as a Senior Executive and Research Director with the regional NGO "South Asia Forum for Human Rights" (SAFHR), directing and coordinating a diverse portfolio of programs, including "Human Rights Audits of Peace Processes," "Women, Conflict, and Peace," "Media in Conflict," and "Rights-based Approaches to Poverty Reduction." Also, during the last decade and a half, she had been the gender advisor, Commonwealth Technical Fund (2004–05), and consultant in projects with UN Women (2010–11, 2012–13, 2014), United Nations Development Programme (UNDP 2014–15), Centre for Humanitarian Dialogues (2011, 2012), and SAFERWORLD (2015, 2016). She has lectured on conflict resolution at Rotary Centre for International Studies in Peace and Conflict Resolution, Chulalongkorn University (2014), *Welthungerhilfe* (WHH; 2014), Lady Shri Ram College (2008–16), and SAFHR: Human Rights and Peace Orientation Course (2000–08).

Her more recent publication *SAGE Series in Human Rights Audits of Peace Processes* undertaken by SAFHR and published by SAGE (2015), is a field-based audit study of peace-making in Northeast (India), Balochistan (Pakistan), Madhesh (Nepal), and Chittagong Hill Tracts (Bangladesh). Among her many books and articles are *Women War and Peace in South Asia: Beyond Victimhood to Agency*, a pioneering study on feminist theorizing and praxis on conflict and peace-building (SAGE 2001), and *Naga Women in the Peace Process* (SAGE 2004).

Contributors

Hana Shams Ahmed coordinates the work of the International Chittagong Hill Tracts Commission. She is a writer, activist, and researcher, and is currently pursuing a master's degree in Sociocultural Anthropology from University of Western Ontario, Ontario, Canada.

Najla Ayubi is a lawyer and former judge in Afghanistan, with extensive experience in judiciary, elections, human rights, and women's empowerment. She holds two master's degrees in Law and Political Science and Post-war Development Studies from the UK.

Anuradha Chenoy is a Professor and former dean of the School of International Studies, Jawaharlal Nehru University, New Delhi. She has written several books and academic articles, including *Militarism and Women in South Asia* and *Maoist and Other Armed Conflicts.*

Neloufer de Mel is a Senior Professor and Head of the Department of English, University of Colombo, Sri Lanka. She is the author of *Militarizing Sri Lanka: Popular Culture, Memory and Narrative in the Armed Conflict* and several essays on gender, culture, film, performance, and disability studies.

Warisha Farasat is a Delhi-based lawyer, with special interest in human rights and impunity issues. She previously worked at the International Center for Transitional Justice, New York and Kathmandu, and Centre for Equity Studies, Delhi.

Bhavani Fonseka is a human rights lawyer and senior researcher with the Centre for Policy Alternatives (CPA) based in Colombo, Sri Lanka. Her work has set precedents in the protection of human rights and challenging the culture of impunity.

Roshmi Goswami is a leading member of the South Asia women's rights movement and the founder member of North East Network. She has worked on women, peace, and security (WPS) issues in UN Women, New York and Delhi, and is a prominent voice on peace and gender justice.

Anuradha Bhasin Jamwal is the Executive Editor, Kashmir Times, and a human rights activist working and writing on communalism, borders, landmines, Kashmir conflict, India–Pakistan peace process, and gender issues. She is the Co-chairperson, India chapter of Pakistan–India Peoples' Forum for Peace and Democracy.

Nighat Said Khan is a socialist feminist activist/academic and is the Executive Director of Applied Social Resource (ASR) Centre, Dean of Studies of ASR Institute of Women's Studies, Lahore, and the ASR Institute for Peace Studies and Peace Activism.

Noreen Naseer is a resident of village Alizai, Kurram Agency, in the Federally Administered Tribal Areas (FATA), and is the faculty member of the Department of Political Science, University of Peshawar, Khyber Pakhtunkhwa, Pakistan.

Swarna Rajagopalan is an independent scholar and author based in Chennai, with research interests in gender, international relations, and security. She is also the founder of the Prajnya Trust.

Huma Safi is a former deputy director, "Equality for Peace and Democracy," and before that she was the Program Manager, "Women for Afghan Women" in Kabul, Afghanistan. She has been working on women's rights since graduating from a Madrasa with a degree in Islamic Studies.

Kumudini Samuel is the Co-founder and Senior Programme and Research Fellow, Women and Media Collective and Executive Committee Member, Development Alternatives with Women for a New Era (DAWN). She is a researcher and works on policy and advocacy with a particular focus on gender, conflict, and post-conflict transitions.

Mandira Sharma is a lawyer and human rights activist from Nepal. Formerly, she was the Executive Director of Advocacy Forum, Nepal. Currently, she is studying for her doctorate at the University of Essex, UK, researching on transitional justice issues.

Gitta Shrestha works as an independent researcher for Wageningen University, the Netherlands. Her core research interests include inequality, social norms, and gender justice in Nepal.

Dina M. Siddiqi is an anthropologist. She teaches anthropology in the Department of Economics and Social Sciences at BRAC University, Dhaka, Bangladesh.

Bishnu Raj Upreti is the Executive Director of Nepal Centre for Contemporary Research (NCCR). He has been engaged in teaching, research, and policy interventions on the issues of conflict and peace.

Index